UNIVERSITY OF NEBRASKA LIBRARIES
UNIVERSITY OF NEBRASKA / LINCOLN
D1320113

AMERICAN EDUCATION

Its Men

Ideas

and

Institutions

Public Education in California

John Swett

ARNO PRESS & THE NEW YORK TIMES
*New York * 1969*

Reprint edition 1969 by Arno Press, Inc.

*

Library of Congress Catalog Card No. 74-89242

*

Reprinted from a copy in Teachers College Library

*

Manufactured in the United States of America

Editorial Note

AMERICAN EDUCATION: *Its Men, Institutions and Ideas* presents selected works of thought and scholarship that have long been out of print or otherwise unavailable. Inevitably, such works will include particular ideas and doctrines that have been outmoded or superseded by more recent research. Nevertheless, all retain their place in the literature, having influenced educational thought and practice in their own time and having provided the basis for subsequent scholarship.

Lawrence A. Cremin
Teachers College

Public Education in California

PUBLIC EDUCATION IN CALIFORNIA

ITS ORIGIN AND DEVELOPMENT, WITH PERSONAL REMINISCENCES OF HALF A CENTURY

BY

JOHN SWETT

AMERICAN BOOK COMPANY
NEW YORK ∴ CINCINNATI ∴ CHICAGO

Public Educ. in Cal.

W. P. I

PREFACE

AFTER my retirement from active public-school service, a number of my friends urged me, as a matter of duty that I owed to my profession, to prepare for publication a volume which should include an outline of my long and varied experience in educational affairs.

Rather reluctantly, I finally ventured on the experiment of writing a book in which the personal narrative should be made the thread for binding together various educational footnotes, including sketches of the common schools and rural academies which I attended in New Hampshire about the middle of the nineteenth century, and also the salient points in the development of public schools in California, the state which opened for me the gate of opportunity.

It has not been easy for me to write about my own work, and I have ceased to wonder why the autobiographies of American public school teachers are so few in number. Born and bred in New England, even the warmth of California sunshine has never quite thawed out that Puritan reticence which is mine by heredity and early environment.

The manuscript copy of this volume has been read, in part or in whole, by more than a score of professional teachers, to whom I am indebted for wholesome criticism as well as for warm commendation. I am under special obligations to Dr. Elmer Ellsworth Brown, United States Commissioner of Education, and to Dr. Nicholas Murray Butler, President of Columbia University, for personal interest in my work. Furthermore, I deeply appreciate the helping hands of the officers and members of the Schoolmasters' Club, and of the California State Teachers' Association.

HILL GIRT FARM, MARTINEZ, CALIFORNIA, 1910.

CONTENTS

CONTENTS

SUMMARY OF THE EDUCATIONAL WORK OF THE AUTHOR

Positions as Teacher and as School Superintendent

1. Teacher of the Buck Street district school in Pembroke, N. H., two winter terms of four months each, in the years 1847 and 1848. (p. 68.)

2. Teacher of the district school, No. 1, in West Randolph, Massachusetts, for two winter terms, in the years 1849 and 1850. (p. 76.)

3. Assistant teacher in Pembroke Academy (N. H.), in 1850. (p. 79.)

4. Principal of Rincon Grammar School, San Francisco, 1853 to 1862. (p. 105.)

5. State Superintendent of Public Instruction, in California, 1862 to 1867, five years. (pp. 146–197.)

6. Principal of Denman Grammar School, San Francisco, 1868 to 1870, and also principal of the Lincoln Evening School. (pp. 198–206.)

7. Deputy Superintendent, San Francisco, 1870 to 1873. (p. 206.)

8. Principal of Denman Grammar School, 1873 to 1876. (p. 218.)

9. Principal of San Francisco Girls' High School and Normal Class, 1876 to 1889, thirteen years. (pp. 219–242.)

10. City Superintendent, San Francisco, 1892 to 1896, four years. (pp. 243–257.)

Author of Public School Reports

Thirteenth Annual Report of the Superintendent of Public Instruction, State of California, 1863. (p. 165.)

First Biennial Report of same, 1864 and 1865. (p. 177.)

Second Biennial Report, 1866 and 1867. (p. 182.)

Reports as Deputy Superintendent of Public Schools, San Francisco, 1871, 1872, and 1873.

Annual Reports of the Superintendent of Public Schools of San Francisco, 1892 to 1895, three reports. (pp. 248, 255.)

Educational Books

History of the Public School System of California (1876), A. L. Bancroft & Co. (p. 226.)

Normal Word Book (1876), Ivison, Blakeman & Taylor, N. Y.

Methods of Teaching (1880), Harper & Brothers. (p. 227.)

School Elocution (1886), H. H. Bancroft & Co.

American Public Schools: Their History and Pedagogics (1900), American Book Company. (pp. 301, 316.)

Joint Author with William Swinton, of: Swinton's Word Book and Word Primer; Swinton's Language Primer and Language Lessons; Swinton's School Composition; Swinton's Elementary Geography and Comprehensive Geography. (p. 209.)

Addresses and Papers

1. Reading and Elocution in the Common Schools; State Teachers' Convention, 1854. Published in the *Pacific*, 1854.

2. Address at the Dedication of the Rincon Schoolhouse, 1854. Published in the San Francisco *Sun*, 1854. (p. 109.)

3. A Plea for the Study of Nature; State Teachers' Convention at San Francisco, 1855. Published in the *Pioneer Magazine*, 1855.

4. School Gymnastics and Object Lessons; California State Teachers' Institute at San Francisco, 1861. "Institute Proceedings," 1861.

5. The Schools and the Commonwealth; San Francisco Teachers' Association, 1862. Published in *The Bulletin*, 1862. (p. 146.)

6. Duties of the State to Common Schools; California State Teachers' Institute, 1863. "Institute Proceedings," 1863.

7. Concerning Common Sense in Teaching; California State Teachers' Institute, 1863. "Institute Proceedings," 1863. (p. 162.)

8. Our State School Law; California State Teachers' Institute, 1865. "Institute Proceedings," 1865.

9. Educational Progress; State Teachers' Institute, 1867. "Institute Proceedings," 1867. (p. 191.)

10. The Annual Reëxamination and Reëlection of Teachers; National Educational Association, Boston, 1872. "Proceedings," 1872. (p. 213.)

11. The Relation of the State to School Books and Appliances; National Educational Association at San Francisco, 1888. "Proceedings," 1888. (p. 236.)

12. Evolution of the American Public School System; California State Teachers' Association, Santa Rosa, 1898. "Proceedings," 1898. (p. 255.)

13. Monograph on the Elementary Schools of California; written for the Cal. Dep't of Educ. in the Louisiana Purchase Exposition at St. Louis, 1904.

14. Concerning Some Common-Sense Ways of Interesting Public School Children in Nature Studies relating to Agriculture, Horticulture, Viticulture, and Farm Life. State Teachers' Association at Berkeley, 1905. "Proceedings," 1906.

John Swett
1910

PUBLIC EDUCATION IN CALIFORNIA

CHAPTER I

The Genesis of American Common Schools

To comprehend clearly the origin and progress of common schools in America, it is necessary to consider briefly the chartered civil rights given by the English government to the Puritan colonists of New England.

The Company of Massachusetts Bay was organized in England by about a hundred influential Puritans for the purpose of making a settlement in New England where the people of their own religious belief should be free from the domination of the bishops of the established church of England. The stockholders in this company purchased from the Council for New England a narrow tract of land bordering on the Atlantic and extending indefinitely westward. The royal charter granted to this corporate company and signed by Charles II (1629) provided for a governor, a deputy governor, and a board of eighteen "assistants." The Company immediately dispatched a vessel which carried away to New England a hundred colonists under the lead of John Endicott, who was appointed governor. These colonists made a settlement at Salem.

In 1630 twelve leading members of the Company, all men of means and of education, including the scholarly

John Winthrop, petitioned the General Court for leave to hold all future meetings of the Company in New England instead of in London, pledging themselves to go with the colonists and there make their home. The request was granted, and the same year the Company fitted out thirteen vessels which carried away nearly a thousand colonists, among whom were Governor John Winthrop and deputy governor Thomas Dudley, together with ten of the board of "assistants." When they reached their destination Governor Winthrop selected a place for settlement on Massachusetts Bay and named it Boston after the city of Boston in the mother country.

The charter of the Company provided an annual election, by the stockholders, of a board of eighteen "assistants," and for an annual election, by the assistants, of a governor and deputy governor, who, with the assistants, were to constitute a "general court," empowered to enact laws, to appoint magistrates, to make grants of land to colonists, levy taxes, and admit settlers to the "freedom of the colony," or, in other words, to give them the right of suffrage in town meeting. When the first colonial election was called, October, 1630, there were only twenty qualified electors in the colony, and of these the old board of assistants, including the governor and his deputy, constituted a majority. The old members of the board of assistants were reëlected for another year, and the assistants reëlected Governor John Winthrop. The General Court then proceeded to admit one hundred and eight colonists as "freemen" qualified to vote in town meeting. As a matter of course all of these new citizens were safe and true men, members of some Congregational Puritan church. The second meeting of the General Court, held May 18,

1631, passed the following order: — "For time to come no man shall be admitted to the freedom of the body politic, but such as are members of some of the churches within the limits of the same."[1]

No magistrate could be appointed by the General Court unless he was a Puritan church member. It followed that the early colonial magistrates or judges were zealous in punishing, or fining, or banishing heretics such as Roger Williams, Anne Hutchinson, John Wheelwright, and the Quakers. But it must be borne in mind that at this time the idea of separating church from state had hardly entered into the minds of men, and suffrage based on manhood was dreamed of only by "visionaries." Year by year the number of freemen in the colony was so cautiously increased that at the end of four years, when the number of inhabitants was upwards of three thousand, the number of freemen was barely three hundred.[2]

This year (1634) marked the beginning of rapid modifications of the civil government in the Bay colony. The new "towns" adjacent to Boston, such as Charlestown, Roxbury, Dorchester, Newtown (now Cambridge), and Salem, claimed the right of sending "delegates," two from each town, to represent their interests at the annual session of the General Court. The privilege was granted, and this marked the beginning of representative government. The

[1] (Massachusetts Records, Vol. I.)

[2] The following is the form of the "Freeman's Oath" as administered by the magistrates in 1634: —

"I do solemnly bind myself that I will give my vote and suffrage as I shall judge in mine own conscience may best conduce to the public weal; so help me God."

It is hard to find in colonial records a finer example of a vital principle condensed into idiomatic English.

next step was to curtail the power of the governor and the board of assistants by a law that no colonial taxes should be levied except by the representative delegates elected by the several towns. Then followed the demand for a written constitution, and a commission was appointed by the General Court "to frame a body of laws in resemblance to a *magna charta*." Following this, came the substitution of written ballots instead of counting votes by a show of hands.

In 1635, the scholarly Puritan statesman, Sir Henry Vane, came over from the English court to cast his lot with the infant colony. The following year (1636) he was elected governor of the colony of Massachusetts Bay. This was the year that the talented Puritan minister, Thomas Hooker, led his whole congregation of a hundred members away from the vicinity of Boston to the beautiful valley of the Connecticut River, and there founded a new town named Hartford, in which the right of voting in town meeting was not limited to members of the Congregational churches. It was during this same year that Roger Williams, another liberal Puritan clergyman, banished from the Bay colony for "heresy," went out into the wilderness among the Indians and founded the Rhode Island colony.

It is in the colonial town meetings for the management of local affairs that we find the democratic side of self-government, differing from the somewhat aristocratic and ecclesiastical organization of the General Court. These meetings, in the beginning, were called whenever required by urgent business or by military necessity, but in general once a year. In the original Anglo-Saxon or Teutonic *tun moote* (town meeting), the sole test of a voice in the proceedings was the ability to bear arms and to fight. The New England town meeting was a partial revival of an institution which, in the mother country, had been merged into the ecclesiastical organization of the established church of England, controlled by the king and the bishops.

The most important officers of the colonial town were the selectmen, three in number, who constituted a board for the general management of local business affairs. They appraised the value of taxable property, apportioned the taxes voted in town meeting for local purposes or imposed by the colonial General Court. The selectmen also collected the taxes, ordered the payment of bills, and acted as treasurers of the public money. There was a town clerk, who kept the town records, recorded the proceedings of town meetings, and kept careful accounts of the receipts and expenditures of public money. There was a constable to arrest offenders; a justice of the peace to try them; a pound keeper to take all stray cattle or horses and put them into safe enclosures; and still another officer was a hog-reeve to take up and impound stray swine. All of these town officials were elected annually for the term of one year.[1]

[1] The one feature that marred the democracy of the early town meeting was the fact that the right of suffrage was restricted to freemen, and no man was made a freeman by the general court unless he could prove himself to be a member of some Congregational church, sound on all the essential points of the Calvanistic Puritan creed. In itself, each little Congregational church was an independent organization that managed its own affairs. Each church elected its own minister by vote of its church members and dismissed him in the same manner. In the beginning, when there was only one church in a small town, the minister was elected in town meeting and paid out of the town treasury. It was hard to draw a dividing line between town and church.

Such was the civil government of the colony of Massachusetts Bay, which in the course of time developed into a representative form of state government.

Turning now from civil government to educational beginnings in the new colony, we find, as we might expect, that these recently transplanted Englishmen modeled their early schools after the grammar schools of the mother country. The Boston Latin School (1635) was started by a subscription list headed by Sir Henry Vane and Governor John Winthrop, but was soon placed under the control of the town selectmen, and thereafter the school was mainly supported by town appropriations. Into this school there entered about a dozen boys who were admitted on the sole condition that they could "read the English language," in other words, at about seven years of age. The curriculum was limited exclusively to Latin supplemented by a little Greek. At thirteen or fourteen years of age the boys were turned out fitted for college. In 1636, one year after the Boston Latin School was "set up," the General Court of the Bay colonies appropriated four hundred pounds ($2000) toward the establishment of a college at Newtown (now Cambridge).

At various intervals during the following decade, grammar schools were set up in Charlestown, Dorchester, Salem, Ipswich, Cambridge, Dedham, and Newbury in Massachusetts, at New Haven and Hartford in Connecticut, and at Newport in Rhode Island. These schools were taught exclusively by men and were attended exclusively by boys. Their primary purpose was to fit boys for college. The major study was Latin, combined with a little Greek. Boys were admitted into the grammar schools at about seven years of age, provided they could read readily in English, which accomplishment it was taken for granted they had acquired at home or in small private schools known as "women's schools," or "dame schools."

The earlier grammar schools were supported partly by tuition fees, partly by town appropriations, partly by gifts, bequests, or endowments. In course of time, it was found that many parents did not desire their boys to study Latin; and reading in English, spelling, writing, and arithmetic were taken as a substitute, so that only a small minority of the pupils remained in the Latin course. Eventually Latin grammar was superseded by English grammar, and little of the original grammar school was left, except the name, which is still applied to the upper grades of the modern elementary graded school.

The conservative town of Boston finally came into line, and in 1682 voted in town meeting "that a committee with the selectmen consider and provide for the teaching of children to write and cipher within this town." Several grammar schools were opened, with one department for teaching writing and ciphering under one master, and the other department under another master, for teaching reading and spelling. Into these new English grammar schools boys were admitted at about seven years of age, or when they could "read the English language by spelling the same." It was one of these double-headed schools that Benjamin Franklin entered when an eight-year-old boy, remaining in it less than two years, which period included all the schooling he ever got. In Franklin's autobiography he says of himself, "I learned a good handwriting, but failed in arithmetic." Franklin's real education was gained in a printing office.

It seemed a matter of course that girls should remain

illiterate, or else must learn to read and write, as in England, in the little private schools known as "dame schools" or "women's schools," in which the tuition fees were a penny a day.

Meanwhile, in 1642, the General Court of the Bay colony passed an act reading as follows:

> "Forasmuch as good education is of singular behoof and benefit to any Commonwealth, it is ordered that the selectmen of every town have a vigilant eye over their brethren and neighbors to see first: That none of them shall suffer so much barbarism in any of their families as not to teach by themselves, or others, their children and apprentices, so much learning as may enable them perfectly to read the English tongue, upon penalty of twenty shillings for each neglect therein."

This law does not seem to have been strictly enforced, but it served as a legal encouragement to the common people to "set up" small schools.

Five years later (1647) the General Court ordered: "that when a town had increased to the number of fifty house-holders, it should then forthwith appoint one within their town to teach all such children as shall resort to him to write and read, whose wages shall be paid either by the parents or the masters of such children, or by the inhabitants in general by way of supply, as the major part of those that order the prudentials of the town shall appoint;" and it was further ordered that "where any town shall increase to the number of one hundred families or house-holders, they shall set up a grammar school, the master thereof being able to instruct youths so far as they may be fitted for the university.' Three years later the Connecticut colony passed a law similar in the main to that of Massachusetts.

The provision for the setting up of grammar schools seems to have been enforced by the magistrates, but the matter of the smaller schools for teaching little children to write and read was, in general, left to the initiative of the common people themselves.

Common Schools in Rural Districts

It is in the records of settlements later than those at the seaports of Boston and Salem that we discover, in embryo, schools differing in type from the schools of old England. In these rural towns of small farms, after the settlers had made a clearing in the forest, they organized a town government, built a meeting-house, and in town meeting voted to hire a minister to preach the gospel. Then, in a few years, they voted in town meeting to build a school-house and hire a man to teach a school to which all the children of the town, without limitation of age or sex, were admitted. Coeducation of the sexes was a necessity, not a theory. There was no printed course of study, but by custom the essential studies were reading, spelling, writing, and arithmetic. These sturdy freemen had a solemn conviction that their children ought to be able to read and write their mother tongue so that they could read the Scriptures and the church catechism. As a matter of business, they ought to know enough of arithmetic "to cast accounts." Such a school was the Hampton school of 1649, previously mentioned, which has an authenticated history in the original records of town meetings.

These primitive schools were sometimes supported by subscriptions, but were soon maintained by a tax voted in town meeting, sufficient to keep them open from three to five months in the year. These "common schools" of the plain people were not charity schools for the children of the poor. They were wholly unlike the endowed grammar schools of England, established for the higher classes. Whether these schools were good or whether they were poor depended almost entirely on the character of the schoolmaster or the temper of the people. Some of the early schoolmasters were college-bred men from over the sea, who, finding themselves unfitted for the hard work of clearing woodlands or building stone walls, took to school-teaching. Such teachers were not limited to the customary studies of reading, writing, and arithmetic. As a matter of fact, they often helped along the big boys, who went to school during the long winters, in English grammar, or algebra, or even in Latin. Along the seacoast, at a later period, these teachers let the most promising boys worry their brains over Pike's Arithmetic, which included algebra through quadratic equations, and geometry through conic sections.[1]

[1] Such a teacher was John Sullivan, a scholarly Catholic Irish gentleman who came over to New England in 1723. After he had gained a foothold, twelve years later, he married Margery Brown, who, as a little girl seven years old, came over on the same vessel that brought John Sullivan. Shortly after their marriage, Schoolmaster Sullivan bought a small farm in Berwick, Maine, and continued teaching school in Berwick, and in Somersworth, New Hampshire. He spoke French fluently and taught Latin well. He seems also to have served incidentally as a lawyer in drawing wills and making out deeds and other legal papers. He taught school until he was ninety years old, and died on his farm in Berwick at the age of one hundred and four years.

The children of John Sullivan and Margery Brown seem to have inherited strong traits of character from both father and mother. Their son, John Sullivan, born in 1740, and educated in schools taught by his father, became a notable figure in the history of New Hampshire, as lawyer, jurist, and Major General in the Revolution. Another son, James Sullivan, born in 1744, became a lawyer, a jurist, and a governor of Massachusetts. One of Schoolmaster Sullivan's grandsons became governor of Maine; another, a senator from New Hampshire, and a third, lieutenant governor of Illinois. Schoolmaster Sullivan was a teacher who honored his profession.

It must be borne in mind by the student of educational history that in colonial times each little common school was a social center hardly second to that of the church. In the rural districts there were no daily papers, and the few weekly sheets in circulation were passed from hand to hand among a hardy yeomanry. There were no public libraries. Books were costly, and the majority of the farmers could not afford to buy them. To many families the Bible, the annual almanac, the New England Primer, and a few schoolbooks furnished their only reading matter. During the long cold winters when there was little farm work to be done, both boys and girls attended school up to the age of eighteen years. Along the seacoast the older boys were engaged during the summer months in fishing for cod on the "grand banks," or along the coast for mackerel. Having no work to do in winter, they went to school, studied arithmetic, and possibly navigation, if the young schoolmasters from Harvard or Dartmouth were competent to teach that branch of practical mathematics. These overgrown vikings of the seacoast were hard to govern, and the school committee preferred to employ robust athletes that could hold their own in a rough-and-tumble attack of the big boys to put the master out of the schoolhouse.

One of the Concord school of philosophers, Mr. F. B. Sanborn, born in the historic town of Hampton, N. H., said in a recent address, that "if there had been no common schools in New England, there would have been no American Revolution." After the preliminary skirmish of Lexington, the hardy yeomanry of New England, who had been drilled in the common schools, promptly answered the call to arms and fought the battle of Bunker Hill. The strong-armed fishermen of Marblehead, Cape Ann, and Cape Cod volunteered in the militia or manned the numerous and daring privateers that were fitted out to prey on British merchant vessels. It was these hardy mariners who manned the boats which safely ferried Washington and his army across East River in the skillfully conducted retreat after the battle of Long Island. These same sailors and fishermen tugged at the oars of boats filled with "ragged Continentals" amid the floating ice of the Delaware, in the darkness of a stormy winter night, when Washington made his brilliant attack on the Hessians at Trenton. The right wing of that little army was commanded by General John Sullivan of New Hampshire, and the advance guard was led by General John Stark of the same state.

The Declaration of Independence, the long war with the mother country, and finally the adoption of the Constitution of the United States, led to a revision of state constitutions, of state laws, and of school laws. The veterans who had served through the war or fought in the ranks of the militia claimed their civil rights and in part got them. The right of suffrage was greatly extended by the relaxation of religious tests and by a reduction of property qualifications. Vermont in New England, and Kentucky in the West, were the pioneer states in establishing manhood suffrage, limited only by the age of twenty-one years. The new nation had, in some measure, cut loose from British precedents in state, in church, and in schools.

It was in 1789 that girls were admitted tentatively into the "English grammar schools of Boston town" by allowing them to go to school at the noon intermission when the boys were absent from the schoolrooms, and on Thursday afternoons when the boys had a half holiday; but no provision had yet been made for teaching either boys or girls to read their mother tongue.

It was in 1789 that the legislature of Massachusetts enacted a law providing that towns could be subdivided into school districts. This law further provided that the course of study should include at least reading, writing, spelling, arithmetic, and "decent behavior." Opposition of the common people to the compulsory maintenance of the old-time Latin grammar schools had by this time become strong enough to secure in the law a provision that no town of less than two hundred families should be "required to maintain a grammar school."

This law of 1789 was amended eleven years later (1800) by empowering school districts to hold district meetings and to levy district taxes for building schoolhouses. In 1817 school districts were made "corporate bodies." In 1827 the law was amended so as to provide that towns having school districts should "choose for each district a 'prudential committeeman' to look after the school and appoint the teacher." At this time geography was added to the list of school studies.[1]

About this time the voters in Boston assumed the initiative in town meeting (1818) by electing a committee "to establish and control primary schools for children under seven years of age." As a result, during the following year, twenty schools were opened, eleven hundred boys and girls were enrolled, and women were appointed as teachers. The Boston "primary schools" were opened

[1] See George H. Martin's "Evolution of the Massachusetts Public School System," D. Appleton & Co., 1894.

one hundred and eighty-four years after the Boston Latin School was established.

This Massachusetts school law was so flexible and so democratic that it was suited both to the temper of the people and to the conditions of pioneer life. The school district became a small political unit in which the common people reigned supreme. The initiative in school matters must be taken by the people themselves. Other New England states followed the lead of Massachusetts. The state of New York enacted similar laws, modified by making the county, instead of the township, the political unit, and by providing for three school trustees in each school district. The New York law, in substance, was enacted by Ohio, Illinois, Indiana, and other states in the northwest. Still later, the main outlines of the New York law were taken as a basis of the law in California, in which state every rural schoolhouse has been built by a school-district tax, voted, not under compulsion, but on the initiative of the people assembled in school-district meetings. This law of 1789, with its long line of amendments, established the district common schools as they existed in 1835 when I began to go to school at five years of age in the town of Pittsfield in New Hampshire.

The Latin grammar schools and the early district schools have been the subjects of undue laudation on the one hand, and of unmerited criticism on the other. The fact is, that in the formative period the private schools, the denominational schools, the dame schools, and the common schools all were suited to the religious, the social, and the industrial conditions of the time in which they flourished, and they all contributed something towards the elementary education of the people. They must be judged by the conditions of the seventeenth and eighteenth centuries, not by the standard of the twentieth century. The early public schools were organized by the plain common people assembled in town meeting. In their formative period they owed little to speculative philosophers or to denominational institutions. With every extension of the right of suffrage they grew stronger, keeping even pace with the progress of civilization, with the broader recognition of the rights of man, and with the increase in wealth and population.

CHAPTER II

MY NEW ENGLAND ENVIRONMENT

In the central part of New Hampshire, about fifteen miles south of Lake Winnepesaukee, among the foothills of the White Mountains, lies the picturesque town of Pittsfield in which were born my father, my mother, and myself. My native town is small in area, containing only eighteen square miles. It forms a part of Merrimac County, which includes a section of the valley of the Merrimac River on which are situated Manchester, the chief city of the state, and Concord, the capital. The early settlers were attracted to this hill region by its fine forests of oak, maple, white pine, hemlock and birch, and by the water power of the Suncook River, a branch of the Merrimac. Near the center of the town rises the long granite ridge of Catamount, shaggy with brush and trees, to a height of 1200 feet above sea level. The stony soil on the hills and rolling swells of glacial moraines was hard to clear, but, when subdued, was fairly productive. For more than half a century lumbering was an important source of profit. The tall white pines were cut and hauled in winter to tide water, a distance of about thirty miles, and sold for masts and ship timber.

One of the early settlers in Pittsfield, John Cram of Hampton, bought a large tract of woodland and built a small sawmill on the falls of the Suncook River, around which was clustered, in a few years, a thriving little village.

The sawmill was followed by a gristmill, a fulling mill, and at a later period by a cotton mill.

Most of the early settlers of Pittsfield came from the town of Hampton, which seems to have been the hive that sent out swarms of hardy pioneers into the wilderness of central New Hampshire soon after the close of the French and Indian War, when there was no longer danger from the incursions of savage foes.

Among these men in search of cheap land for homesteads were my grandfathers, Thomas Rogers Swett and Abraham French, and my great-grandfather on the maternalside, David Knowlton. In the early Pittsfield town records there are found many family names, all English, that appear in the still earlier Hampton records; such as Batchelder, Brown, Blake, Berry, Cram, Drake, Dow, Dearborn, French, Garland, Green, Jenness, Lane, Leavitt, Marston, Norris, Page, Perkins, Prescott, Swett, Smith, Sanborn, Tilton, and Towle. The names of small towns in southern New Hampshire, settled largely by emigrants from Hampton, show unmistakably that the early settlers came originally from the southwestern shires of the mother country over the sea, and they read like an extract from a geographical gazetteer of old England: "Hampton, Dover, Portsmouth, Exeter, Stratham, Epping, Nottingham, Salisbury, Durham, Epsom, Chichester, Canterbury, Pembroke, Newmarket; and crossing the line into Massachusetts, "Newbury," Ipswich, Essex, Gloucester, Marblehead, Boston, Plymouth, Yarmouth," etc.

Turning to the town records of Pittsfield, I find that in 1772 it was voted "to build a meeting-house of the same bigness of Hampton Falls meeting-house," and "to raise some money this year for preaching";

also "to hire Jonathan Brown to teach a school six months at nine dollars a month." Presently the town built a schoolhouse which, like the meeting house, was "of the same bigness" as the schoolhouse at Hampton Falls.

Now the town of Hampton, bordering on the seacoast and also on the Massachusetts line, is notable in the early annals of common schools. It was settled in 1632 by "liberal" Puritans from Boston, Salem, and the surrounding towns of Massachusetts Bay, who pushed out into the province of New Hampshire, some of them in search of cheap land for homesteads, and a few of them under compulsion on account of holding "various heretical doctrines." The Hampton town records "on the 2 of the 2 month, 1649," show that the "selectmen" made an agreement with John Legat "to teach and instruct all the children of or belonging to our Towne both mayle and femaile (wch are capable of learning) to write and read and cast accounts (if it be desired) as diligently and carefully as he is able to teach and instruct them, and in consideration thereof we have agreed to pay or cause to be payd to the said John Legat the sum of Twenty pounds, in corn, cattle, or butter att price current."[1] At the time of this contract, Hampton was under the jurisdiction of Massachusetts.

A few years later the town records of Hampton show that a property tax was ordered in town meeting for the support of this school. Still later, when the population had increased, a "Latin grammar school" was ordered by vote in town meeting as a supplement to the "common

[1] History of the Town of Hampton, by Joseph Dow. 1893. Salem, Mass. Printed by the Salem Press Publishing and Printing Company.

school." This school was taught for half a century by various graduates of Harvard College, many of whom were clergymen. When the age of academies began to dawn Hampton Academy was founded in 1810.

After an extended examination of town histories and records it is evident to me that the town of Hampton can fairly claim the honor of beginning in New England one of the first typical colonial common schools, which placed all children, boys and girls alike, on a common footing of equal rights to an education in reading, writing, and arithmetic. When the succeeding generations in Hampton pushed out into the border wilderness of New Hampshire and Maine to found new settlements, they followed the example of the mother town, and this was why the schools of my native town provided from the beginning for the coeducation of the sexes and for the teaching of reading, writing, and arithmetic.

The historical records of New Hampshire show how it came about that this feeble rural settlement opened the doors of its first school in 1649 to "all the children of or belonging to our Towne, both mayle and femaile." It seems that Rev. John Wheelwright of Lincolnshire, England, landed in Boston, May 26, 1636, and was admitted to church membership in that town in June following. Now, John Wheelwright was a brother-in-law of Mrs. Anne Hutchinson, and this fact placed him under the suspicion of holding Antinomian doctrines, and he thought best to remove to Mount Wollaston (now Quincy), where he became pastor of a church. But he soon preached a "fast-day sermon" for which he was called "into Court" and adjudged guilty of "sedition and contempt." At the next meeting of the General Court nine months later,

Mr. Wheelwright was "disfranchised and banished" and ordered to leave the jurisdiction of the Court within fourteen days. So he departed with some of his church members and formed a new settlement at Squamscott (now Exeter) in New Hampshire, and became pastor of a new church (1638). But in 1642 the people of Exeter and Hampton placed themselves under the jurisdiction of Massachusetts, and Mr. Wheelwright was forced to remove to Wells, in the province of Maine, whither he was followed by many of his church members. Finally, in 1654, the people of Hampton presented a petition to the General Court praying that the sentence of banishment be no longer enforced. The request was granted, though indirectly and with much circumlocution.

Furthermore, the first pastor in the town of Hampton was the Reverend Stephen Bachiler, a liberal Puritan, who in 1632 had settled at Lynn. On account of his zeal for popular rights he was soon suspended from the ministry, and ordered to depart from the town. In 1638 he became pastor of the small church at Hampton. In fact, many of the original settlers of Hampton moved away from Boston and Salem because the right of suffrage in those early theocracies was strictly limited to members of the Congregational church. Among other occasional visitors to the liberals in Exeter and Hampton there was the notable dissenter, Mrs. Anne Hutchinson, known among the strict constructionists of that day as a "theological fire-brand." In the days of Ralph Waldo Emerson, Mrs. Hutchinson would have been classed among the transcendentalists. The "liberals" were numerous in Hampton, which fact probably accounts for the admission of girls into their first common school. It is worthy of note, also, that in Hampton, from the beginning, there was no religious limitation of the right of suffrage.[1]

It was in the common schools of Hampton that four generations of my ancestors received their scanty education. In a town settled almost exclusively by Puritan emigrants from Hampton, my father and mother attended district schools like those of the mother town. It was in such schools that my father was for several years a teacher. It was in one of the old-time district schoolhouses that I was introduced at five years of age to Noah Webster's spelling book. Furthermore, following my father's example, I became a teacher in the district schools of New Hampshire and Massachusetts for four winter terms, during the time when I was working my way through an academic education.

My Puritan Ancestry

My ancestry, so far as I can definitely trace it, runs back to the records of the General Court of the Massa-

[1] The far-reaching impulse of this Hampton primitive common school is illustrated in the education of Daniel Webster, whose father, Captain Ebenezer Webster, was a lineal descendant of Thomas Webster, who settled in Hampton in 1636. Captain Ebenezer Webster was a hardy farmer, Indian fighter, and pioneer who, after the close of the French and Indian Wars, pushed his way from Kingston to the utmost verge of civilization in the province of New Hampshire, and built a log house in the town of Salisbury. He was a leader in town affairs, and in due time he and his neighbors started a common school similar to the typical Hampton school. In order to accommodate the sparse and scattered population, this school was held in three different parts of the town, under the same schoolmaster. Ebenezer Webster was bent on giving his youngest son, Daniel, the best possible education, and so the boy followed Master Thomas Chase, and afterwards Master James Tappan, from school to school, sometimes traveling several miles, and sometimes put to board with some farmer nearer the schoolhouse. It was schoolmaster Tappan who discovered talent in the boy Daniel, and who urged his father to send him to Dartmouth College.

chusetts Bay Colony, which shows that John Swett, of Devonshire, England, was admitted to the freedom of the Colony, May 18, 1642.[1]

John Swett, Nathaniel Weare, and eighty-nine other freemen were granted tracts of land in the town of Newbury, Massachusetts, on the seacoast near the New Hampshire line. To this land grant, made December 7, 1642, the colonists immediately repaired. Savage's Genealogical Dictionary says that "John Swett of Newbury brought with him from England his sons, Stephen, Benjamin, and Joseph, and perhaps others."

Benjamin Swett married Hester, daughter of Nathaniel Weare, Senior, and in 1663 removed with his brother-in-law, Nathaniel Weare, Junior, to Hampton, and settled

[1] John Fiske, in his "Beginnings of New England," makes a rough estimate that about one-sixth of the Puritan influx to New England came from the southwest seacoast counties of England, viz.: Devonshire, Dorset, and Somerset. Of the people of Devonshire, Woodrow Wilson, the historian, writes:

"For a time, all that was most characteristic of adventurous and sea-loving England was centered in Devonshire. . . . Devonshire lies in the midst of that group of counties in the southwest of England in which the Saxon mastery did least to destroy or drive out the old Celtic population. There is accordingly a strong strain of Celtic blood among its people to this day, and the land suits with the strain." . . .

"For itself, Devonshire had the great harbor and roads of Plymouth, and innumerable fishing ports, where a whole race of venturesome and hardy fishermen were nurtured. All the great sea names of the Elizabethan age belong to it. Drake, Hawkins, Raleigh, and the Gilberts were all Devonshire men; and it was from Plymouth that the first fleet went out which beat the great Armada on its way to shipwreck in the north. The men who first undertook to colonize the New World for England were bred to adventure, both by books and by the sea air in which they lived." *New England Genealogical and Antiquarian Register*, 1852. Vol. VI. p. 49–62. "The Swett Family." Also *Savage's Genealogical Dictionary of the First Settlers of New England*, p. 240. Boston: Little, Brown & Co., 1862.

on the "Falls Side." They both grew to be men of affairs.

Mr. Swett was chosen selectman and commissioner of county rates, but his chief service was in drilling the militia and in fighting Indians. He was successively elected ensign, lieutenant, and chaplain. In June, 1677, he was made commander of an expedition against the Indians in the province of Maine. This force, consisting of ninety men aided by two hundred friendly Natick Indians, landed at Black Point in Scarborough, where there was a fortified garrison Captain Swett and Lieutenant Richardson moved out of the fort to attack the enemy, but fell into an ambuscade prepared by the wily foe. The friendly Indians stampeded, and the whites, fighting bravely, retreated to the garrison house. Lieutenant Richardson was killed early in the fight. "Captain Swett," says Williamson's History of Maine, "fought the enemy hand to hand, displaying upon the spot and on the retreat of two miles, great presence of mind as well as personal courage in repeated rallies of his men, in his exertions to bring off the dead and wounded, and in defense of his rear, upon which the savages hung with destructive fury. At last, wounded in twenty places, exhausted by fatigue and loss of blood, he was grabbed and thrown to the ground and barbarously hacked to pieces at the gate of the garrison. With this intrepid officer fell sixty of his men, forty English and twenty Indians."

Captain Benjamin Swett left a family of eleven children, — five boys and six girls. His widow married a Mr. Greenleaf of Newbury and took with her to that town the younger children, leaving in Hampton the four older sons,

— Benjamin, John, Joseph, and Moses. Joseph, the most notable of these, took an active part in town affairs, and was elected representative to the Provincial Assembly (1708). He had a family of eight children, three of whom were sons, — Benjamin, Nathan, and Moses. His eldest son, Benjamin, born in 1710, married a daughter of Bonus Norton of Ipswich, and had three children, — Stephen, Sarah, and Thomas Rogers. This youngest child, Thomas Rogers Swett, only three years old when his father died, was put out at an early age as an apprentice to learn the trade of fuller and clothier. He learned "to read and write and cipher" in the common school at Hampton Falls. When sixteen years of age, he enlisted as a private in the New Hampshire quota of militia, called out in what was known as the "Rhode Island campaign." Though two years under the legal age of eighteen, he was enrolled, June 26, 1777, under the name of Thomas Swett, omitting Rogers, his middle name, in Captain Joseph Parson's company, Colonel Joseph Senter's New Hampshire regiment, and was mustered out with the regiment in January, 1779. In his old age he was placed on the Revolutionary pension roll of New Hampshire. After his discharge from the army he worked for several years at his trade, and then settled in Pittsfield, N. H., where he built a fulling mill on the Suncook Falls.

When his mill was swept away by the "great flood," he traded the mill site for the Drake farm on the edge of Pittsfield village. He was engaged at times in buying beef cattle in New Hampshire, and selling them in the Boston market. He had a family of ten children, — two by his first wife, Abigail Cram, who died in 1789, and eight by his second wife, Betsey Knowlton. All these, six sons and four daughters, were educated in the common schools. All grew up to maturity, were married, and had children.

The names of this large family run as follows, in order of birth: — By his first wife: Eunice, 1787, and John, 1789; by his second wife: Moses, 1792; David, 1794; Thomas Rogers, Junior, 1797; Eben, 1799; Daniel, 1802; Mary, 1805; Betsey, 1807; and Sarah, 1809. Eben Swett, the fifth son, was my father.

Few of the Swett family became wealthy, but in the hard struggle to earn a living in early days they all managed to keep their heads above water. Though of direct Puritan descent, they had a marked tendency to liberal ideas. Samuel Swett of Boston, a lineal descendant of John Swett of Newbury, published a "History of Bunker Hill Battle," and various other historical documents. Leonard Swett, born in Turner, Maine (1825), was a grandson of John Swett of Buckfield, Maine, and great-grandson of Dr. Stephen Swett, who settled in Gorham in 1770. He went west and became, in Illinois, the most notable lawyer and politician that appears in the records of the Swett family. Sophie Miriam Swett and her sister, Susan Hartley Swett, of the Swett family that settled in Maine, are known as authors and magazine contributors. The mother of Frank Swett Black, governor of New York in 1897–98, was daughter of my uncle, Moses Swett, of Hollis, Maine.

My maternal grandfather, Abraham French, was born in Stratham, near Hampton Falls, in 1758. Abraham was left fatherless at the age of seven years, and his mother with six young children had a hard struggle to support them. He was apprenticed at an early age to learn the trade of joiner and cabinet maker, but he attended the common school in Hampton Falls during the winter terms, and learned "to read and write and cast accounts." When the large meetinghouse, erected by vote of the town of Pittsfield, was nearing completion, he was sent for to do the finishing work of the interior. He packed his tools on his back and traveled the whole distance on foot. He liked the town so well that he bought a farm on the edge of Pittsfield village, married Hannah Lane (1795), and settled down for life. The house on this farm was built as a parsonage for Christopher Paige, a minister of the Congregational church. In this house my grandfather and his wife reared a family of eleven children and sent them to the common school to be educated. The fifth child of this family, Lucretia French, was my mother.

My grandfather French was a shrewd man of business, who carried on his farm, ran a sawmill, dealt in lumber, and managed a carpenter shop for making furniture and the cases of old-fashioned stately eight-day clocks. I remember him as a genial old man, who had a keen sense of humor, who smoked his pipe, drank his mug of cider, and took cheerful views of temporal affairs, notwithstanding the severe Calvinism of his religious creed. It was in his workshop that I learned to use a lathe, on which I turned my own tops when a boy. He died in 1850, aged eighty-two years.

My grandmother French, I remember as a venerable old lady, small in stature, nervous in temperament, and skilled in housekeeping. She delighted in reading the Bible, Scott's Commentaries, and various volumes of theological sermons. She was a devoted member of the Congregational church and regularly attended its meetings, while her husband as regularly went to the Calvin-Baptist church; yet there was no discord in the family on that account, for each was tolerant of the other, and both made their faith evident in good works. She visited my bedside once when I was a small boy, sick with a fever, and talked very kindly to me. She said: "You must not be afraid to die. Life is a vale of tears, and those who die young are better off than those who live to be old." I remember that I thought I wanted to get well and would rather take the chances. The Lane family records show a long list of substantial farmers, mechanics, tradesmen, long-lived and thrifty; also a few teachers, several ministers, and a large number of Congregational deacons.

My grandmother's brother, Ebenezer Lane, who settled in Pittsfield at an early date, was a teacher, a farmer, and a surveyor, educated in Phillips-Exeter Academy. He was elected to various town offices, was sent to the state legislature, and was a man of marked ability and character. After his death, when his personal property was sold at auction, I "bid in" his surveyor's compass, chain, and other instruments, and with this outfit surveyed and plotted the Swett farm. My strong liking for trigonometry and surveying, when at school, was perhaps owing to a thread of heredity running back through my grandmother to the Lane family.

David Knowlton, one of the early settlers that came from Seabrook near Hampton, was by trade a blacksmith and farmer, and by "profession" an elder in the Freewill Baptist church. He bought a tract of woodland, high up on the slope of Catamount, cleared it, and built a farm-

[1] Lane Genealogies, Vol. I, by Rev. Jacob Chapman, Exeter, N. H., News Letter Press 1891.

house. Then he organized a Freewill Baptist church of six members, built a small meeting house on one corner of his farm, and was ordained as a preacher of the gospel. He preached to that mountain congregation for more than twenty years, refusing any salary, and supporting his family by the work of his own hands in his blacksmith shop and on his rocky little farm. He is described as a man of powerful physique and commanding presence. He was not college bred, but was endowed by nature with the gift of public speaking and with a religious enthusiasm that never flagged. He died in 1815, at seventy-four years of age. His wife, Mary (Green) Knowlton, died three years later, at seventy-four years of age, and was buried by his side in the small church burial ground near the old Quaker burial ground on Catamount.

Elder Knowlton had ten children, only five of whom lived to maturity and were married. His two sons, Ebenezer and David, became Freewill Baptist preachers of marked ability. His daughter, Betsey, married Thomas Rogers Swett, my grandfather.

Betsey Knowlton grew up under strong religious influences, and made her fervent piety manifest in training a large family of boys and girls in the way they should go, so well that when they grew up they did not depart from it. My grandmother inherited intellectual ability and an emotional temperament, traits which she transmitted to one of her sons, Eben, and to her three daughters. When she was married to my grandfather in 1791, at twenty-one years of age, she became stepmother to two children, — Eunice, four years old, and John, two years old, — whom she cared for as lovingly as for her own five sons and three daughters. She lived to see all of her children grow to manhood and womanhood; she saw them well married and settled in life; and then, somewhat broken with the care of a large family and the domestic duties of a farmer's wife, she rested from cooking, spinning, weaving, and knitting, folded her worn hands, and passed peacefully away in the seventieth year of her age. I was ten years old when I sadly followed with the mourners and saw her body laid to rest in the grave. I have always cherished her memory, and I am glad in my old age to pay this humble tribute to my grandmother, Betsey (Knowlton) Swett.

My grandfather Swett I remember as a stirring old man, quick in temper, small in stature, with a full head of flowing white hair. He still had in the house the heavy old flintlock "queen's arms" musket that he had shouldered in the army. He was rather an aggressive man, fearless, independent, and a stubborn disbeliever in devils, witches, ghosts, and other current superstitions of his time.

I distinctly recall a discussion between him and his brother Stephen, which I overheard when I was eight or nine years old. My grandfather stoutly defended his Universalist belief until his brother, a rigid Calvinist, turned to him and said, "Well, I would not trust the salvation of my soul on any such flimsy platform as you stand upon." My boyish sympathies ran with my grandfather. I remember, too, that he liked to have some one read to him from "The Trumpet," the Universalist weekly paper, and when something pleased him he would exclaim, "That's God's truth." He died in 1847, at the advanced age of eighty-eight years. His grave in the village burial ground near the town hall is marked by a headstone recently placed there by one of his grandsons, bearing the inscription, "A Soldier of the Revolution."

CHAPTER III

MY BOYHOOD HOME, EARLY SCHOOL DAYS, AND THE AGE OF HOMESPUN

THE New England farmhouse which was once my home is yet standing on what was long known as the Drake-Swett homestead. The eastern boundary of this farm is the Suncook River, which washes the base of Catamount. The house commands a view of Pittsfield village; of Mt. Kearsarge, rising blue in the western horizon; and of the "Ossipee hills," that stand like granite sentinels guarding Lake Winnepesaukee, that beautiful sheet of water which the Indians rightly named the "Smile of the Great Spirit."

Near the close of the eighteenth century Simeon Drake bought a tract of heavily wooded land on the edge of Pittsfield village, and built on a little eminence a spacious two-story house, a barn, and other outbuildings. Then he made a clearing for a farm on the lateral moraine of a glacier that, ages before, had moved slowly down what is now the channel of Suncook River, grinding granite into soil, and mixing it up with cobblestones and bowlders of all sizes. The heavy stone walls still remain as monuments of the hard labor by which the land was brought under cultivation.

My grandfather, Thomas Rogers Swett, made a trade with Simeon Drake by swapping a mill site and water-power right on Suncook River for the Drake farm. Samuel

G. Drake, son of Simeon Drake, the pioneer, was born in Pittsfield (1798). He removed to Boston, where he became a well-known book dealer, author, and publisher. One of his many books is "Drake's History and Antiquities of Boston" (1852). His son, Samuel Adams Drake, born in Boston, is the author of many popular books on New England scenery and history.

In the Drake-Swett house my father, Eben Swett, was born (1799), and here he died (1842). Here I was born July 31, 1830. Here lived for many years my cousin, David Knowlton Swett, and here he died (1896). Since his death the place has changed hands several times; but though the exterior of the farmhouse has been modernized, the original framework of huge pines, hewn out with the broadax, remain without change, and its timbers are still as sound as they were a century ago. The place is now known as the "Sculkook Farm."

It was into this historic house that my father took his young wife after his marriage in 1829. A two-story wing was added to the original farmhouse, so that there was ample room for two separate families.

It was my misfortune to be an only child, but the place of brothers and sisters was partially filled by the five children of my uncle, Thomas Rogers Swett, Jr., who lived in a house near by, on a part of the original Swett farm. My cousin, David Knowlton Swett, about my own age, was my playmate for ten years.

The earliest recollections of my childhood include pictures of my mother, busy in spinning woolen yarn on a large spinning wheel, or in weaving cloth on the great loom in the large chamber of the second story. I recall frequent visits to the rooms of my grandmother, who often invited me to sit up to her table and drink sage tea from her curious little blue china teacups. At one end of the kitchen there was a row of "dressers" well stocked with pewter plates and platters which shone in my eyes as if made of massive silver. The tall eight-day clock, the great fireplace with its crane, pothooks, and kettles, — I see them still. My grandmother often allowed me to look at the pictures in the large well-worn family Bible, and sometimes she read aloud to me interesting Bible stories.

Of my first summer at school I have only hazy recollections, but I retain a vivid picture of the antique schoolhouse on the edge of the village near the mill pond and cotton factory, and of the long unpainted desks rising like seats in a theater on each side of a central level floor, at one end of which there was a huge open fireplace. One of the first things I learned at school was the name of the president of the United States, Andrew Jackson. One day, for whispering to another boy, I was ordered by the teacher, Miss White, to sit on the back seat with a row of big girls who laughed at me. At another time Miss White unjustly accused me of telling her a lie, and I hated her ever after. On my way to school we passed along the edge of the mill pond where the dragon flies, known to us as the "Devil's darning needles," were a constant source of terror to me because the big boys said they would sting us and then sew up our eyelids. We had no nature study in school in those days.

About this time a kind friend living in Dover, Miss Lucy Ham, sent me five bound numbers of *Peter Parley's Magazine*, which proved for several years a source of delight. The first piece of verse that I committed to memory from these books was a poem of ten stanzas entitled "The Sailor Boy's Story," which I recited at home to admiring visitors. The piece began as follows:

> "I am a little sailor boy,
> And would you know my story?
> I've sailed across the ocean blue,
> And seen it in its glory."

The following summer the school was again taught by Miss White. I have dim recollections of Webster's Spelling Book. I had learned to read at home before I was sent to school, and therefore made rapid progress in both reading and spelling.

In 1836 my father and mother moved into Pittsfield village to take charge of the large "corporation boarding house" connected with the cotton factory. At that time the operatives in the factory were almost exclusively daughters of farmers living in Pittsfield and the surrounding towns. The times were hard, and this was the only way they had of earning money. I did not like life in the village. In 1837 there came the great commercial panic which swept over New England like a tornado. I remember well the general talk about hard times. My father continued to carry on the farm, and my mother worked hard in managing the boarding house, but the business proved unprofitable on account of the high prices of foodstuffs, and we all moved back to the farm, much to my delight.

While we lived in the village, the old schoolhouse on the river road was torn down, and the school was held for a year in the academy building. The only distinct recollection that I have is, that one day I boldly made a protest against too long a lesson assigned in Emerson's

Primary Arithmetic, whereupon the reasonable teacher cut it down one-half. Our reading book was the "Progressive Reader," of which I can remember vividly only one piece, and that was an extract which treated on the properties of metals. From this lesson I learned that "iron is ductile, that is, capable of being drawn out into wire;" also that "gold is malleable, that is, it can be hammered into thin sheets called gold leaf." I recall also a story about the Good Samaritan illustrated by a woodcut. I remember that my father bought for me a small book of stories about Indians and Indian wars in colonial times, and the reading and re-reading of this precious volume was the beginning of a lifelong taste for American history. I discovered in my father's library two bound volumes of the *Penny Magazine*, which contained illustrated descriptions of most of the famous sea fights in the War of 1812. I recall in particular the accounts of the capture of the *Guerrière* by the *Constitution*, of the *Macedonian* by the *United States*, and of the *Java* by the *Constitution*. The stories of these great naval victories I read and re-read until I knew them by heart; and as I studied the rude woodcuts of the disabled British frigates, my heart swelled with patriotic pride. One thing troubled me, I did not know exactly how to pronounce the name of the British frigate — the *Guerrière*.

Next winter the school was held in the new brick schoolhouse, situated on a bluff from which we had a view of the village, the cotton mill, the gristmill, the mill pond, and Catamount. Abel Berry, the schoolmaster, a graduate of Dartmouth College, was a young law student who was paying his way by teaching school. The school was now crowded with big boys and big girls, some of them from sixteen to eighteen years of age. I began to pick up ideas by listening to the recitations of the older pupils.

The schoolmaster boarded at my father's house, and I was allowed to go with him to the evening spelling matches held once in two weeks. I soon ranked as a good speller. The master was a ready talker, and he and my father were engaged many long winter evenings in discussing politics, religion, and books. I was allowed to be present, and from these long conversations I learned far more than I acquired from my school study of textbooks. When the winter term closed, the master went "out West" and opened a law office.

Our next teacher during the summer term was Miss French, a beautiful and accomplished lady, who won all our hearts by her gracious manner. She made lovely wax flowers and presented one to each member of our class in Peter Parley's Geography. She sometimes allowed me and my dearest friend, Tom Nutter, to study our lessons outside of the schoolroom, under the shade of a big maple tree near the school. Happy days were those, and we all did our best to learn our lessons.

The regular term of three months was supplemented by a private school, continued for six weeks, during which time we each paid a small tuition fee for the teacher. This was in accordance with the usual custom at that time in most New England schools. During my eight years of attendance in the common school I was kept at school about eight months in each year.

Miss French was succeeded by Ruth Leavitt, a veteran teacher, famous for drill and discipline. Her successor was Sarah Batchelder, the daughter of our near neighbor,

Colonel Batchelder. She sang in the church choir, and taught us two very simple children's songs, which included all of my training in music in the common school. I liked her very well, but thought more of her younger sister, Abbie Batchelder, "the prettiest girl in school," who had a train of youthful admirers among the small boys.

And now there came, during the winter term, a law student, Enoch Eastman by name, over six feet in height, with the muscles of an athlete and a swarthy complexion like that of Daniel Webster, whose mother was an Eastman. There were two big boys, about twenty years old, who constituted a class in Comstock's Natural Philosophy, and I immediately established myself as a silent partner and outside member of the class. This giant master did something more than hear textbook recitations. He talked, he explained, he illustrated, he even laughed. I never missed a lesson, and a lifelong interest in physics began in this surreptitious listening to the words of this great teacher. How genial he was! Arithmetic was made easy, grammar was sweet to the taste, and the whole world seemed delightful. When school closed this ideal teacher also went out West to open a law office.

I was now old enough to attend with my father the evening meetings of the "Pittsfield Lyceum," in other words, a debating society. My study of politics began in hearing a long debate on the question, "Ought Texas to be admitted into the Union?" This discussion was carried on for several meetings by two able lawyers, the minister, schoolmaster Eastman, and my father. I still have in my possession my father's written argument in the affirmative, which is a clear and forcible paper. At my father's house the subjects of politics and religion were frequently under discussion, and these conversations, to which I was a silent listener, constituted no small part of my education.

Monroe Berry, educated in Pittsfield Academy, was the teacher during the next winter term. Him I remember with pleasure because he graciously granted my request to allow me to study Goodrich's History of the United States, though I was the only pupil in the class. With this history I was delighted. The part that thrilled me most was a detailed account of the battle of Bunker Hill. At this time I was studying Smith's Grammar, Adams's New Arithmetic, Colburn's Intellectual Arithmetic, Smith's Geography, Webster's Spelling Book, and Porter's Rhetorical Reader. At the end of the term this teacher went out West.

In addition to the limited number of books that fell into my hands, I found in the garret a file of Dudley Leavitt's Almanacs, and some files of the *New Hampshire Patriot*, a weekly political paper, edited by Isaac Hill, a stanch supporter of Andrew Jackson and his policy. I remember to this day a campaign doggerel on the United States Bank, beginning as follows:

> "Bah! Bah! Nicholas, have you any cash?
> Have the five and thirty millions wholly gone to smash?" etc.

It is hardly necessary to add that I became a Democrat, opposed to a national bank.

At another time I found a roll of "Coffin Handbills," issued during the Jackson presidential campaign, in which "Old Hickory" was charged with the murder of six militiamen. This campaign document was illustrated by a row of six black coffins. As both my father and my grandfather were Jackson democrats, this roll of campaign literature, instead of being distributed, had been carefully stowed away in a hidden corner of the old farmhouse.

It was about this time that my father was reading Combe's "Constitution of Man," and I have a vivid recollection of conversations between him and schoolmaster Eastman about this book. In particular, it was impressed upon me that sickness is the result of violations of the laws of nature, and not of a special Providence, mysteriously designed for our own good.

About this time, while foraging in the old garret for reading matter, I came across a well-worn copy of "*The New England Primer, Or an early and pleasant Guide to the Art of Reading, Adorned with Cutts*," a little book that was extensively used in the colonial common schools for more than a century. It was a rare prize, which I regarded with a singular kind of wonder. It began with the alphabet, followed by five pages of words for spelling, which began with words of one syllable like "age, beef," etc., and ended with "a-bom-in-a-tion, ed-if-i-ca-tion," etc. Then there came an illustrated alphabet, each letter being adorned with a rough woodcut and accompanied by a rude couplet in rhyme. Some of these verses have stuck in my memory through life. Here are three of them, running as follows:

A. "In Adam's fall,
We sinned all."

D. "The Deluge drowned
The Earth around."

F. "The idle fool
Is whipped at school."

Then followed a rude woodcut of the "burning at the stake of John Rogers, a martyr of Smithfield, England."

Next there appeared a condensed lesson in Biblical history, running in part as follows:

Who was the first man?	Adam.
Who was the first woman?	Eve.
Who was the first murderer?	Cain.
Who was the first martyr?	Abel.
Who was the oldest man?	Methuselah.
Who was the meekest man?	Moses.
Who was the strongest man?	Samson.
Who was the wisest man?	Solomon.
Who was in the whale's belly?	Jonah.

The chief piece of resistance in this primer for children was "*The Shorter Catechism*, agreed upon by the Assembly of Divines at Westminster," which filled up twenty-five solid pages of metaphysical theology. I read the first question, "What is the chief end of man?" and the answer, "Man's chief end is to glorify God and enjoy him forever." Most of the remainder I skipped because I failed to understand what it all meant. The New England Primer ended with an eight-page "Dialogue between Christ, A Youth, and the Devil," all in rhyme that passed for poetry.

It was Webster's Spelling Book that finally succeeded the New England Primer in the common schools in New England. Noah Webster himself, born (1758) on a small farm near Hartford, Connecticut, was sent to the common school and well trained on the New England Primer. He was fitted for Yale College by a clergyman, and was graduated from Yale in 1776. After his graduation his strict Puritan father handed him an eight-dollar bill in Continental currency, worth four dollars in silver, saying, "This is all I can afford to give you; take it and earn your own living." Naturally enough he began by teaching in a private school for ten years, but meanwhile finding time to study law and to write a number of schoolbooks, one of which, Webster's American Spelling Book, (1782) had a greater popularity and a longer lease of life than any other elementary schoolbook published in the United States. It is pleasant to remember that the income from this book enabled him to support his family during the long period that he was engaged in compiling that monumental book, Noah Webster's Dictionary. For many years, about the middle of the nineteenth century, the sales of Webster's Spelling Book averaged a million copies a year.

Among numerous other schoolbooks, Noah Webster tried his hand on "The Little Reader's Assistant," published at Northampton, Mass., 1791, at the time he was a schoolmaster in that town. It was a book of one hundred and forty-eight pages, beginning with a series of short stories relating to the history of our own country. Remembering the New England Primer which he studied when a small boy, he put into the middle of this book a catechism, but it was a "Farmer's Catechism" instead of the "Assembly Catechism." I cannot resist the temptation of quoting a few sentences from this first attempt, a century ago, to introduce eight pages about agriculture into a schoolbook.

"THE FARMER'S CATECHISM"

Q. What is the best business a man can do?

Ans. Tilling the ground or farming.

Q. Why is farming the best business?

Ans. Because it is the most necessary, the most healthy, the most innocent, and the most agreeable employment of men.

Q. Why is farming the most innocent employment of men?

Ans. Because farmers have fewer temptations than other men. They have but little dealings with others, so that they have fewer opportunities to cheat than other men. . . .

Q. What is the great art of cultivating the land to advantage?

Ans. It consists in raising the greatest quantity of produce on the smallest quantity of land with the least expense and labor.

My Common-School Training as a Whole

In looking back on my eight years' attendance in a village school, I feel that I was fortunate in falling, each winter term, under the instruction of a superior class of men, some of whom were graduates of Dartmouth College. These teachers made a stronger and deeper impression on me in every way than was made by the young women who taught the summer schools.

In those days it was the teacher's chief duty to hear textbook lessons, and the chief end of the pupils was to memorize the textbook and assimilate the matter as best they could. It was assumed that whatever a child could repeat from memory, he could also understand by intuition.

We had no nature study, no drawing, no singing, no composition writing. But we learned to spell correctly, to read well, and to write a legible hand. We were thoroughly drilled in Colburn's Intellectual Arithmetic, and poorly trained in written arithmetic, which we pursued on the individual system. Whenever we "got stuck on a hard sum," we were allowed to ask some older boy to show us how to do it. We worked as hard as we could, and our chief aim was to get through the book. With each new teacher we began the textbook with addition, and never ciphered further than cube root or alligation. John Batchelder, the oldest boy in school, was my coach in arithmetic. He was a descendant of the Batchelders of Hampton, of tough English stock. When he became of age, he emigrated to Illinois, bought a farm, and ten years later persuaded his younger brothers to follow his example.

One vital defect in our study of arithmetic was that we had no training whatever in accuracy. I am certain that no one of our teachers ever once mentioned the importance of careful and accurate work. There was no blackboard in school, and no teacher ever gave us any drill outside of the printed pages.

In geography the teacher seldom asked us a question not printed in the book; seldom ventured on any kind of an explanation, or gave us a supplementary idea. In front of the schoolhouse there ran a beautiful river, but no teacher ever called our attention to it. Right before our eyes a picturesque mountain rose to the height of twelve hundred feet, but no teacher ever mentioned it, or ever suggested that we should climb to its summit and see how the surface of the earth looked.

We were well trained in textbook grammar and parsing, but we had no exercises in writing our mother tongue. The teachers kept no record of checks or credits. We had no written examinations, but in spelling and Colburn's Mental Arithmetic we recited in class, and were stimulated by trying to get to the head of the class. We were so thoroughly drilled on Webster's Spelling Book, in oral spelling and pronunciation, that, in after life spelling with me became automatic, with little occasion for reference to a dictionary. One good result of this general method of memorizing textbook lessons without explanation was a fixed habit of finding out by myself the meaning of the printed page, and as in after life my education was largely obtained from books and reading outside of schools, this habit became of vital importance to me.

The school discipline was reasonably strict, but not severe. Of corporal punishment there was very little, and that only in cases of insubordination. I was never whipped and was seldom reprimanded in school. Never once in my school life was I "kept in" after school hours to study an unlearned lesson. I always liked to study, and I had a strong Puritan sense of duty. I was never absent from school except for sickness. Truancy from school was unheard of, fighting was unknown. We had ample grounds for playing ball. We had in summer the Suncook River for a swimming pool, and in winter the neighboring mill pond for a skating rink. Coasting and snowballing were our winter amusements. On the whole, we enjoyed life, liked to go to school, studied our lessons, and memorized books. Our only special training in morals and religion was the morning opening exercise in reading the New Testament, each pupil reading in turn a single "verse." Neither note nor comment was made by the teacher.

But my home training was a most important supplement to my school instruction. My father taught me to write, and gave me occasional lessons in arithmetic. I was neither petted nor indulged, though always treated with kind consideration and sterling common sense. Though never overworked, I was required to do my share in the daily chores about the house and farm. On Saturdays I was allowed to visit some of my numerous cousins, or to go a-fishing in the Suncook River. On Sundays I always went with my father and mother to the Congregational meetinghouse, and enjoyed the going. The church was a social institution, and my chats with other boys during the "noon intermission" were more attractive to me than were the long theological discourses of the minister. After attending church, my father and mother often went out, in summertime, to walk in the woods or pastures, and took me along. There was nothing of the old Puritan hardness in our way of life. On Sunday morning my father read aloud a chapter from the Bible and made a family prayer, and this was the only religious service in the family. Even the custom of saying grace at meals had gone out of use. I was not drilled on the Assembly Catechism, nor shut up in the house on the Sabbath, nor prematurely crammed with metaphysical theology.

In fact, during my boyhood I was surrounded by liberal influences. My grandfather Swett was a sturdy disbeliever in witches, ghosts, and devils, and to him and my father I owe a special debt of gratitude that my young life was not darkened by superstitious beliefs. Though my father was a religious man, he declined to join the church because he could not subscribe to all the dogmas of the creed. My mother was a church member, but was never troubled about theological metaphysics. My grandfather Swett was a Universalist; my grandmother Swett was a Freewill Baptist; my grandfather French, a Calvin Baptist, and my grandmother French, a Congregationalist. I attended many revival meetings, camp meetings, and "protracted meetings," but none of them made any deep impression on me. Yet I was a serious-minded boy who thought about religion, but was in revolt against dogmatic Puritan theology. Some years later a series of tract-sermons, by William Ellery Channing, fell into my hands, and thereafter I called myself a Unitarian, though for years I generally attended the Congregationol church.

I have a vivid recollection of one incident which affords a striking illustration of the old-time manner of introducing to young boys the subject of religion. Our minister, a profound and solemn theologian, asked the boys of his society to meet him one Sunday afternoon in the vestry of the meetinghouse. After making a prayer, the minister plunged at once into his subject. He called up the first boy and said: "Thomas, do you think you have experienced religion?" "Yes, sir," was the conventional reply. Similar questions were put to each boy in turn, and each boy answered, "Yes, sir." It happened that I was the last boy in the line. The boy next above me was known as the wickedest boy in the school, but he told the minister that he had been converted at the last camp meeting, and that he had repented of his sins and was now a Christian. At first I thought that I would tell the truth and say, "No, sir;" but when the minister called on me and said in a solemn tone, "John, have you any reason to think that you have experienced a change of heart?" my courage failed me. I could not face the disgrace of being the only unregenerate sinner in the class, and so answered in a faint voice, "Yes, sir." I went home from that meeting ashamed of myself because I had lacked the courage to tell the truth. This was the first cold-blooded, deliberate lie that I can remember of telling, and I cannot help feeling at this remote time that the minister led me into temptation.

Up to the age of twelve years my life had been one of unclouded happiness, but now there fell upon me the darkness of a great bereavement. My father was taken down with an attack of typhoid fever, and after a few days of delirium passed away from us at the early age of forty-three years. After his death, for many weeks I wandered around the farm, refusing to be comforted. The burden of a great anxiety fell upon me, for I realized that I must look out for myself and make my own way in the world.

My father had always treated me with tenderness, consideration, and justice, seeming to have an intuitive perception of the shyness of a boy's nature. He trained me to work, but gave me ample freedom for play. He looked on the sunny side of life, and his manifold kindness to me made me contented, happy, hopeful, and obedient. He never had occasion to whip me, and I can recall only one reprimand. He had received a good common-school education, supplemented by a number of terms at an academy, and by teaching for several winters in district schools. His strong taste for reading educated him all through his life. He was for years the town clerk of Pittsfield, and was repeatedly elected as one of the three selectmen. He was genial in manner, social in disposition, temperate in his habits, and just in all his dealings. He was a man given to religious thought, and was for many years the teacher of a large Bible class of adults in the Congregational church. He took an active interest in the village Lyceum, or debating society, in the common schools, and in all other social and town affairs. His library was a limited one, but was larger and better than that of most other farmers in town. In his business affairs he was careful and prudent, but was not over-economical, and money-making was not a passion with him.

The Age of Homespun

A good illustration of the manner in which a New England farmer lived near the close of the "homespun age" is afforded by one of my father's account books, which begins with the year of his marriage (1829) and continues for five years. Every item of expense and income is here entered in detail. The balance of receipts and expenses runs as follows:

Year ending	Receipts	Expenses
Nov., 1830	$ 123.85	$118.41
1831	372.57	222.80
1832	182.40	134.85
1833	187.69	228.71
1834	235.33	137.16
1835	324.36	123.24
	$1426.20	$965.17

In no year, except in 1833, did the family expenses outrun the income, and the total of small savings during the six years amounted to $461.03. The account book from 1835 to the time of his death was unfortunately lost. The items of the above account show that the family lived chiefly on the products of the farm. Wheat and corn supplied the breadstuffs; beef, mutton, pork, and poultry were home products; tea, coffee, sugar, and spices were imported luxuries. The woolen clothing worn in winter was chiefly of domestic manufacture. My own winter clothing, up to the age of twelve, was spun and woven by my mother, and the cloth sent to the fulling mill to be fulled and dyed. My mother was an expert weaver of both woolen and linen cloth. She knit woolen stockings for the family, and also for sale in the market for the purchase of gowns and millinery. In all families knitting was the steady occupation of women during the long winter evenings. This old account book shows the prudent management by which I was left, after my father's death, with means to enable me to acquire a fair academic education. My father's estate was appraised at fifteen hundred dollars.[1]

[1] It seems fitting to close this chapter with a quotation from Horace Bushnell's "Secular Sermon" on the "Age of Homespun," delivered at the centennial celebration of Litchfield County, Connecticut, 1851.

"In these olden times, these genuine days of homespun, they supposed, in their simplicity, that thrift represented work, and looked about seldom for any more delicate and sharper way of getting on. They did not call a man's property his *fortune*, but they spoke of one another as being *worth* so much, conceiving that he had laid it up as the reward or fruit of his deservings. The house was a factory on the farm; the farm, a grower and producer for the house.

"It was also a great point in this homespun mode of life, that it imparted exactly what many speak of only with contempt, a closely girded habit of economy. Harnessed all together in the producing process, young and old, male and female, from the boy that rode the plow-horse to the grandmother knitting under her spectacles, they had no conception of squandering lightly what they had all been at work, thread by thread, and grain by grain, to produce. Men of patrimony in the great world, therefore, noticing their small way of trade or expenditure, are ready to charge them with meanness, simply because they knew things only in the small. Still, this knowing things only in the small, it will be found, is anything but meanness. It will be found that children brought up in this way, to know things in the small, what they cost and what is their value, have, in just that fact, one of the best securities of character, and most certain elements of power and success in life. When the hard, wiry-looking patriarch of homespun, for example, sets off for Hartford or Bridgeport, to exchange the little surplus of his year's production, carrying his provision with him, and the fodder for his team, and taking his boy along to show him the great world, you may laugh at the simplicity, or pity, if you will, the sordid look of the picture, but, five or ten years hence, this boy will probably enough be found in college digging out the cent's worth of his father's money in hard study; and some twenty years later, he will be returning in his honors, as the celebrated judge, or governor, or senator and public orator, from some one of the great States of the Republic, to bless the sight, once more, of that venerated pair who shaped his beginning and planted the small seeds of his future success."—*Work and Play*, by Horace Bushnell. New York: Charles Scribner, 1864.

CHAPTER IV

PITTSFIELD ACADEMY; MR. EDWIN F. SHERMAN, THE IDEAL PRINCIPAL; MY VACATION WAGES

THE earlier endowed academies in New England were established, like the Boston Latin school, for the special purpose of fitting boys for college. They were denominational institutions, designed in the main to perpetuate the orthodox religious faith of the fathers. Among these were the Dummer Academy at Byfield (1762); the Phillips-Andover Academy in Massachusetts (1780); and the Phillips-Exeter Academy in New Hampshire (1781).

Soon after the adoption of the Constitution, the New England states, in common with other states in the Union, entered upon what is called the "age of academies." The decadent grammar schools died out by slow degrees, and were replaced by small rural academies, most of which were under denominational control, though, in general, somewhat liberal in spirit. Most of these secondary schools were supported by tuition fees, though the buildings were generally erected by subscriptions or by small bequests. These new academies provided a classical course to fit boys for college, and also a general elective course for both boys and girls, intended as an outfit for the ordinary pursuits of life.

For half a century these academies supplemented the district common schools by giving great numbers of young men and young women a fair equipment for their work in life. After the academies had fulfilled their mission, they also went into decadence soon after the middle of the nineteenth century. The rapid increase in wealth and in population, the rise of manufacturing towns, villages, and cities, the general advancement in science and in literature, together with the spread of liberal ideas and the rising tide of democracy, all united in gradually bringing about the general establishment of high schools supported by public taxation, in which young men and young women were placed on a footing of equality in education. Thus, in the course of two centuries, the colonial dame schools, with their petty tuition fees of a penny a day, had developed into free primary schools; the Latin grammar schools had been largely superseded by the English grammar schools, in which English grammar was taught instead of Latin; the academies were largely superseded by free high schools with both a classical course and an English course of study.

It was in accord with the spirit of the times that, in 1829, half a century after the first common school in Pittsfield had opened its doors to all the children, both "mayle and femaile," the people contributed lumber, labor, and money for the erection of an academy building. Everybody lent a hand. The building was dedicated in 1830, the year in which I was born. The population of the town at this time was a little less than one thousand inhabitants, — a homogeneous people, exclusively of English Puritan descent. They were neither rich nor poor. Agriculture was the leading occupation. The small farms ranged in value from one thousand to three thousand dollars. The farmer freeholders worked hard, lived frugally, and stood in town meeting on a broad footing of democratic equality in respect to property as well as to

The Old Academy, 1845

The Swett Homestead

suffrage. The richest man in town was supposed to be worth from five to ten thousand dollars.

The academy opened in October, 1830, with an attendance of forty-eight students, seventeen young women and thirty-one young men. My grandfather, Abraham French, was a member of the first board of trustees. In the course of time several small bequests were made to the school, which served to keep the building in repair. This institution was maintained for sixty-five years as an academy, and was then transformed into a free public high school.

After my father's death, my mother and I continued to live on the farm for nearly a year. I went to school and took care of the cattle during the winter. In the following spring the farm was leased, and my mother and myself went to board with my uncle, John F. French, who lived on the French homestead on the edge of Pittsfield village. My grandfather and grandmother French lived in the main house, and my uncle and his wife in the added wing, the families being entirely separate. Individualism was too strong to admit of coöperative housekeeping. My uncle, educated in common school and academy, managed the farm in summer, and worked in winter at making shoes for the Lynn manufacturers. His wife, Aunt Ruth, one of the smartest of housekeepers, besides doing her housework, earned ready money by binding shoes for the Lynn manufacturers. In this pleasant home my life began to brighten.

It was into Pittsfield academy that I entered in the fall term of 1844, a sensitive, diffident, thoughtful, studious boy, who had no marked talent, but who read every book that he could get hold of.

The preceptor, or principal, of the academy was Edwin

F. Sherman, a graduate of Dartmouth College, and a law student. He was an ideal teacher, who knew how to waken boys and girls into intellectual life. He talked with us; he explained things; he was human. He took a lively interest in our games of ball out of doors, as well as in our lessons in the schoolroom. I can picture him to this day as he stood at the blackboard explaining some problem in arithmetic or algebra, in manner easy, graceful, and animated. My studies were Porter's Rhetorical Reader, Adams's Arithmetic, Day's Algebra, Smith's Grammar, composition, and declamation. I have preserved to this day a complete file of my compositions during this first term; and I hold in memory extracts from Webster's speeches, which I declaimed with fear and trembling on that high academy platform before the eyes of the assembled students. We were required to write a composition every other week, but without a hint, suggestion, or word of advice from the teacher as to what we should write about, and without any instruction whatever in "the art of writing the English language with propriety," which was assumed to have been learned by studying Smith's Grammar. In my youthful dearth of ideas I consulted my cousin, Matilda Swett, several years older than myself, who had attended the academy and had learned how to write compositions. She selected "Spring" for a subject and under it wrote two or three sentences for a beginning. I added three or four sentences of my own, ending with the following philosophic aphorism: "Spring reminds us of the springtime of our life, when we should study to improve ourselves instead of spending our time in idleness."

After this first collaborated composition I fell back on my own resources, selected less abstract subjects, and succeeded better. I have now before me on the table a file of these exercises in good preservation. The subjects range as follows: "A Husking;" "Town Meeting Day;" "Indian Corn;" "The Early Settlement of New England;" "A Militia Training Day." These papers contain few misspelled words and few blunders in grammar. The improvement in each succeeding composition shows that I derived some benefit even from unguided attempts in writing. We were required to go upon the platform and read our compositions before the assembled school, and this public reading was dreaded more than the laborious act of writing.

We were also required to be prepared with declamations, but no hint whatever was given as to what kind of selections we should make, and no training whatever was given in elocution. How it happened I do not know, but I began of my own accord to select, from Lovell's United States Speaker short extracts from the speeches of Daniel Webster. Our drill book in oral reading was Porter's Rhetorical Reader, which we read and re-read until I knew many of the gems of literature by heart. The many short extracts from Milton's "Paradise Lost" stick in my memory to this day. It seems to me that those Friday afternoon exercises in composition and declamation constituted a very important part of my earlier training, for when I began my lifework I was required not only to express my thoughts in print but to speak from the public platform. During this first term at the academy, I was a silent outside member of a class of older students in Abercrombie's Mental Philosophy; for I was an attentive listener to the recitations, which were made interesting by the anecdotes and by the illustrations of Mr. Sherman. Next term I began to study Comstock's Natural Philosophy, which I pursued with intense interest, reciting in a large class instructed by the "preceptress," a sister of preceptor Sherman.

In 1844 my mother became the second wife of William Berry, whose first wife was my mother's sister, Mary French. By this marriage I was introduced into a family of three cousins, two of whom were boys, one a year younger than myself, the other one year older. We three boys attended school together.

After teaching two years, Mr. Sherman left us to begin the practice of law in the city of Lowell. We all regretted to have him go. His successor was a theological student preparing for the ministry. He was in every way a contrast to Mr. Sherman. He was stiff in manner, was never seen to smile, and he made no explanations. I studied hard but without my former enthusiasm. In an old memorandum book I find the following entries: "March 1, 1845. Spring term at the academy. Forty scholars. My studies are Andrews's Latin Grammar and Reader, Davies's Geometry, Day's Algebra, Comstock's Chemistry, parsing in 'Young's Night Thoughts.' "

During the summer vacation I worked out as a hired boy on the farm of Smith R. Berry on Catamount, and received, according to an old memorandum book that I kept, $7.75, for thirty-four days' work. This rate of wages now seems low, but it was the current rate of 1845. This sum was sufficient to buy my books for the next term at the academy. My memorandum shows that during the autumn term my studies were Latin, Burrett's Geography of the Heavens, chemistry, algebra, and geometry; that I had not missed a day; and that I was in excellent health. At the end of this term our teacher silently flitted away to a theological school. He was a good man, but was lacking in tact.

Our next principal was a law student, a graduate of Dartmouth. He was a scholarly man but an indifferent teacher, who heard our book recitations but neither criticized nor commended us.

During my attendance in Pittsfield Academy I read all the books I could borrow, but the number was small. In this school there was no library whatever, not even an English dictionary for reference. The first dictionary I ever used was Leverett's Latin Lexicon. Rollins's Ancient History fell into my hands and I waded through every dreary page of it. Then came Josephus, and next an antique history of England which I discovered in my grandfather's bookcase. The Boston *Journal* was my weekly newspaper.

At this period of my boyhood I began to entertain dim hopes of being able to go to Dartmouth College, though I said nothing about it. None of my relatives or friends had ever given me a word of advice about going to college or about what I should do to earn a living. After my father's death I was left to decide things for myself.

After the close of the spring term I went to work for my uncle, Charles French, who had rented the Swett farm. While helping him repair a piece of stone wall I sprained my back so severely that I was disabled from work. The change from school to farm work had been too sudden. Up to this time I had been tough, hardy, and strong, but this accident handicapped me for life. I went home and sent for Dr. Warren, but his treatment gave me no immediate relief. I felt a constant desire to draw a long breath, but was unable to get it. I lost my appetite, became weak and low-spirited, and was a wretched invalid during the whole summer. For several months, on account of weak eyes, I could not even read; but during that depressing period my mother placed me under a great debt of gratitude by her patient kindness in reading aloud to me. This weary period of invalidism arrested my growth at a critical period of my life and left me with impaired digestion and broken health.

In the cool weather of autumn I began to gather strength, and fortunately my aunt, Mrs. Mary (Swett) Brewster, who resided in Salem, Massachusetts, invited me to make her a visit of three months. With a change of surroundings and a cheerful family of cousins, my spirits returned and my health improved. The old city of Salem greatly interested me. My cousins attended Master Lackey's famous grammar school for boys. After a visit to the school I fully realized the severity of discipline which had been handed down from early Puritan times. I visited Gallows Hill, where witches were hanged in the dark days of this typical Puritan town. On Sundays I listened to the sermons of Dr. Worcester, a typical Congregational minister. My uncle, Ira A. Brewster, was a lineal descendant of Elder Brewster, one of the Pilgrim Fathers. My aunt Mary, an intellectual woman, was deeply interested in the antislavery movement.

The following winter I remained at home, reading and studying by myself. The succeeding spring and summer I worked out with the neighboring farmers as a hired hand in planting, plowing, and haying. I was not robust, but I always managed to keep up with the other hands, making up in will power what I lacked in muscular strength.

Here is a report of my work and wages in detail, taken from a little pocket memorandum book which I kept at that time, and have carefully treasured ever since:

AN ACCOUNT OF MY WORK IN 1847.

April	By 3 days' work at Wm. Lane's	$ .75
	2 days' work at Col. Batchelder's	.80
May 21	2½ days' planting at Col. Batchelder's	1.00
May 24	1 day's driving cattle, Isaiah Berry	.25
May 26	3 days' planting, Isaiah Berry	1.25
June 4	2 days' work on road, Isaiah Berry	.83
June 5	1 day's planting, J. B. Berry	.42
June 10	2 days' hoeing, John French	1.00
June 17	5½ days' shingling for Wm. Lane	2.75
June 25	3½ days' hoeing at Wm. Lane's	1.75
July 3	3 days' haying at Col. Batchelder's	1.50
July 5	1 day's hoeing, Abram French	.50
July 6	1 day's haying, Col. Batchelder's	.50
July 18	6 days' haying, Isaiah Berry	3.00
July	4½ days' haying, Wm. Lane's	2.25
July 23	1½ days' haying, Wm. Lane's	.75
Aug. 7	4 days' haying, Isaiah Berry's	2.00
		$21.30

CHAPTER V

STUDENT AND TEACHER

WITH a little hard-earned money of my own, and a small amount added by my guardian and stepfather, I made up my mind to attend the fall term of the academy at Pembroke, on the Merrimac River, six miles south of Concord. This institution, among the earliest of endowed academies in New Hampshire, was founded by the Reverend Abel Blanchard (1818) with a bequest of twenty-five hundred dollars. Though not largely endowed, it has maintained its existence up to the present time, and has fitted large numbers of students for Dartmouth College. This school had a classical course to fit students for Dartmouth College, and elective English courses for other students. When I appeared before the preceptor, Jonathan Tenney, a graduate of Dartmouth, I told him my story, and with him selected my studies, omitting Latin on account of the weakness of one of my eyes, the result of scarlet fever. My elective studies included rhetoric and composition (Parker's Aids to Composition), Davies's Algebra, Davies's Geometry, and Cutter's Physiology. In pursuing rhetoric and composition under the personal instruction of Principal Tenney I began to learn how to express my thoughts in writing. The students organized a debating society and started a weekly manuscript paper, of which I was made editor-in-chief. From our scanty means we also contributed money to buy books, and made the beginning of a small library; for up to this time there had never been a volume in the library room. It had not been supposed that any books except school textbooks were desirable. Pembroke Academy, like Pittsfield Academy, was open to young women, and their attendance made the meetings of our debating society doubly interesting.

And now there began a new phase of my education. One day, near the close of the term, a school trustee from a neighboring district applied to preceptor Tenney for a teacher during the coming winter term. On Mr. Tenney's urgent recommendation and advice I entered into an engagement, at "ten dollars a month and board," to teach the Buck Street school, situated two miles from Pembroke Academy, on the banks of the Suncook River not far from its junction with the Merrimac. Up to this time I had never thought of becoming a teacher; but I bought a copy of "The School and the Schoolmaster," by George B. Emerson and Alonzo D. Potter, and began to study methods of teaching. To prepare for the examination necessary to secure a certificate, I made a cram on arithmetic, grammar, and geography. In due time, in company with several other candidates, I appeared before the school committee, which consisted of the Reverend Abraham Burnham and Deacon Vose. We were asked to define "arithmetic, multiplication, a fraction," and to reckon interest on a promissory note for a given time. In grammar the chief question was: "Into what four parts is English grammar divided?" We were each asked to spell orally two or three words, and to pronounce "gewgaw." We were then required to file with the board of examiners a certificate of good moral character from some minister who knew us. With this our examination was ended. My certificate ran as follows:

This certifies, that we have examined Mr. John Swett in respect to his qualifications to teach the various branches required to be taught by a schoolmaster in the district schools in this State, and are of opinion, that he is qualified according to law.

(Signed) FRANCIS VOSE,
A. BURNHAM,
Superintending School Committee of Pembroke.

PEMBROKE, NOV. 24, 1847.

My boarding place was in the family of the school trustee, which consisted of himself, an elderly bachelor, Rodney Carlton by name, and two sisters, elderly maiden ladies, named respectively Achsa and Amelia. The established price for boarding a schoolmaster was six dollars a month, which sum was drawn from the town treasurer by the trustee himself, thus making sure of his payment.

The schoolhouse was a neat and comfortable one-room building, in which I found assembled about thirty pupils, the youngest of whom was eight years old, and the eldest, twenty-one years. But most of them were pupils of marked ability, and it was a pleasure to teach them. The school was without maps or charts, or even a dictionary for reference. As no pupil had ever seen a school globe, I asked one of my big boys, Horace Towne, who worked in a mill where there was a lathe for woodwork, to turn a six-inch globe for me. I ruled this globe for meridians and parallels, outlined carefully the continents, oceans, and large islands, fitted in the poles, and varnished the whole. This inexpensive piece of apparatus I used in all my classes in geography with good results. I took it with me when, afterwards, I went to teach in Massachusetts, where I found a school also destitute of a map, chart, globe, or reference dictionary. If I was not skilled in psychological methods, I was full of enthusiasm tempered by common sense. My whole ambition centered on my school, and the people appreciated the fact.

There was no occasion to resort to corporal punishment in maintaining discipline, for I succeeded in interesting the pupils in their work. I skated with the big boys on the mill pond and took part with them in snowballing. The schoolhouse had no ventilator, and I immediately borrowed tools and arranged a window to lower from the top. An economical taxpayer, who thought this involved an unnecessary waste of fuel, nailed up the window at night; but I drew out the nails and lowered it again. When I last saw that schoolhouse, many years afterwards, the window was still lowered.

One morning, on my way to school, I bowed to a farmer driving past, who sang out, "My boy, who teaches your school this winter?" "A cross old man by the name of Swett," I replied. He told this story at the grocery store, and "Old Swett" passed into a proverb in the district, though I was then only seventeen years old.

The people of this district were so well pleased with my teaching that they hired me to continue the term for six weeks longer, paying my wages by subscription. To me the winter's work was worth more, as an educative power, than any one year at the academy, because it developed character and strengthened self-reliance and decision. When the term closed, the people insisted on a conditional promise that I would return and teach their school the following winter. I returned to Pembroke Academy and pursued my studies under Mr. Tenney's instruction during the spring and summer, and then went back to the Buck Street school and taught during the winter term of

JOHN SWETT
AS A YOUNG TEACHER AGED SEVENTEEN
From an old daguerreotype, 1847

four months, supplemented by a rate-bill term of six weeks. In the printed town reports my school received "honorable mention" as one of the best in town, for each of the two years.

Many of the pupils in this school afterwards attended Pembroke Academy for a few terms, and they emigrated to the West, where they made good records. One of them, Irad Cochran, went to California, and thence to New Mexico, where he became a wealthy ranch owner. He shipped his live stock to his younger brother, another of my boys, who became the successful manager of a stock-yard in the city of Chicago. Another promising boy, Horace Towne, married the most scholarly girl in school, a sister of the boys just mentioned, and emigrated to California, making a success in life. Three other pupils moved with their father and mother to Illinois.

Manual Training on a Farm

In the spring of 1848 I began a three months' course of manual training on the farm of one of my numerous uncles. This interchange of academy, school-teaching, and farm work was continued for several years, not from special love of manual labor, but as a physical training which I thought my constitution needed. Nevertheless I chafed under the lack of mental stimulus, though I found time on rainy days to keep up my reading in literature and history. Some books I bought, others I borrowed. A complete file of the New York *Knickerbocker Magazine* was placed in my hands by Mrs. Martha (Cilley) Berry, and was carefully read from beginning to end. This reading was the foundation of a lifelong taste for magazine literature. Some years later I became a sporadic contributor of fugitive articles to the *Knickerbocker Magazine*, and some other publications. The New York *Weekly Tribune* and the Boston *Weekly Journal* gave me news of the world and the politics of the time. Shakespeare, Scott, and Burns, constituted a part of my reading in literature. There never was a day that I did not find at least half an hour for reading. On rainy days, when there was no outdoor work, I read most of the time. It was at this time that I began to find floating around in the newspapers a few of John G. Whittier's poems, quite a number of which I committed to memory as I worked alone in the field.

During this season I received the customary wages for farm work,— eight dollars a month. My uncle, Enoch French, was a house carpenter, who, when a young man, had worked at his trade in the city of Boston. He was a man of marked intelligence and of genial manner. His son, John Cate French, about my own age, had learned to make Lynn shoes, and was at work with another man, Elder Harvey, in a small shoe shop on the farm. I was entirely at home in this pleasant family and my cousin seemed to me like a brother. This cousin of mine, after an attendance for several terms at Gilmanton Academy and at Pembroke, organized the New Hampshire Fire Insurance Company at Manchester, and became one of the notable business men of the state.

In the autumn of 1848 I gladly returned to academic study at Pembroke. A classmate and myself tried the experiment of hiring a room and boarding ourselves, as a measure of protection against the conventional boarding-house diet of hot biscuit and pie. Aided by frequent relays of provisions from home, we thrived on a Spartan diet, but did not repeat the experiment a second term. What little skill I acquired in cooking proved useful to me a few years later. Athletic exercises were not in vogue in the academies of this period, though military drill was introduced into a few schools. For exercise I took long tramps over the surrounding country. In fact, many schools of that period recognized the existence of mind only, and ignored the body as of little worth. Dr. A. D. Mayo, speaking of the schools, academies, and colleges of this period in New England, characterized them as "slaughter pens of young men." It was during this term that I made my first appearance in print by contributing several articles of prose and verse to the Boston *Cultivator* under the signature of "Jack." The debating society flourished, and I continued to edit the manuscript paper.

My studies this term, according to the best of my recollection, were Davies's Trigonometry and Surveying, rhetoric, chemistry, geology, and astronomy. I also took special lessons in elocution under Professor Wilson, who had been trained by Professor William Russell. Mr. Tenney was preceptor, Mr. McKean, associate principal. In the study of geology I took unbounded satisfaction, making long tramps over the country for the purpose of collecting minerals. Hitchcock's Geology was the textbook. More than any other natural science, geology has had for me lifelong attractions. Wherever I have traveled I have made a study of geological features, and through modern textbooks have kept abreast of the marvelous development of this science. Trigonometry and surveying I took hold of with delight, probably on account of a thread of heredity running back to my grandmother French's family, the Lanes.

I learned textbook chemistry, supplemented with a course of lectures and experiments by a professor of chemistry from Concord. Of astronomy I learned enough to awaken an interest that led me to become a reader of later textbooks, thus following up the rapid advances made in modern astronomy. Burrett's Geography of the Heavens was the textbook in use.

Besides the "orthodox" academy which I attended, there was in Pembroke a "liberal" institution known as the "Gymnasium," or "Military Institute," which was at that time under the management of Captain Alden Patridge, formerly of the Vermont Military Academy. There had been for some years a bitter feud between these two academic institutions, and the students were not on speaking terms. By some accident I made the acquaintance of three students in the military school, — Joseph C. Morrill, Thomas McConnell, and John F. Rowell — and we soon brought about an era of good feeling by extending an invitation to the students of the rival school to attend one of the meetings of our debating society. The students came in full blaze of uniforms and brass buttons. This meeting led to an interchange of courtesies. In turn, they invited us to a dance. Thereafter there was peace as long as we remained at school, but soon after we left the old feuds were revived. Thomas McConnell, Scotch-Irish by descent, was a gigantic Vermonter, six feet three inches in height, who presented, in military uniform, a most imposing figure. After leaving Pembroke he emigrated to California, where he became a wealthy farmer and stock grower.

Teaching in Massachusetts

In the winter of 1849–50 I secured a school in West Randolph, a town adjacent to Quincy, about fifteen miles from Boston. This engagement I owed to the kindness of Nehemiah C. Berry, an attorney-at-law, who resided in West Randolph and had a law office in Boston. He took an interest in me because, when a boy in Pittsfield, he had been a pupil in the district school taught by my father.

Accordingly, I filed my certificate of good moral character from the Congregational minister of Pittsfield, passed an oral examination before Aaron Prescott, chairman of the school committee, and secured a certificate valid for the winter term. When I entered the law office of Mr. Berry, one of the school committee, he was examining Greene's First Lessons in Grammar, then a new book, which he said the committee would adopt. He handed the book to me, and I welcomed it as an improved method of teaching English grammar.

West Randolph was then, and is now, a thriving town entirely devoted to the manufacture of shoes. My school was "District No. 1," at the south end of the village. The schoolhouse, in size and plan, was a counterpart of that on Buck Street in Pembroke, New Hampshire. My first innovation was to borrow some tools and provide for the lowering of a window from the top to secure ventilation. I found the school numbering from thirty to forty pupils, ungraded, and in scholarship somewhat behind the pupils of my New Hampshire school, from the fact that the endowed Stetson High School in the town had taken off the older pupils. My pay was sixteen dollars a month and board. I boarded in the family of John Belcher, the district trustee, or "prudential committeeman," who drew from the town treasury eight dollars a month for my board. As was the custom at that time, I built the fire and swept the schoolhouse. School was opened, as required by law, with the reading of the New Testament without note or comment by the teacher. The school was provided with a record book of attendance, designed by Horace Mann, and supplied by the State Board of Education. I recall nothing of interest in the uneventful course of the winter term. There was one girl of promise in the school who ciphered through Greenleaf's Arithmetic. As this book was new to me, I spent many wearisome evenings in working out the puzzling problems in "miscellaneous examples" at the end of the book. Had I failed on any one of these, my reputation as a scholar would have been ruined.

During the winter I had the good fortune to attend a course of lectures by Ralph Waldo Emerson, Theodore Parker, and E. P. Whipple. Ralph Waldo Emerson was the first great thinker that I had ever heard speak, and his lecture on "Power" impressed me so strongly that I took brief notes and afterwards wrote out all of it I could recall. This report I still have among my papers. It is hardly necessary to mention that, after hearing this lecture, I read all newspaper reports of Emerson's lectures, and bought each succeeding volume of his essays as it appeared in print. To me, as to hundreds of other New England boys, Emerson was an inspiring power. Theodore Parker's lecture led me to read many of his published lectures and sermons. E. P. Whipple's lecture on "Webster, Clay, and Calhoun" was a masterpiece of political and personal characterization. This lecture, some years later, appeared in a volume of "Whipple's Essays." About this time I attended a theater for the first time in my life and saw that great actor, the elder Booth, as Shylock in "The Merchant of Venice."

During this term I attended a teachers' institute held for two days in a neighboring town. Most of the time was devoted to discussing methods of teaching arithmetic, particular emphasis being placed on a new method of finding the least common multiple of numbers by resolving them into prime factors. There were no lectures, and the proceedings were uninteresting and unprofitable. Teachers' institutes, inaugurated by Horace Mann, were then in their infancy. Not a word was said about Horace Mann, or the great reforms which he had advocated during the eight years that he was secretary of the State Board of Education. Indeed, at this time, Horace Mann was regarded by many of the old-type schoolmasters as a dangerous educational fanatic.

Near the end of the term two members of the examining committee passed half a day giving my school an oral examination. One member of this committee was the master of the Stetson High School, and he examined my second class of three pupils in arithmetic. His first and only question was, "Give an explanation of the reason for inverting the divisor in division of fractions." The explanation given by the pupils was the identical explanation given in Greenleaf's Arithmetic, but it was pronounced unsatisfactory by the questioner. I took sides with the pupils, and the matter was dropped. The committee reported the school well taught and in good condition.

After the close of my school, in accordance with a suggestion from my physician, I made a visit to a former

Pembroke student by the name of Bailey, who lived at Rockport on Cape Ann. His father was a fisherman, through whose influence I secured, after several weeks' delay, a chance to "work my way" on board a mackerel schooner during the season. While waiting, I made a visit to Provincetown, and explored a part of Cape Cod. Our first trip was a run of three weeks off the coast, during which time we caught only a few barrels of fish. The sea air was bracing, but the diet, consisting mainly of hot shortcake, — a compound of corn meal, lard, and molasses, — was enough to ruin the digestion of an ostrich. On the Fourth of July, when the schooner put into Rockport, I told the captain he could have my "lay" of the mackerel, and that I would not go out on the next trip.

I was glad to return to Pembroke during the fall term of the academy. My revered friend, Mr. Tenney, had been succeeded by Nathaniel Hills, a graduate of Dartmouth, a quiet, thoughtful, and faithful teacher. He persuaded me to take charge of certain classes in the preparatory department for three hours daily, under the high-sounding title of "associate principal." The management of the elocutionary and composition exercises was also assigned to me. Preceptor Hills also asked me to hear the recitations of a class of three young ladies who wanted to study chemistry. I told him that my knowledge of that subject was limited, and that I was not competent to teach it. "Never mind," he said, "you know more about it than they do, and as there is no chemical apparatus, all you will have to do is to hear them recite their textbook lessons. Besides, there is no one else to take the class. It is a case of necessity." I took the class. No great harm was done. Two of the girls cared nothing about the subject but took it because it was the conventional thing to do. The third young lady was a student, and she probably derived some benefit from the textbook.

My roommate this term was John B. Sanborn, a splendid specimen of robust manhood, who began fitting for college when twenty-two years of age. He had an iron constitution and could study fourteen hours a day. We two constituted the entire class in Logic and in Butler's Analogy. We had ample time for discussion, and we often differed from the textbooks and the teacher. I took special lessons in French from the preceptress, Miss Carr, and special lessons in elocution from Professor Wilson. For the rest, I did some reading in English literature, though debarred from reading by lamplight on account of the weakness of one of my eyes. I took charge of the closing exhibition, wrote a burlesque farce entitled "The Mesmerizer," and took the leading part in the play. On the valedictory, which was assigned to me, I put forth my best efforts, because I felt a presentiment that I should not again return to Pembroke.

School over, I at once started off on a long foot tramp in the hill regions of New Hampshire. I passed through Salisbury, where I saw the Webster farm; climbed Mt. Kearsarge, and slept one cold night on its summit in the open air under a granite ledge; visited a friend in New London; tramped around the Ossipee Mountains and Lake Winnepesaukee; visited a school friend at Nottingham, and then walked home through Deerfield and Epsom to Pittsfield.

During the winter of 1850 I was again employed to teach the school in District No. 1, West Randolph, at sixteen dollars a month with board. There was a new committeeman, John Wales, in whose family I found a delightful home. Before beginning school it was necessary for me to pass another oral examination and to file another certificate of good moral character. My certificate ran as follows:

RANDOLPH, 30th November, 1850.

This certifies that Mr. John Swett of Pittsfield, N. H., has been approbated as a teacher in the school of District No. 1 in this Town for the winter term, of this current municipal year, to whom we have given duplicate certificates.

AARON PRESCOTT,
Chairman of School Committee.

My school ran smoothly, with not a ripple to break the unvarying monotony. At this period schools were kept in session five and a half days in a week, and I could find no opportunity to make even a trip to Boston. During this winter I heard a great deal of talk about Horace Mann, who had been appointed as congressman from the Plymouth district to fill the place made vacant by the death of John Quincy Adams. I remember vividly the excitement caused in the old Bay State by his speech in Congress, made soon after Webster's famous seventh of March speech in the United States Senate. Of his great work as an educational reformer I knew little at that time. "Horace Mann, like so many of the great men of the Puritans, was modeled on the type of the Hebrew prophets," says William T. Harris. It was left for me many years later to read Horace Mann's official reports and to comprehend in some measure the sweep of his flaming enthusiasm.

One day, as the term was drawing to a close, my school was visited by a dignified gentleman who quietly sat in his chair and looked on for half a day. After expressing great satisfaction with my manner of teaching, he offered me a ten months' school at Ipswich, with a salary of two hundred and forty dollars a year and board. The offer was a tempting one, but I declined it. I was slowly beginning to face the future. Debarred from the college course by delicate health and a chronic weakness of one of my eyes, I could see no inducement whatever to engage longer in teaching. After the close of my winter term I bade good-by to Randolph and returned to my home in an uncertain and unsettled state of mind. Finally I determined to go to Oregon or California by way of Cape Horn, and my Pembroke school friend, Joseph C. Morrill, agreed to go with me; but my mother, unknown to me, pleaded so hard with him not to go, that he yielded to her entreaties, and the project fell through. It was probably fortunate for both of us that our plan was given up, though I did not think so at the time.

After this failure I decided to begin the study of medicine, the medical profession being the only one for which I had any inclination. But when I called on our village doctor and asked if I could begin to read medical books in his office, he said he was making arrangements to go to California for a two years' absence, and he thought I had better go along with him and study medicine after our return. Accordingly I tried to secure a ticket on the same steamer with him, but failed, as the tickets had all been sold long in advance. There was nothing for me to do but bide my time, and I decided in the meanwhile to attend Russell's Normal Institute at Reed's Ferry, on the Merrimac River, a few miles below the city of Manchester, where I remained for six months during the spring and winter terms. The course in rhetoric, grammar, composition, and elocution, under the instruction of Professor William Russell, was of inestimable value to me. The full notes of many of Professor Russell's lectures and exercises on rhetoric, composition, and word study are still treasured relics of my school days. Dana P. Colburn gave the method lessons in arithmetic. Attention to good reading and the study of English literature was a characteristic feature of this institution. Here I read two books of Virgil, took lessons in French from Anna Russell, and edited the school paper.

For several years I had been a contributor of fugitive pieces of prose and verse to the Boston *Cultivator*, an agricultural weekly journal having a literary department in which young writers were invited to try their apprentice pens. I have a bulky scrapbook of these early contributions which are still of interest to me, as showing a gradual improvement in style. As a supplement to my academic drill in rhetoric and composition, this miscellaneous work led up to a fair degree of readiness in writing. I am glad to find that the pieces of verse, as I look at them now, though not in any sense ranking as poetry, neither "broke the legs of melody nor docked the tail of rhyme."

Professor William Russell was born in Scotland. He had graduated from Glasgow University, and was one of that notable group of educators that clustered around Horace Mann during his great work in educational reform. He was one of the editors of the first school journal published in Boston, and one of the active promoters of state normal schools. He was the author of a number of excellent schoolbooks, among wh'ch are Russell's Normal Training, Russell's Elocution, Studies on Words, and the American

School Reader. Under his tuition I was brought into personal contact with the most enlightened educational thought of that time. For many years in after life I continued to receive from him letters of approval and encouragement.

At the end of the spring term the honor of giving the valedictory was conferred on me. An extract from this address on "Scholarship and Action" is of incidental interest to myself as showing how I looked at the world when twenty-one years of age, at the close of my academic education. It also affords an illustration of the florid rhetoric of youth.

> The true scholar must be a doer as well as a thinker. All great men shaped each burning thought into some glorious deed. He who thinks but never acts, who stores up knowledge which he does not use, is no more a scholar than an ass loaded down with an Alexandrian library. When the scholar goes into the world, he is measured by what he *does*, not by what he knows. Those who take the lead, who hold responsible stations, who mold public opinion, are not always the men of the greatest acquirements in book knowledge; they are men of action, who, like Andrew Jackson, do not hesitate to take the responsibility. Life is a struggle for power; the members of society are engaged in a continual contest for mastery. Every newcomer is met at the threshold of society; there is a conflict of man with man, and he who can bring his knowledge to bear with the greatest ease will gain the victory. Hence, the mere book student often finds himself overreached by those who are far inferior in point of attainments. Let the student, then, strive, not so much to pile up facts in the storehouse of memory, as to acquire the power of ready thought.

Soon after leaving Russell's Normal Institute I made another effort to get started for California. This time my former roommate at Pembroke, John B. Sanborn, agreed to go with me, and we tried to secure steamer tickets by way of Panama, but failed on account of the mouth College and to study law. Five years later he emigrated to St. Paul, Minnesota; he became a leading lawyer there, and served with distinction in the Union army during the war, retiring as brevet Major General of volunteers. I decided to go to California in a sailing vessel, " 'round the Horn," hoping that a long sea voyage might improve my health and strengthen my eyes. During the summer I persuaded Joseph C. Morrill, of the Pembroke Military Institute, to go with me by offering to advance him part of the money for his outfit. We secured our passage in the ship *Revere*, paying for our fare two hundred dollars each.

I had no intention of teaching in California, as I confidently expected to return in three years and take up the study of medicine; but I took the precaution to secure from Professor Russell a general letter of introduction which might be used in case of necessity. It was fortunate that I did so, for, unknown to me, my six months' training under William Russell had determined my life work.

CHAPTER VI

GOLD MINING DAYS IN CALIFORNIA

On the fifteenth of September, 1852, the merchant ship *Revere* sailed out of Boston Harbor, bound for San Francisco, with seven cabin passengers, Mr. Morrill, myself, and five others, — a man with his wife and three children. The voyage of four and a half months was tedious and monotonous. We put into no port, and sighted land in the distance only twice, — once off Cape St. Roque, and once off Cape Horn, until we caught sight of the "heads" at the entrance of the Golden Gate.

We beguiled the close imprisonment of a long sea voyage in various ways. The first month out we talked with one another and read all the literature aboard the ship; then I took to reading Shakespeare and Scott, and to writing long letters for the Boston *Cultivator*.

One hundred and thirty-five days after the *Revere* was towed out of Boston Harbor, a San Francisco pilot stepped on board of her, and we heard that Franklin Pierce had been elected president and that Daniel Webster was dead.[1]

[1] At the time of the presidential election in 1852 I was off Cape Horn, and consequently lost my vote, which would have been cast for Pierce had I been at home in New Hampshire, where I had often heard him make pleasing political speeches. My first vote for president of the United States was cast for John C. Fremont in 1856, since which time I have never missed an election, and have not failed to cast my ballot for the regular candidate of the Republican Party. Neither have I ever failed to vote at every state election, or city election, or special local election. Generally, too, I have turned out to vote at primary elections.

JOHN SWETT
AT TWENTY-TWO YEARS OF AGE

Reproduced from a daguerreotype taken in Boston in 1852, shortly before he started for California "'round the Horn."

Next day, February 1, 1853, I went ashore and wandered about San Francisco with the mingled sensations that come over a country boy when he finds himself an unknown atom of humanity in a bustling city. I called on the Reverend S. H. Willey, pastor of the Happy Valley Presbyterian Church, and presented a letter of introduction to him from a Congregational minister in New Hampshire. I was kindly received and was given a letter to Mr. J. W. Douglas, editor of the *Pacific*, a religious weekly publication. He secured a promise from me to send him occasional articles, and the files of that paper for 1853 to 1858 show that the pledge was kept. I called on the city superintendent of schools, Thomas J. Nevins, to secure some statistics about the public schools, telling him that I was a teacher and a correspondent for an Eastern newspaper. My reception was rather chilling, and I got little information that I wanted.

After a week's stay in San Francisco, without making any effort to find employment, I took the Sacramento River steamer, *Thomas Hunt*, for Marysville, on my way into the mines, not with the expectation of "making a strike," but with the hope of getting health from the rough life and hard work of gold mining. On my way I called on Dr. O. P. Warren, the Pittsfield physician with whom a year before I had planned to go to California. He had taken up a squatter's claim of one hundred and sixty acres on what he supposed was government land, six miles south of Marysville on the "slough," near the "Hock Farm" of General John A. Sutter. I found him living in a squatter's shanty, practicing medicine among the surrounding settlers, most of whom were suffering from chills and fever. He had great expectations of the future value of the land, in which he was doomed to be disappointed. His quarter section proved to be part of the Sutter grant, and a year later he moved to San Francisco and resumed medical practice. He never returned to Pittsfield, but a year or two later sent for his family, and lived in San Francisco and Oakland to the day of his death.

After a short visit with Dr. Warren, I left with him my books and other superfluous baggage, packed my blankets on my back, and started on foot for the little trading post of White and Nutter at Potter's Bar on the North Fork of Feather River, about thirty miles from Marysville. On my way I passed through Oroville, then a deserted mining camp, once famous for its rich diggings in '49 and '50.

When I reached my destination, I was warmly welcomed by my two friends, Thomas W. Nutter and James E. White, with whom I had attended common school and academy in Pittsfield. They were keeping a trading post of miners' supplies, and were evidently doing a good business. The outlook they gave me was not particularly encouraging. It had been a hard winter of heavy rains in California. The Sacramento valley had been flooded, and Sacramento City was a scene of desolation. Provisions of all kinds were scarce and high on account of the difficulty of transportation. Thousands of miners were out of work and out of money. A heavy storm came on and the rain poured down without cessation for five days. The river rose forty feet in two days, and poured through the rocky canyon of the Feather River with terrific fury, bringing down uprooted pine trees and driftwood from mountain flumes. The Sacramento valley became an inland sea, and Sacramento City was flooded for the second time during the year.

After this rainstorm was over, I secured a miner's outfit and went to the Morris Ravine, a decayed mining camp five miles distant, which had yielded, in the days of '49 and '50, several millions of dollars from its rich placer diggings. This ravine lies between two basaltic table mountains and was evidently the channel of an ancient river before the period of the great lava flow in this mountain region. The diggings had been "worked out" in early days, but a few miners still remained, mostly engaged in working over the "tailings" a second or third time. I soon came across a good-natured Dutchman, six feet two in height, who kindly allowed me to spread my blankets in his cabin and cook my meals at his fireplace.

Then I looked around to find work. Hearing of a Scotchman two miles out of camp who wanted a partner to help sink a prospecting shaft, I immediately hunted him up. He admitted me into partnership on equal shares. We began work at once, he digging in the shaft while I ran the windlass, hauling up sand, gravel, and water in a large bucket. We sunk a vertical shaft fifteen or twenty feet, to "bedrock," and struck gravel that promised to pay for working. Heavy rains came on and stopped work for a week. Then we began to run a drift from the bed of the creek toward the shaft where we had struck gold. Joe Donaldson, my partner, was now taken down with a severe attack of chills and fever, and as he had no medicine I set out on foot to Marysville, forty miles away, to get a supply of quinine that I had left with Dr. Warren. On my return with medicine, Donaldson was soon able to resume work, and for a week we took out of our claim an average of two dollars a day.

One day, Donaldson being sick, I worked alone, struck a "pocket," and cleaned up eighty dollars, the first and last strike I ever made in mining. Of course I divided this sum with my partner. This strike so elated me that I stopped work earlier than usual. It was fortunate that I did so, for in half an hour after I left the drift the bank caved down and buried the mouth of the tunnel under twenty feet of earth. Had I remained at work a little longer that day, I should have been instantly crushed out of existence. We afterwards cleared off the débris, but the claim paid so little that we soon gave it up.

In a pocket memorandum and account book I find a few entries that show the daily routine of my life at this time.

April 11, two of us worked all day and cleaned up $6.00.
April 12, $3.00.
April 14, Donaldson sick, worked alone, $1.00.
April 15, alone, 50 cents.
April 16, two of us, $3.00.
April 18, bank caved in. Three days' work in clearing off dirt.
April 21, three of us, $20.00.
April 22, another cave of the bank, claim given up.
April 23, face and hands swollen from the effects of "poison oak."
April 24, 25, 26, 27, 28, 30, laid up in misery.
May 1st, 2d, 3d, 4th, unable to work.

On May 5, in company with George B. Davis and Dennis Hite, two New Hampshire men, I began washing out the old "tailings" along the creek. Our board cost us about fifty cents a day each. Our diet consisted chiefly of tea and coffee, stewed beans, bread, and occasionally a little beef or ham. Potatoes were a luxury we could not afford, as they cost from fifteen to twenty cents a pound. Butter was unknown; even pork and beef were hard to get and high in price. We baked our bread in a large iron Dutch oven and stewed our beans in a camp kettle. I soon learned to make bread equal to the very best French bread. Our bill of fare was short, but the diet was substantial and wholesome and we thrived upon it. Most of the cooking fell to me because I proved to be the best cook. My memorandum runs as follows:

May 5, 50 cents; May 6, 75 cents; May 7, 50 cents; May 8, 50 cents; May 9, not even color; May 10, 50 cents; May 11 to 15, nothing.

We gave up our claim and went to the Potter Ravine, where we camped out, slept on the ground, and cooked our meals in the open air over a camp fire.

On the first day the three of us washed out $3.40; May 22, three of us cleaned up $54.00, a good day's work; May 24, worked alone, the other two men being sick, cleaned up $10.00. May 25, three of us, $4.00; May 26, three of us, 25 cents. Claim worked out, no more water. May 31, packed blankets to Morris Ravine and worked with Davis and Hite. June 1, three of us, $29.00; June 3, three of us, $3.00; June 4, $6.00; June 5, water gave out.

After the failure of water there was no further surface mining to be done in that region for six months, or until the return of winter rains. Under the sharp spur of necessity four of us — Davis, Hite, Burroughs, and myself — planned a prospecting tour to the headwaters of the Feather River, far up in the mountains. As Burroughs was a veteran miner, we made him our guide and leader. He knew of a river "bar" that had never been worked out. We rolled up our blankets, tied on our picks and rations, and slung the whole over our backs, each weighted down with forty pounds of baggage. Shade of Don Quixote! What a party of innocents we were! How we reached our imaginary El Dorado is best told by a few extracts from my home letters in the Boston *Cultivator*.

BOARD RANCH, June 6, 1853.

At the close of a hot day, after footing it for twenty-five miles under a burning sun over a dusty road, the little ranch where we are resting, nestled among the trees, seems very inviting. I send these "home letters," instead of keeping a diary. My nervous energy has mostly gone into the heels of my boots, leaving very little to ooze out at the point of a pen. Early this morning I left the Norris Ravine bound for the mountains, to see the white elephant. . . . On our way we passed through Bidwell's Bar, a little trading post for miners, where there is a ferry for crossing the Feather River. The miners have worked up through the center of the town, undermining houses and streets. This place is the center of travel into the "Northern Mines."

JACK.

June 8, 1853, Little Grass Valley — We are on the south fork of the Feather River, about seventy-five miles from Marysville. Yesterday the road along the divide ran through one continuous forest of sugar pines and firs, straight as gun barrels, and more than a hundred feet in height. Passing through Forbestown, where a thousand miners were at work, we met a large number coming down from the mountains in search of work. We reached snow this afternoon, and its cool carpet was very grateful to our blistered feet. In this little valley the snow is just melting away and the green grass is springing up. The frogs are croaking, and everything reminds me of New England.

JACK.

— LITTLE RICH BAR, MIDDLE FORK OF FEATHER RIVER, June 11.

Leaving Grass Valley early this morning, we crossed the south fork and followed a mule trail to the Middle Feather. On the dividing ridge between these rivers we passed over large snowfields from ten to twenty feet deep. We missed the trail, struck into Onion Valley, and followed down the creek to the Middle Feather, about three miles above our point of destination. Then we worked our way down the rugged canyon of the Feather, climbing high ridges and plunging down ravines, clinging like monkeys to the jagged points of slate. After three hours of slow and toilsome progress we reached Little Rich Bar and stood on the fabulous diggings to which our gray-headed guide had taken us, in one of the wildest, roughest, and most desolate sections of the Sierra Nevada Mountains. But we found there twenty-five miners who had taken up every foot of land on the small river bench or bar.

The miners shared their supper with us, but not their claims. Next day my partners were too stiff and sore to move out of camp. Having been accustomed to long foot-tramps, our forced march did not disable me, though I was the least robust of the party. So I started out alone to prospect along the river. The geological formation of this section consisted of granite and slate intersected by veins of quartz. I washed out many pans of sand and gravel along the river channels, but secured only a few tiny scales of float gold, not worth working. Rich Bar itself is a shelf or bench at a bend of the river, thirty or forty feet above high-water mark. It must have been at one time the bed of the stream. A few of the claims seemed to be paying well, but most of the miners were sinking shafts and had not struck the bedrock on which gold is found. Provisions are now brought by mules, but until within a few days the miners packed on their own backs all their supplies from Little Grass Valley, twelve miles distant. For several days we prospected along the river but found nothing, not even the color of gold. Then we tried to buy a claim, but prices were too high for our capital. I told my partners that I was tired of chasing rainbows to find a pot of gold, and that I had made up my mind to go to San Francisco. They wanted to go higher up into the mountains, and we parted company.

JACK.

— VALLEY OF THE FEATHER RIVER, NEAR MARYSVILLE, July 5.

DEAR MR. EDITOR:—I went into the mountains expecting my stay would be short. But how did I get here? Well, one morning I came to the conclusion that I had seen the elephant and the circus, and I began a retrograde movement, leaving my partners to hunt for grizzly bears. I rolled up my blankets, packed them on my back, left my pick, pan, and shovel with my friends, and started out alone. It is easier to get into a scrape than it is to get out of one. It is easier to go down into the deep canyons of Feather River than it is to climb out of them. After toiling up the rude trail for three miles to the divide, I found the snow melted off, and there were no traces of a pathway. I struck out first in one direction, then in another, and found myself lost in the chaparral. I wandered blindly around until nearly sunset, when I stumbled across a miner's rough cabin, and in the cabin a solitary miner who bade me welcome to a supper and a bunk. In the morning he went with me to the trail, pointed out the direction, and I have held him in grateful remembrance ever since. I may as well mention here that my partners came over this same trail a week later.

JACK.

On my way out of the mountains I picked up a job for two days at Buffalo Ranch, mowing and raking hay in a little hayfield on a small patch of level land. On the first day of July I reached the cabin of my friend Dr. Warren, on Sutter's Slough, near Marysville, and on July 12 I took passage on the steamer *Senator* for San Francisco.

Thus ended my five months' stay in the mines. I should gladly have remained there longer if I could have found any way of making a living. As it was, I had a small emergency fund of about one hundred and twenty-five dollars carefully strapped around my waist to be used in case of sickness. As I look back on these mining days my only regret is that they did not last longer. They toned up my health and strength and gave me a taste of pioneer life, something for which I had an hereditary longing when a boy. During all this time I had been a regular correspondent of the Boston *Cultivator*, and my letters and other articles, carefully preserved by my mother in a scrap-book, make a bulky volume. In addition to the *Cultivator* letters, I made numerous contributions of prose and verse to the *Pacific*, a weekly paper published in San Francisco, the organ of the Congregational church, and sent several contributions of prose and verse to the *Knickerbocker Magazine*.

The fact was that in 1853 the rich surface or placer diggings had been worked out. The whole state was overrun with men tramping in search of work. The days of rich strikes and reckless dissipation had come to an end. The men that I worked with were steady, temperate, and economical, from force of habit as well as from necessity. Of course there was some of the driftwood of humanity floating around in the mines, as well as in the cities, but the great majority of the miners were steady, hard-working men, struggling for a competence to enable them to return to their homes in the East. As for myself, I was exposed to no temptations whatever. I used neither whiskey nor tobacco. I never played a game of cards, even without stakes. I lived on a diet of Spartan symplicity. In our camp there was little profanity and no vulgarity. So far as moral conduct was concerned, all of us lived up to the rigid standard of an old Puritan community, save that we did not go to church on Sunday, there being neither minister nor meeting within twenty miles of us.

I am tempted to close this sketch of my life in the mines by "some verses" written in the Morris Ravine and published in the Boston *Cultivator*.

ROUND THE CAMP FIRE

Leave the "sluice" and "tom" untended,
  Shadows darken on the river,
In the canyon day is ended,
  Far above the red rays quiver.
Lay aside the bar and spade,
  Let the pickax rest from drifting,
See how much the claim has paid,
  Where the gold dust has been sifting.

Tell no tales of wizard charm
  In the myths of ages olden,
When the sorcerer's potent arm
  Turned at will all things to golden;
Pick and spade are magic rods,
  Toil and industry diviners,
Drawing gold from sand and sods
  Touched by brawny arms of miners.

Stretched around the supper fire,
  Hear the iron kettle steaming,
While the sharpness of desire
  Lulls into luxurious dreaming;

On the "oven" heap the coals
Till it seems a dragon waking,
For a dozen hungry souls
Wait for bread within it baking.

On the ground the tin plates spread,
Pour the tea out, strong and stronger;
From the "Dutchman" draw the bread,
We can wait for it no longer;
Roll it out upon the ground,
Pray the gods to be propitious,
Never loaf before was found
With an odor so delicious.

Break it up with brawny hand,
Pass it round with labor's blessing;
Now the waiting men look bland,
Hungry miners need no pressing.
Pass the ham around this way,
Quick! before it all is taken,
Hang philosophy, we say,
If we only save our *bacon!*

Spread the blankets on the ground,
We must toil again to-morrow;
Labor brings us slumbers sound
No luxurious couch can borrow.
Through the dark-topped, sighing pines
Watch the moon "with white fire laden,"
Fall asleep to dream of mines,
Home, or wife, or child, or maiden.

As the needle, frail and shivering,
On the ocean wastes afar,
Veering, changing, trembling, quivering,
Settles on the polar star,
So in souls of those who roam,
Love's magnetic fires are burning;
To the loved ones left at home,
Throbbing hearts are ever turning.

FEATHER RIVER, 1853 JACK.

Looking for Work

When I arrived in San Francisco I hunted up my school friend, Joseph C. Morrill, whom I found at work on a milk ranch on the outskirts of the city of San Francisco. Then I applied to an intelligence office, and was sent to work for Thomas Hayes, who had a large vegetable garden in Hayes's Valley, near the present site of the John Swett Grammar School. For thirty days I was kept at spading, hoeing, weeding, and planting, from six o'clock in the morning until seven in the evening. My boss was a tough and muscular Irishman, and it nearly broke my back to keep up with him. One month's experience in gardening was quite enough; I thanked Mr. Hayes for his kindness, took my wages, twenty-five dollars, packed my blankets, and moved on as a tramp in search of work.

Next I went to the old Mission of San José, carrying a letter of introduction from the editor of the *Pacific* to Mr. E. L. Beard, the owner of the Mission ranch. He kindly set me at work immediately, and here I remained for two months. Among the twenty or thirty men at work on this farm were two college graduates, four teachers, and one lawyer. One of the large rooms in an old adobe house was fitted up with bunks for a sleeping room; but it was swarming with millions of bloodthirsty fleas, and after a trial of one night I slept in the open air, on the ground under a fig tree in the old Mission garden. But even there the fleas followed me.

After working a month, hearing that a district school near Alvarado was in want of a teacher, I hunted up the head trustee, — a Congregational minister from New England, — passed an examination exactly like those that I had passed in Massachusetts, and secured a certificate; but a young woman living in the district got the school, and I went back to work. Soon after, my friend Mr. Morrill, who had just been appointed teacher of the Spring Valley school in San Francisco, wrote to me to come to the city and pass an examination for a certificate, as he thought I could secure a school. Accordingly I went to the city, was orally examined, in company with a dozen other men, in reading, spelling, arithmetic, and grammar, and was given a certificate, "valid for one year, if not sooner revoked." I called on William H. O'Grady, superintendent of public schools, and applied for the first vacancy that might occur. The credentials which I filed with the superintendent read as follows:

(1) Merrimack Normal Institute.

Mr. John Swett has been, for several years, a member of this Seminary, and has been uniformly distinguished by exemplary deportment, assiduous application, rapid advancement, and high attainments. Mr. Swett's noble talents and his excellent habits indicate emphatically the individual whose success is sure in the peculiar duties and business of instruction. We part with him reluctantly; and we can but hope that he will obtain such a position in life as his merits entitle him to fill. I may add that Mr. Swett's influence on younger minds cannot fail of encouraging the best results on the disposition and character, as his own traits of personal character have won the universal esteem of teachers and students here. He carries with him our best wishes for his prosperity in whatever career of life he may enter.

William Russell,
Principal.

Merrimack, N. H., 21st July, 1852.

(2) Letter from N. C. Berry, Esq.

To whom it may concern: —

The subscriber is very well acquainted with Mr. John Swett of Pittsfield in the County of Merrimack and State of New Hampshire. I knew his lamented father. He was an excellent teacher, and in my school days I was faithfully flogged by him at school. Thanks to him for it, and peace to his ashes. And now here is a worthy and only son of him. He has been bred to letters and fitted for a teacher of youth in some of our best New England academies. He has a thorough knowledge of the English language, acquired by long and persevering study. I am informed that he has a good knowledge of the Latin language, but how extensive that knowledge is I am at present unable to say, never having had an opportunity, personally, to examine him in this department. During the years of 1849 and 1850 I employed him to instruct a large and interesting school in Randolph, Mass. He succeeded in giving the best satisfaction, and in bearing off the palm for keeping the best school, from a dozen of his associates in the same town; for confirmation of this statement, reference is had to the printed report of the School Committee of those years. He has been an associate teacher in the Pembroke Academy for some time past, and as I learn with entire success. He sustains an excellent moral character, with habits and a deportment suitable for a teacher of youth. Whatever institution of learning shall have the good fortune to employ him for an instructor, will find him all that he pretends to be, and one among *the very few* of his profession who are in fact qualified for their business.

N. C. BERRY,
Attorney and Counselor at Law.

Office, 20 Court Street, Boston, Mass.

(3) Letter from the Editors of the Boston *Cultivator:*

OUR DEAR YOUNG FRIEND: — It is with sorrow that we hear of your intention to leave the land of your birth for the untried scenes of the golden sands of Eldorado! and this feeling is, we confess, not entirely disinterested, for from the day of your first "Communication" for the columns of the Boston *Cultivator* have we considered you one of the very best contributors, and to whom we were indebted for a large amount of excellent and original matter, both prose and verse.

Will you accept our best thanks for your valuable services in the cause of the *Cultivator*, and our fervent prayers for your health and success in your future undertakings. Nothing will afford us greater pleasure than to hear of your prosperity, while the pages of the *Cultivator* will stand open, ready to receive with thankfulness whatever you may please to consign to our care. May God bless you, our dear and young friend, and if it be in our power to serve you, please command us, and believe us most truly and affectionately yours,

OTIS BREWER, *Proprietor,*
JAMES PEDDER, *Editor,*
Boston Cultivator.

BOSTON CULTIVATOR OFFICE, 13th September, 1852.

(4) From Nathaniel Hills, Principal of Pembroke Academy, 1850.

This certifies that the bearer, Mr. John Swett, has formerly been a member of the Pembroke Academy in this place. As a scholar he always took a high standing in the numerous classes with which he was connected. More recently he has been employed as a teacher in the same institution, the duties of which office he has discharged with much credit to himself and entire satisfaction to the board of Trustees and members of the Academy. He is a young man of great energy of mind, possessed of a good moral character, and is cheerfully recommended as a young gentleman worthy the confidence of all such as may wish to employ him as a teacher.

NATHANIEL HILLS,
Principal.

PEMBROKE, N. H., November 16, 1850.

(5) From the Reverend Samuel H. Willey, Pastor of the First Presbyterian Church, 1853.

SAN FRANCISCO, NOV. 1, 1853.

To the Hon. Board of Education, San Francisco: —

I herewith forward the name of *Mr. J. Swett* to you as candidate for the place of teacher in a City school.

I will not add a word in commendation of him, as the accompanying letters are amply sufficient on that point.

I believe him to be a teacher possessing merit of the first order, and consequently take pleasure in presenting him as candidate for a school in my adopted City.

I am, gentlemen,
Yr. Obt. Servt.,
S. A. WILLEY.

Having secured my certificate, I returned to farm work at the Mission of San José. An extract from one of my home letters to the Boston *Cultivator*, dated San José Mission, September 13, 1853, shows my outlook at that time: —

One year ago to-day I left New England for the shores of the Pacific. I came here, not with the hope of gaining wealth, not with high expectations, but with the hope of regaining health. I have had some dark days and some sunny days, but have never been disheartened. The year has been a long one, for we measure time, not by hours and days, but by events. I looked forward to a "good time coming." Like Mr. Micawber, I am waiting for "something to turn up."

Yours truly, JACK.

Not long after this letter was written something *did* turn up, for I received a letter from Mr. Morrill stating that I was appointed as an assistant teacher in the public school on Washington Street in the basement of the Baptist church, of which Mr. Ellis H. Holmes was principal. Then I thanked Mr. Beard for his kindness in giving me employment, and took an order on a commission house in San Francisco for the amount of my wages, fifty dollars, together with one hundred and twenty dollars that I had deposited in his office for safe keeping while I was at work for him. After some delay in cashing this order, I was fortunate enough to secure my money from Mr. Beard's agent a few days before the announcement of his failure. Mr. Beard was an able business man, but he carried on extensive farming operations, and a sudden fall in the prices of wheat and other farm products swept him down in the general wreck.

I arrived at San Francisco only to find that the Board of Education had decided not to assign me as an assistant in the Washington school, holding out the hope, however, that I would be appointed to the first vacancy in the department. Mr. Morrill and myself rented two small rooms, furnished them with primitive simplicity, and set up housekeeping, taking our dinners at the restaurants and cooking the other meals ourselves. During a month of waiting I visited the various public schools, made some good friends, and busied myself in writing letters for the Boston *Cultivator* about scenes in San Francisco. Among these letters I find in my scrapbook a realistic picture, in rime, of weather conditions at the beginning of the rainy season in California. It is dragged out of obscurity only to show that, though I was waiting on the anxious seat, I managed to keep up my spirits.

RAINY DAYS IN SAN FRANCISCO

I

The San Francisco streets to-day
Are in a sloppy, muddy way,
And dripping mortals sadly say,
  "The weather's bad!"
Go into any public place,
A frown lies scowling on each face;
Of fun there is not left a trace,
  'Tis very sad!

II

A Chinaman stepped in a hole —
He looked and acted very droll —
And, burrowing like a blinded mole,
  Sank out of view;
All save his tail of braided hair,
Which stood a solemn warning there
To all who moved in upper air,
  To mind their queue!

III

A drayman drove into the mire
And cursed his team with heathen ire.
Down, down he went, his eyes on fire,
  Till quenched in water;
He met the fate of Phaeton,
That reckless driver of the sun,
Who rushed his horses on the run
  To wreck and slaughter.

IV

An organ grinder killing songs
With power of forty thousand gongs —
These grinders should with fire and tongs
Be chased to Hades —
Fell down a man-trap yawning wide,
And music with its master died;
A pandemonium was his pride,
And there his shade is!

V

A Yankee, so the papers said,
Was fished up out of water, dead;
They thought the vital spark had fled
And stole his money —
He started up in wild surprise;
Exclaiming as he tried to rise,
"Don't pick my pockets, darn your eyes,
The weather's funny!"

VI

The newsboys hurry through the showers,
At morning and all other hours,
Crying with more than mortal powers,
"The Daily Times!"
Under the eyes of all they meet
They thrust their wet and dripping sheet —
It makes the misery quite complete —
Such howling crimes!

VII

The reeking sheets contain no news,
They seem made up of rain and dews,
The printer must have had the blues
Or else the "hypoes";
But then such horrid rainy weather!
It makes folks all grow glum together,
And geese and goosequills drop a feather;
— Blame not the "typoes."

1853 JACK.

CHAPTER VII

THE MAKING OF A GRAMMAR SCHOOL IN SAN FRANCISCO

My opportunity came soon in an unexpected manner. The principal of the Rincon School, who had been in charge of the school only sixty days, had some serious troubles in matters of discipline; the big boys rebelled, and he suddenly resigned. The superintendent assigned me to the vacancy in November, 1853. Naturally enough the ringleaders of this small school of sixty boys and girls tried their hand on the new teacher, but the decisive manner in which one was punished on the spot, and another ordered out of school not to return, quelled an incipient mutiny, and there was no further trouble about order and discipline. This school was at that time held in a small rented house, planted in the middle of a sand bank on the corner of First and Folsom streets. To the original shanty there had been attached a shed-like addition for the primary children. There was neither blackboard nor map in this primitive schoolroom. The only apparatus consisted of a wooden water pail and a battered tin dipper, from which the children drank water brought from a well not far distant, the owner of which allowed the boys to draw one bucket of water a day. There was a small table for the teacher, and one rickety chair. The school children furnished their own ink bottles, their pens, and their paper. Compared with this wretched makeshift of a schoolhouse, the Pittsfield school building in which I learned to read and write and cipher was a palace. My department numbered thirty boys and girls, and the primary room in charge of Miss Bain had about the same number.

The organization of the city schools under state law had begun about two years before this time with the appointment, by the common council, of a board of education and a city superintendent, Thomas J. Nevins, who came to San Francisco from New York City as agent of the American Tract Society.

But the preliminary efforts to start a public school had begun in 1847, when the town council (Ayuntamiento) built a small one-room schoolhouse on a corner of the town plaza (now Portsmouth Square). In this building a few citizens, assembled in "town meeting," elected the first public school committee in California, consisting of seven members. A school was opened early in 1848, with six pupils taught by Thomas Douglass, a graduate of Yale. This was a public school, supported by tuition fees, but indigent children were to be admitted as charity pupils, the town council agreeing to pay four hundred dollars a year towards its maintenance. The discovery of gold broke up this school soon after it opened, and schoolmaster Douglass drifted away, with hundreds of other gold hunters, into the mountains.

In December, 1849, Mr. and Mrs. John C. Pelton arrived from the state of Maine and opened a private tuition school, "free to the children of the poor," which was made a free public school by ordinance of the common council, April 8, 1850, and John C. Pelton remained in charge of it until September 25, 1851, when it was reorganized under the state law, by a new city ordinance which provided for a city board of education and a city school superintendent.

One of the first teachers elected by this new board was James Denman (December 17, 1851), a graduate of the State Normal School at Albany, New York. In 1852 Ahira Holmes, a graduate of the Massachusetts State Normal School at Bridgewater, and William H. O'Grady from Middlebury College, Vermont, were added to the list of principals. In 1853 the following additional school principals were elected: Joseph C. Morrill, of the Pembroke Military Academy, New Hampshire; Henry P. Carleton, of Massachusetts; and myself, from Professor William Russell's Merrimack Normal Institute in New Hampshire. At this time the salary of principals was fifteen hundred dollars a year, — a small compensation, considering the cost of living at that time.

William H. O'Grady succeeded Mr. Nevins as city superintendent. There were now seven schools, with a total enrollment of fifteen hundred pupils and an average attendance of about eight hundred. These early schools were all held in rented buildings roughly fitted up for school purposes. The school appropriations made by the common council were wholly insufficient for the needs of a rapidly growing city. Meanwhile there sprang up numerous denominational and private schools, — Catholic, Episcopal, Presbyterian, German, and French. As might have been expected in a city with a cosmopolitan population drawn from every state in the Union and from most of the European nations, the common-school spirit was relatively weak, and it required heroic work on the part of teachers and educators to bring public opinion up to a liberal support of the common schools, which were for a long time regarded by a strong minority of citizens as "charity schools" for the education of children whose parents were too poor to pay tuition fees in private and denominational schools.

We were all young teachers then, and we took hold of our work in earnest, ambitious to play our part in the development of a great city. There was no printed course of study and we had free play for our individuality. As we were not handicapped by written examinations, we classified pupils according to their ability or their own individual needs. A year or two later some of us had classes in natural philosophy, and I had a class of older pupils in natural history.

Mr. Denman and myself worked harmoniously together, and there was a generous rivalry between our two schools, which were in adjoining districts. We looked after the nomination and election of the best citizens we could find that were willing to accept the unpaid honor of serving on the board of education. At the close of each term we held public examinations and exhibitions, and invited parents and reporters of the press to attend, thus making known the existence of our schools to the general public. The congenial work of teaching and the exciting bustle of business in a large city formed an agreeable contrast to the isolation of a migratory life in the mountains. My health had been reëstablished and my muscles hardened; my eyes had become strong once more, and I made good use of them over the rich book treasures of the Mercantile Library Association, of which I have now been a member for more than half a century.

As my school was crowded into a shanty, I began at once to stir up the citizens in my district to the need of a larger and better building. The father of one of my schoolboys, Mr. Hutton, a public-spirited merchant, made a proposition to the board of education, stating that he would build on one of his own lots a two-story frame building capable of seating three hundred pupils, provided the city would lease it for two years at a reasonable rent. His offer was accepted and the house was built on Hampton Place, near Third Street, between Folsom and Harrison streets. On the 22d of August, 1854, the new building was dedicated in the presence of a large assemblage. The exercises were reported in full by the city press. There were songs and recitations by the school children, and remarks by the mayor-elect, S. P. Webb, Superintendent O'Grady, the Reverend John E. Benton, General John Wilson, and Alderman Talmadge. Having been invited by Superintendent O'Grady to deliver a written address, I took advantage of the opportunity to make a strong appeal to the people in support of a system of public schools. The address was well received by the audience, was complimented by the press, and published in the *Sun*, then a leading daily paper. As this was my first public address in California I quote from the files of the *Sun* a few paragraphs, to show how I then looked at things.

The opening of a schoolhouse is an occasion which well deserves a public commemoration. In ancient times, the heathen temples were dedicated to the gods, with games and festivals and the rejoicings of assembled multitudes; and it is quite as appropriate that the humbler edifices of the common school should be consecrated to learning by the songs of children and the presence of parents. It is natural that teachers, parents, pupils, and citizens should all exult together in the dedication of this building. This schoolhouse should be consecrated to the spirit of order. Efficient discipline is essential to a public school. The children in Sparta all gathered round the public table and ate the black broth common to all. In the common school of to-day one table is spread for all, with no dainties for pampered pets, and no distinctions of rank, or birth, or fortune.

As teachers we ask the coöperation of fathers and mothers in enforcing strict discipline in accordance with the rules of common sense. We would teach children that the greatest lesson of life which they have to learn is that of self-government, and that if they fail to learn it, we propose to aid them with strong school discipline.

The importance of the common school as a national institution cannot be overestimated. The system of free schools, indeed, is an essential element of our free government. Our safety lies in the ballot box, and that rests directly upon the common schools; for uneducated men have always been made and always will be made the tools of political demagogues. The common schools have been justly termed "The People's Colleges," for in them the great majority of the men and women of this country receive their education. We need the living sympathy of the people in favor of free public schools for the education of all classes of children. Of wealth there is enough and to spare; strong hands and earnest hearts must use it. This State is filling up with inhabitants from the four quarters of the globe. All the elements of greatness are here — intellect, talent, genius, energy,— and a restless activity that knows no precedent. But the heterogeneous atoms lie in one chaotic mass, to be molded into symmetry by some controlling power.

The spirit of the Rincon School is best shown, perhaps, by the press reports of its public examinations, exhibitions, and May festivals. This record begins with an examination held in December, 1854, three months after the school was installed in the new building. Mayor Webb, Superintendent O'Grady, together with Frederick Billings and J. B. Moore, members of the board of education, were in attendance, and awarded a prize book to Robert Wilson for the best declamation, and a similar prize to Margaret Dayley for the best recital of poetry.

The *Sun* reported the proceedings as follows:

An exceedingly interesting exhibition of the pupils of the Rincon School was held yesterday afternoon. Mr. Denman was present with his elder pupils from the Bush Street School. The salutatory by Master Frank Hutton was in verse, which was written for the occasion by Mr. Swett, whose success as a teacher has been of the most gratifying character.

At the conclusion of the excerises, as announced on the program, one of the young ladies of the school approached Mr. Swett and placed in his hand a gold hunting watch and chain, which she begged him to accept as a token of the affection and respect of his pupils. The watch was accompanied by a note expressive of this regard, which was signed by some fifty or sixty of the scholars of the grammar department. The interest manifested in the public schools is of a very encouraging and gratifying character, and always secures a large attendance on any of the public exercises. This school numbers three hundred pupils, — one hundred in the grammar department, one hundred in the intermediate, and one hundred in the primary.

At the end of the next term, April 27, 1855, the Rincon School held a public examination and exhibition which was fully reported by the press. One report reads as follows:

An examination of the Rincon School on Hampton Place took place before the board of examiners and a large number of spectators yesterday afternoon. Specimens of drawing were exhibited, declamations, dialogues, singing, and reading by classes, and many other interesting exercises followed. Remarks were made by Mayor Webb, Alderman Moore, Mr. Sherman, Mr. O'Grady, and Rev. John E. Benton.

Following this examination, the school held its first May-Day Festival at Russ's Garden, which was situated only five blocks distant from the schoolhouse. The owner of this pleasure resort, Mr. Russ, had four children in the Rincon School, and consequently leased to us the large pavilion and playgrounds at a nominal price. The program of the day included songs, recitations, declamations, dialogues, the crowning of a May Queen, dancing, and a collection contributed by the parents. The affair was in every way a great success. The receipts from the sale of admission tickets amounted to four hundred and twenty dollars; the expenses, including a fine orchestra, were two hundred and sixteen dollars, leaving a balance of two hundred and four dollars, of which one hundred was applied to part payment on a school piano, and one hundred and four dollars for gymnastic appliances. Afterwards the pupils raised by subscription for the piano fund one hundred and thirty-seven dollars, which, added to the one hundred dollars appropriated from the proceeds of the exhibition, made two hundred and thirty-seven dollars. The piano cost three hundred and fifty dollars, and the school was still in debt.

The Annual Reëxamination of Teachers

At the end of the year, December, 1854, all the teachers in the school were reëxamined "according to law," for the purpose of ascertaining if we knew enough to teach our schools for another year. Our examination, wholly oral, was similar in all respects to that of the previous year, and both were patterned after the primitive examinations which I had passed in New Hampshire and Massachusetts. Each of us was asked one question in each of the following studies: reading, spelling, arithmetic, grammar, and geography. The board of education was made up exclusively of men from New England, and they held faithfully to old-time precedents. The mayor of San Francisco, *ex-officio* chairman of the board, was from Salem, Massachusetts, of which famous Puritan city he had once been mayor; Frederick Billings was a prominent lawyer from Vermont; William Sherman had been a teacher in Rhode Island; J. B. Moore was a young lawyer from Concord, Hew Hampshire; and William H. O'Grady, the city superintendent, was from Vermont. Mayor Webb, true to his Yankee instincts, put the following question, which for a quarter of a century had been a kind of *pons asinorum* in school examinations in New England: "Give an analytical explanation of the reason for inverting the divisor in division of fractions." This proposition was put to Mr. Holmes, whose strong point was mathematics; and the fun of it all was, that this veteran teacher was flustered and after several trials gave it up, saying, "I know well enough but can't explain it." The certificate which I received has been carefully treasured as a relic of the "old régime." It reads as follows: —

CERTIFICATE

We, the undersigned, the Committee appointed for the examination of Teachers of the Free Common Schools of this City, do certify that we have personally examined Mr. J. Swett, and are satisfied that he is of good moral character and of sufficient learning and ability, and has a competent aptness and fitness for teaching. We therefore grant to him this our Certificate of Approval, which shall continue in force one year, unless sooner revoked by the Board of Education.

S. P. WEBB,
FREDERICK BILLINGS,
WILLIAM SHERMAN,
JACOB B. MOORE,
Committee.

SAN FRANCISCO, November 4, 1854. W. H. O'GRADY, *Supt.*

These annual reëxaminations were continued during the nine years that I was principal of the Rincon School. The story of how they were finally broken up will be told in a future chapter. After 1856, written examinations came into vogue. Not only were we reëxamined annually, but we were also reëlected annually, for the term of one year only. It was these twin humiliations that eventually drove me to seek a more independent field of action. But in this connection I cannot refrain from mentioning one famous examination held in 1860. That was a red-letter day. The president of the board himself prepared most of the questions. He was a man of inordinate self-conceit, who once remarked to me that he could teach more in one day than any teacher in the city could teach in six months. His geography questions, a fair example of the others, ran as follows: —

1. Name all the rivers of the globe.
2. Name all the bays, gulfs, seas, lakes, and other bodies of water on the globe.
3. Name all the cities of the world.
4. Name all the countries of the world.
5. Bound each of the States in the United States.

We were allowed only one hour for answering these very short questions. I recall one tall Texan who had worried through the arithmetic examination. When he got hold of the geography questions he examined them leisurely, and, stalking up to the chairman's table, handed back the questions and drawled out: "If the board want me to prepare a primary geography, they must pay me for it." He took his hat and disappeared. At the end of the hour some were still at work on the first question, some on the second question, a few on the third, and one on the fifth. As for myself, I got through all the questions by answers brief and condensed, naming the more important rivers, bays, countries, etc., and bounding the United States as a whole, — but I gained nothing by generalizing my answers. When the report was made, we all stood exactly alike, sixty per cent. Twenty years afterwards I hunted up these papers from the musty records of the board of education as a matter of curiosity, and found out how we were credited.

Trouble in the Schools

The first board of education in 1851 adopted a resolution requiring the teachers to open school by reading the Bible and by prayer. This rule was drafted by Thomas J. Nevins, the city school superintendent, who copied it from the school regulations of the city of New York. When a new superintendent came into office in 1853, the rule was no longer rigidly enforced. Mr. Denman and myself thought that under the conditions of a cosmopolitan city, in which there were large numbers of the children of Catholics and Jews, it was an unwise policy to continue the reading of the Bible as a school exercise. But when the fusion of parochial schools with the public schools was effected in 1854, the question about the reading of the Bible in school broke out anew. The organization of the Know Nothing party greatly intensified the feeling on this point. It was finally settled, many years later, by allowing no religious exercises whatever in the city schools.

In November, 1854, school directors and a school superintendent were elected by direct vote of the people. Previous to this time the school board had been appointed by the common council, and the school superintendent had been elected by the board of education. The new board consisted of eight members, one from each ward, with the mayor, C. K. Garrison, *ex-officio* president. The Democratic party ticket was elected by a sweeping majority. Mr. E. A. Theller was elected school superintendent. He was neither a teacher nor an educator, but he took an active part in politics. Among the members of the board were Ferdinand C. Ewer from Nantucket, and

Elisha Cook, a prominent lawyer. Mr. Ewer, some years afterwards, became a popular Episcopal clergyman in New York city.

The board proceeded to reorganize and reform the schools by fusing the Catholic parochial schools for boys with the existing schools. This was done in consequence of an amendment to the state school law of 1853, which required the teachers in parochial and convent schools to pass an examination and secure a public-school certificate as a condition of drawing the public money. The nuns and sisters of the various convent schools for girls declined to submit to an examination; but the teachers in parochial schools for boys passed examinations, were appointed teachers, and were paid out of the school fund. For two years previous to this action there had been more or less discussion by the press as to the policy of apportioning public money to the support of sectarian schools. Through the columns of the *Pacific* and of the daily papers I had taken a hand in opposition to this division of the school fund. As a matter of course, when the consolidation of parochial schools and public schools went into effect, I was marked for decapitation. My official head was saved only by the determined stand in my favor taken by Ferdinand C. Ewer, a stanch Democrat, who held an office in the Custom House, and also edited the *Pioneer Magazine*, to which I was a contributor. I knew nothing of all this until several years afterwards, when Mr. Ewer gave me the inside history of the movement against me. Several other teachers, however, were "dropped out" to make room for teachers from the parochial schools.

Business Depression and the Vigilance Committee

In 1853 there had been a business boom, and speculation ran riot. But in 1854 there were heavy business failures, and in 1855 a great financial collapse began. There were one hundred and twenty-seven failures, amounting in all to eight millions of dollars. Two great banks, Adams & Company, and Page, Bacon & Company, suspended payment and became hopelessly insolvent, spreading ruin among thousands of depositors. Many other smaller banking institutions were involved in the general crash.

The business failures were intensified, and perhaps were partly caused by the corruption of the city government, which is thus graphically described by Theodore H. Hittell in his History of California:

> The political and social corruptionists of San Francisco included not only the usual criminal classes in general, but also regular experts in ballot-box stuffing, and, worst of all, those kinds of politicians who employed, abetted, and, by their recognition, gave encouragement and a sort of character to manipulators of fraudulent elections. Bodies of men frequently marched from precinct to precinct on election day, repeating their votes and swearing them in by perjured testimony.
>
> But what may be called the very perfection of election fraud and rascality was reached in the invention and at length frequent use of what were called "double improved back-action ballot boxes," which were so constructed with false sides that any number of tickets could be hidden in them in advance, exposed at the proper time, and counted so as to made majorities exactly as might be desired.

The facts thus accurately set forth were known to all citizens of San Francisco who took any interest in political affairs. There was no hope of redress except by force, because the whole election machinery was in the hands of the roughs and their abettors. It was under such conditions that James King of William started a daily paper, the *Evening Bulletin* (October, 1855), which boldly expressed the feelings of the indignant and despairing better class of citizens. Personally fearless and independent, he dared to tell the truth. A month after the first issue of this paper, William H. Richardson, United States marshal of California, was assassinated on the street by a gambler named Charles Cora. The assassin was tried but not convicted, four jurymen voting for acquittal, one for manslaughter, and seven for murder. From 1849 up to this time — seven years — there had been in San Francisco over a thousand homicides and only one legal execution.

Mr. King continued his reform editorials until he was shot down on the street by James P. Casey, a supervisor from the eighth ward of the city, — a ward notorious for its ballot-box stuffing and for fraudulent election returns. Casey was arrested and confined in the county jail. The intense popular excitement led to the immediate formation of what is known in history as the Vigilance Committee,— an organization of citizens formed for the purpose of enforcing law and justice. The leader of the movement was William T. Coleman, from Kentucky, one of the leading business men of the city. Fifteen hundred citizens were soon enrolled and organized into companies of one hundred men each, who elected their own officers. This number was soon increased to twenty-five hundred men. On the last night of the enrollment I stood in line until midnight, when the enrollment closed, because no more volunteers were wanted. There were a hundred men in line ahead of me, and thus I failed to become a member of the Vigilance Committee. An executive committee was elected and a thorough organization was soon completed.

Cora and Casey were taken from the county jail by an armed force, conducted to the rooms of the Vigilance Committee, tried in due form, and convicted of murder. James King of William lingered six days after he was shot before he expired. On the day of the funeral, Cora and Casey were hanged in front of the rooms of the Vigilance Committee. At a later date two other murderers were executed. A score of roughs were tried and banished from the state. After four months of active work the committee was disbanded.

Educational Activity Outside of School

During the exciting years from 1854 to 1856 it is not to be supposed that I did nothing but drill school children in reading, writing, and arithmetic. I contributed to the press occasional articles on school topics that were under discussion. Turning to my voluminous scrapbook, I find many of these articles clipped from the newspapers. The *Pacific* at that time was a well-conducted, influential weekly paper of large circulation, both in the city and in the mines. It was the official organ of the Congregational churches, but it was liberally edited with marked literary ability and was open for the discussion of educational matters. The headings of some of my articles in the *Pacific* run as follows: —

Examination of Public Schools; Against the Separation of the Sexes in Public Schools (three articles of two columns each); On Juvenile Depravity in San Francisco; Against the Apportionment of School Moneys to Denominational Schools; etc.

By a rule of the board of education all teachers were required to attend a normal school held on Saturday forenoon of each week from nine to twelve o'clock. I find in the old files of the *Pacific* an address which I read before one of these meetings, from which I quote a few paragraphs to show the professional spirit of half a century ago:

> The question addressed to the teacher is, not how much do you know of *books*, but what do you know of *men* and *things;* not can you scan Virgil, but can you write strong English; not can you make eloquent speeches, but can you talk common sense. A living man is asked for, not a walking library. The isolated teacher cannot become a skillful one. As well expect a solitary man on a lonely island to attain high civilization. A child cannot be well educated at home; he needs to enter a class and gain healthful vigor by buffeting with playmates and equals.
>
> Association in some form is the soul of modern progress. We constitute the advance guard on the shores of the Pacific, cut off from the main body of American teachers. Let us organize and work together. Let us make our influence felt in leading public opinion in school affairs. The press is open to us; let us use it. All we need is common sense and uncommon energy. Let us meet together as seekers after truth. That our meetings may be the means of advancing each of us in the scholarship of teaching, that they may make us more skillful, more earnest, more liberal, is my desire, and, I doubt not, yours. It is only the little-minded that despise little things. Remember with Plato, "Men cannot propose a higher or holier object for study than education and all that appertains to education."

At a state teachers' convention, called by the state superintendent of schools, December 26-28, in San Francisco, besides taking an active part in discussions I read a paper on "Reading and Elocution as a Means of Culture in School," which was published in full in the *Pacific.* At a following convention I read a paper on the "Love of the Beautiful," which was published in full in the *Pioneer Magazine.* I sent occasional letters to the Boston *Cultivator* concerning affairs in San Francisco, and an occasional contribution to the *Knickerbocker Magazine*, which was then in its decadence. Meanwhile, I was a busy reader of books on science, history, and literature, drawn from the Mercantile Library.

The Rincon School Grows Larger

Early in 1856 the Rincon School was so overcrowded that the building was enlarged by the addition of a wing which gave us five additional classrooms, and, strange to say, a large office for the principal and the teachers. This office room I carpeted and furnished at my own personal expense, amounting to four hundred and fifty dollars, and it became a reception room for parents and visitors. From the proceeds of a May festival the school yard was fitted up with the beginning of a gymnasium, and I myself led the gymnastic class of boys half an hour daily during the noon intermission, and sometimes in the morning before nine o'clock, or at the forenoon recess. The girls were drilled daily in the schoolroom in free gymnastics and in the use of wands. In the springtime I often took the pupils out for walks on the hills of the Potrero, which were then a garden of wild flowers. I encouraged the boys to play ball, and on Saturdays invited them to go with me on long tramps over the sand hills to the beach and the "heads," often walking from ten to fifteen miles during the day. The boys took along for lunch a supply of bread and also raw beefsteaks, which we broiled on long sticks over a camp fire. Excursions of this kind the boys never have forgotten. As I meet some of them, forty years later, they always give my hand a hearty grip and exclaim: "I'm glad to see you. Say, didn't we have jolly good times together when you took us out over the sand hills?"

The good will of the larger boys I gained by becoming their leader in athletics and excursions, and they aided me in securing firm discipline in school hours. I took the older pupils on visits to foundries, machine shops, and flour mills. The school was under strict discipline, but I seldom resorted to corporal punishment, and then only in cases of the most flagrant insubordination. The corporal-punishment roll did not exceed half a dozen cases a year. The military drill in marching into and out of school, keeping step to music of the piano, and the habit of obedience in gymnastic drill, naturally led to good order in the schoolroom. Once a week, at least, I had a plain talk with the pupils on honor, truthfulness, courage, and other virtues, ending by reading some short story or anecdote illustrating some one of these topics. Politeness also received due consideration. In this way there grew up in the school in time an unwritten code of manners and morals.

At the annual city election in 1855, the Know Nothing party elected a part of its ticket and brought into the board of education several able members, among whom was William Sherman, a man of marked executive ability. He was elected president of the board in 1856, when he began his work by taking the preliminary steps towards securing a city high school, which was established, after much opposition, in 1856, under the name Union Grammar School, though it had a high-school course of study. In the month of April he personally conducted an oral examination of the highest grade class in each of the city schools. His examination of my school lasted all day and was thoroughgoing. He was accompanied by James King of William, editor and manager of the *Evening Bulletin*, the recently established reform paper. Mr. King was a close observer and I will let his editorial report tell the story:

Of the examination yesterday, we must say it far exceeded our expectations and was perfectly satisfactory as to the fidelity of the teachers and the proficiency of the scholars. The exercises in reading elicited unbounded admiration from all present. The girls all read well, but to our surprise the boys at this school excelled in this department of the exercises. It was a pleasure to listen to them. The examination of the philosophy class was the closest and the severest ordeal of the kind we have ever witnessed. The examination, made by Mr. Sherman of the board of education, was of the most searching kind, and the answers of the pupils evidenced a thorough acquaintance with the principles of the science which they had been studying. The questions were not alone such as might be found in the books, but were of every imaginable kind. In a variety of examples where the laws of nature were supposed to be suspended, the answers to the questions put evinced no little thought and reasoning on the part of the pupils. The answers in several cases elicited the hearty applause of the audience.

The official public examination conducted by President Sherman was followed by an elocutionary exhibition held in the assembly room of the schoolhouse, especially intended for the fathers and mothers that wished to see their children act their parts in reading and speaking. The program which is pasted in my scrapbook runs up to No. 30 in the list of readings, recitations, declamations, and dialogues. It took much patient drill to make forty boys and girls fit "to speak in public on the stage." This training I did myself, all except the preparing of the May Queen, to which my assistant teachers attended. The selection of suitable pieces was no small task, but this special training was never allowed to interfere with the regular work of teaching. It was all done before or after school hours, or at recess or intermissions. In nearly every such exhibition I wrote two or three original pieces — prose or verse — fitting the occasion. But if the work was hard, the reward was great. I came to know my pupils, and they in turn became attached to me.

May-Day Festival

On May 2, 1856, the Rincon School closed the term with a May festival at Russ's Garden, held for the purpose of raising money to buy additional calisthenic and gymnastic appliances. In addition to songs, readings, declamations, and dialogues, the boys, led by their principal, gave a gymnastic exhibition on the garden ground, which included exercises on the horizontal bar, on the rings, and with clubs, wands, and dumbbells. The opening number was a piece of "verse" written for the occasion by the principal, and recited by the May Queen.

THE MAY QUEEN'S WELCOME

Friends, parents, and children, merry welcome to all!
My rule is supreme in this beautiful hall;
The happiest queen that reigns under the sun,
I command you to join in the frolic and fun!

Dear subjects, from lessons I set you all free,
Neither schoolma'am nor master dare contradict me;
And puzzling committeemen, sober and glum,
Within my dominions will never dare come.

Poor students, with weary and woebegone looks,
Whose hearts are as dry as a bundle of books;
Escape from confinement, grow merry and gay,
And come to the free school of laughing Miss May.

Brave boys, from the schoolroom I turn you all out
To grass, like young calves, to cut capers about;
Sweet girls, you may romp till each ruddy cheek glows
With a color that vies with the red of the rose.

My books are green fields and lovely wild flowers,
My playgrounds, the hillsides; my schoolroom, the bowers;
The birds, my musicians; my harps, the green trees;
My scholars may laugh and play just as they please.

Dear "old folks!" just think of your merry May-days,
When you, handsome boys, met the girls in their plays;
When plump little maidens, with coquettish arts
And sweetest of glances, tormented your hearts!

Dear fathers and mothers, were not you once young?
The sweet songs of youth, were they not by you sung?
Hearts still are the same as in good days of old,
The same pleasant story forever is told!

The girls meet you here with the sweetest of glances,
The toes of the boys ache to join in the dances;
And, mothers, if you do not join with us, too,
I'll tell the old tale of our fathers and you!

So, young folks and old folks, join all in the fun,
The dancers are waiting, the talking is done;
We'll meet you again on some future May-day
When we need a dollar which you have to pay.

James King of William, editor of the *Bulletin*, himself wrote about the exercises as follows, in part:

It was nearly twelve o'clock when we arrived at the large pavilion, before reaching which we could distinctly hear the voice of one of the boys who was speaking. The declamation was very good indeed. To hear Frank Soule's poem on "The Press" recited as it was by Master William Gillis was well worth a trip to the Garden. Several performances not on the program were introduced with pleasing effect, and among the rest were declamations from scholars from the Nonantum and North Beach schools. After the exhibition was through, a recess was had to allow the children to refresh themselves with a cold lunch, and here occurred another item worth mentioning. In announcing the fact, Mr. Swett added that "after the children were served, there would be room and plenty to eat for the grown people." This announcement of reversing the usual order of things was received by the "grown-up" ones with unbounded satisfaction, the impression being that as this was a *children's* festival the children should be served first, and this spirit was kept up throughout. It was announced that the dances would at first be confined to the children of Mr. Swett's school, then those of the other schools present would be invited to join, after which the older persons generally would be invited to join in. The May Queen and her attendants led off, and in succession as more room was made, others joined in, until finally the large floor was crowded with young and old, and all enjoyed themselves to their hearts' content. The scene presented to the view, as the many little ones were whirling in graceful measures, was enough to convert the strictest Presbyterian that ever lived. We left at about half-past five, and even at that hour a large number were keeping up the festivity. From all the teachers, and from as many of the scholars as we could speak to, we received a hearty welcome, which we shall never forget.

What little doubt we ever had of the propriety of boys and girls going to the same school was all dispelled. We go in for it with all our hearts. At Mr. Swett's school the other day, we were pleased to notice a little act of gallantry on the part of one of the boys. The reading class was standing near a window curtain which kept waving back and forth over the book of a school-girl, when the nearest boy stepped forth and fastened back the curtain. The act was done without ostentation. It was a simple act, possibly a trifle, but that boy acted the gentleman, and the influence of that sweet girl already had its effect in that room. What wonder that the girl's "report" stood so high, or that the boy's answers to the questions put to him evinced such close application to his studies! Let the boys and girls go to the same school, we say. Place them in the same room and the same classes.

These were the last editorial comments on schools ever written by Mr. King. Eleven days later, on May 13, 1856, he fell on the street, a short distance from his office, mortally wounded by a pistol shot from the hand of an assassin.

School Examinations

In August, 1856, at the close of the quarterly term, the Rincon School held the usual public examination. The *Alta California* reported as follows, in part:

As is his usual custom, Mr. Swett held a sort of review or examination of the classes in arithmetic, grammar, and geography, followed by reading and declamation exercises. There has been added to the school grounds, through the efforts of Mr. Swett, an excellent gymnasium, in which the larger boys are exercised daily by the teacher, who appears to be as familiar with gymnastics as he is with the regular school studies.

When we arrived at the school yesterday, it was the hour of the midday intermission, and we found about fifty boys in the yard going through with their various exercises of the gymnasium, while in the schoolroom the girls were engaged in dancing up and down the aisles and in front of the desk. The improvements which have been added to Mr. Swett's school cannot be too highly spoken of or too highly commended. They are what should be supplied to every school in the city.

In October, 1856, the Rincon School, being in want of more money for gymnastic appliances, gave an elocutionary exhibition in Musical Hall, then the largest in the city. The readers and speakers included the older pupils that had been under training for two years, and the selections for reading were of marked literary merit. I shall let the report of one of the morning papers give an account of the exercises.

The room was densely crowded, every seat was occupied, and numbers were compelled to go away. The pupils occupied raised seats on the back of the stage, which was tastefully decorated. The program arranged by Mr. Swett was excellent, and the rendering of the various pieces reflected the highest credit both on the scholars and their teacher. It is proverbial, however, that Mr. Swett is one of the most successful schoolmasters in the city, so no one was surprised at the excellence of the entertainment. We have no space for particular notices of those who took part. After the exercises were over, the pupils, teacher, and audience adjourned to Assembly Hall near and enjoyed themselves in the graceful mazes of the dance until the small hours of the morning.

Financially, the exhibition was a success. The receipts from the sale of tickets amounted to five hundred and seventy-three dollars; the expenses for halls, music, and printing were one hundred and ninety dollars, leaving a balance of three hundred and eighty-three dollars for school purposes. This sum paid up in full the debt on the school piano — one hundred twelve dollars and seventy-five cents; the debt on school incidentals and the gymnasium, one hundred twenty-one dollars and seventy-five cents, leaving a balance to the credit of the school of one hundred forty-nine dollars and fifty cents.

Leave of Absence

It must not be supposed for an instant that my time was mainly devoted to public examinations and exhibitions. The school now numbered five hundred pupils, and every room was crowded. The whole work of supervision fell upon me, and in addition to this I had the entire instruction of the highest class. The regular routine work in the ordinary school studies went on with the regularity of clockwork. The public examinations and exhibitions were the means used to bring the parents into sympathy with the work their children were doing and to make known through the press the existence of public schools. I had struggled first to gain a foothold, and then by strenuous effort to win recognition as a teacher. I felt that I needed a rest, and my mother was entreating me to make her a visit. Besides, I had a strong desire to visit the best Eastern city schools and learn something more about teaching and school management. I applied to the board for a four months' leave of absence, and my request was granted. Hearing of this, my pupils gave me a surprise by placing in my hands the following letter:

San Francisco, April 18, 1857.

Mr. John Swett,

Dear Sir: — Having learned of your intention to visit the Atlantic states, we desire to express our regard and esteem for you as a teacher, and we respectfully tender to you a complimentary party to be given to you at the close of the present term, at such place as you may be pleased to name.

With feelings of sincere esteem we remain,

Your Scholars and Friends,

(Signed) LIZZIE THORNTON,

Lucy Atwood, F. B. Lyle, A. F. Lyle, Mary Shafter, Annie Hucks, William Gillis, Frederick Russ, Henery B. Russ, Clara Cummings, Anna Chalmers, Mary J. Little, Emeline Anderson, Minnie Elliot, and seventy-eight other pupils.

Of course I named Russ's Garden as the place, and we set about arranging a program which included a few recitations, songs, declamations, the crowning of a May Queen, and a good social time. The large pavilion was crowded with parents, pupils, and friends, and the occasion was one to be long remembered. The receipts from the sale of tickets amounted to five hundred and forty-four dollars; the expenses for pavilion, music, printing, and incidentals were one hundred and fifty-four dollars, leaving a balance of three hundred and twenty dollars, which was turned over to me by the finance committee of pupils.

My Trip to the East

I took passage in the steamship *Golden Gate* for New York by way of Panama, paying two hundred and fifty dollars for a through ticket. The steamer was crowded with more than a thousand passengers. I had the lowest of three berths in a small inside stateroom. The fourth night out I retired early; the two men occupying the higher berths came in late, closing both the door and the window. About midnight I woke with difficulty from a deathly stupor of suffocation. I am satisfied that if I had not made a mighty effort to rouse myself I should have been reported in the morning as "dead from apoplexy."

That night of bad air in a coffin-like stateroom laid the foundation of a throat trouble that lasted for several years. During the remainder of the voyage I slept on the cabin floor under the table.

On my arrival in New York I visited several large public schools and was received most courteously by the teachers. In Boston I stepped into a large grammar school for girls and presented a letter of introduction from the president of the board of education of San Francisco. The principal, who was hearing a recitation in history glanced at my letter, waved me to a chair, and went on with his class. He was evidently in ill humor, for he badgered the girls mercilessly, and at the end of the hour told them to take the same lesson for the next day, threatening them with detention after school if the lesson were not thoroughly learned. Then he took his hat, remarking as he passed me that he was going to his lunch, and without another word he stalked off, leaving me sitting on the platform. It is hardly necessary to say that I made no further visits to the Boston schools.

I visited Professor William Russell at Andover, Massachusetts, and found him giving a drill in elocution to a large class of theological students. I presented to him a small gold nugget, about the size of a robin's egg, the last remnant of a few specimens that I had dug out of a drift in the Morris Ravine. After this meeting I never saw him again, but I received from him many kind letters of counsel and encouragement.

In Providence I passed two delightful days in the Rhode Island State Normal School, then in charge of Dana P. Colburn, whom I had met when he was a teacher of methods in arithmetic in William Russell's Merrimack Normal

Institute in New Hampshire. I recall vividly Mr. Colburn's drill of his class in geometry, which seemed to me the perfection of the art of teaching. I had the good fortune also to hear Professor S. S. Greene, author of Greene's Grammar, give a lesson in language that I still recall with delight.

My mother welcomed me home with joy, but her grief was great when I was forced to let her know that I had returned only to make her a visit, and that my life work lay in California. In my native village I found myself a stranger. I visited the brick schoolhouse and the old academy, but went away saddened to find that all the boys who went to school with me had moved away to Boston, or had gone out West, or to Texas, or to California. I bade my mother a tearful good-by, went to New York and secured a steamship ticket for San Francisco *via* Panama, for which I paid two hundred and seventy-five dollars. The steamer was overcrowded, and some of the passengers were attacked with a type of ship fever before we reached San Francisco. Two strong men, friends of mine, died a few weeks after their return. I escaped with my life, though I had a severe attack of fever and a bad hemorrhage of the throat. But hard training in the gymnasium, combined with a rigid hygienic diet, finally restored me to health.

On my return in August, both teachers and pupils gave me a warm welcome, and I was glad to take up my congenial work once more. The board of education this year published a printed course of study, with the usual rules and regulations, taken from eastern reports. The schools were now classified as primary, grammar, and high schools. Previous to this time they had been known as primary, intermediate, and grammar departments, after the manner of the New York city schools. John C. Pelton became city superintendent, and William Sherman, president of the board of education. Written examinations were required for admission to the high school.

At the end of the term, in 1858, the school closed for the summer vacation with an examination and a May party which netted two hundred and twenty-nine dollars.

While my work in teaching was pleasant, the position of a public school-teacher at this time was no bed of roses. Overbearing and conceited men often made their way into the board of education and played the part of petty tyrants over school-teachers. The places of all teachers in the school department were declared vacant at the end of each year, and in secret session the board of education elected new teachers or reëlected the old ones. Some school directors had friends for whom places had to be provided, even if competent teachers were left out of the list. Then at the end of the year we were required to pass a long and tedious written examination in order to determine our fitness "to teach a common school one year." Meanwhile, I pursued a steady course of reading and study to make up in some measure for lack of a college training. I did more than my share of preparing papers for educational meetings and in contributing to the press on educational matters.

Superintendent of the Unitarian Sunday School

In 1860, at the urgent request of Thomas Starr King, I accepted an appointment as superintendent of the Sunday school connected with the First Unitarian Society, in which I had been engaged for a year as teacher of a small class.

I did not desire this appointment, but I felt willing to make any personal sacrifice to be of service to the talented preacher and lecturer who was pastor of the society of which I was a member. This Sunday school was a very large one, and was provided with a well-selected library. Horace Davis, afterwards Congressman, and president of the University of California, was the librarian at the time I was superintendent. Starr King was deeply interested in the public-school system of California, and I found in him a warm friend and wise adviser. In 1860 he delivered an address at the dedication of the new high-school building, in the course of which he spoke as follows, in part:

> The spiritual forces must be started soon in States like this, and trained to ten times their present vigor, or we shall be unable to wield the majestic armor and implements of our science and materialistic culture. Every time I enter a school building I travel back to the time twenty years ago (when I was a *young* man), when my name was enrolled in the army of instructors. During the three years of service appointed to me in that department, I learned so much of the difficulties and responsibilities of the office, that the stepping into a pulpit seemed like passing into an easier sphere of duty. We do not pay our social reverence wisely as yet, even in our most advanced and thoughtful communities.

Dedication of the Rincon Schoolhouse

The Rincon School had outgrown the rented building on Hampton Place, and in 1860 the board of education purchased a lot on Vassar Place, three blocks distant, and proceeded to build a schoolhouse, neither larger nor better than the old one. It was a very plain two-story house with four classrooms on each floor, each room seating from forty to fifty pupils. On the upper floor the rooms were divided by large sliding doors, so that the four rooms could be thrown together on public occasions. The doors were partly made up of glass windowpanes, so that the principal could keep his eye on the assistant teachers. Some years later I saw in the city of Philadelphia several antique schoolhouses on a similar plan, which had been erected when the Lancastrian system was in vogue. This poorly planned, cheap building was dedicated as if it had been a palace. On December 22, Forefathers' Day, the exercises were made memorable by an address by Thomas Starr King. On the morning of that day I received from Mr. King the following characteristic note:

December 22, 1860.

My dear Friend: — My sermon is not finished, but I will not disappoint you.

My wife will ride nearly to the schoolhouse with me, if the carriage will accommodate. I am sorry that I cannot stay all the evening.

Yours sincerely,
T. S. King.

Dr. Tuthill, the brilliant literary editor of the *Bulletin*, reported the proceedings, part of which I quote:

FOREFATHERS' DAY

The Rincon School Housewarming

Those who attended the Vassar Place School housewarming on Saturday night, will remember it for years to come — if not for what they saw, heard, or did there, then for the drenching they experienced getting to or from it.

The afternoon had been pleasant enough; the haze that early in the evening eclipsed the stars and moon was presumed to be only a fog, until suddenly, about eight o'clock, the wind rose, and the rain came dashing down in full-grown drops. Far the larger portion of the Rincon scholars were already gathered to their festival, dressed in their Christmas rig; and but for the irrepressible gayety of people of their age, the first rattle of rain on the window — it came so violently yet steadily, not with the impertinent air of a shower that knows it must dry up in an hour, but with the steady blows of a storm that is in for a whole night's frolic — would have started in every breast the question: "How shall we ever get home without drowning?"

The house was brilliantly illuminated, and all its rooms were thrown open. In the upper floor — the glass doors thrown back — as many as could comfortably squeeze into the seats were gathered for some exercises that should be commemorative both of Forefathers' Day and of the inauguration of a public Schoolhouse.

The Reverend Mr. Willey was first called — one of the earliest friends of the school. He spoke very briefly, but right to the point — the use of the school to a Christian people, the attention due from a Christian people to the school, the equal demand of the Pilgrim Fathers for schoolhouse and meetinghouse, the joint influence of the two in making our country what it is.

Then the Reverend Mr. King was introduced. Obedient to the rule of the occasion, "Be short," he too spoke briefly. With a few bold strokes he etched the picture of the *Mayflower* landing her famous passengers two hundred and forty years ago, on a day such as this evening represented, as well as weather could in California, the December weather of New England. Then for a moment glorifying this particular edifice, he traced back its history, and showed that its foundation stones came out of the *Mayflower's* hold; following down its genealogical tree, and found its roots twining around and burrowing under Plymouth Rock. Gathering up the lessons of the day and of the history of the principles that were planted in Massachusetts soil, he held them up a moment, that the old and young, the overcoated and muffled, and the gayly dressed little folk might see them — and then Mr. King retired.

The principal, Mr. Swett, followed. The thought that he enforced was this, that public education is the safeguard of the Union. In conclusion he recited the following original verses:

NEW ENGLAND MEMORIES

I

Let us talk together, brothers, of the good old Christmas times,
When sleigh bells on our northern hills rang out their merry chimes;
  That northern land — our native land — is shrouded now in snow,
  But round its blazing firesides warm hearts are in a glow;
No biting frosts, no cutting winds, no wintry snows can chill
The hearts that loved us long ago, the hearts that love us still;
  As the year brings back Thanksgiving and Pilgrim Fathers' day,
  Our hearts are turning homeward to Massachusetts Bay.

II

God bless the rough old granite land, and Plymouth's sea-washed rock,
And guard all wandering children of the hardy Pilgrim stock.
  New England's wealth lies treasured, not in golden stream nor glen,
  But in priceless souls of women and heroic hearts of men.
Our footsteps wander from her, but our pride is still to know,
We keep the steady habits that she gave us long ago;
  The ties that bind us to that land, nor time nor space can sever,
  Our homes are on Pacific's strand, our hearts are hers forever.

III

Across the Rocky Mountains, from Massachusetts Bay,
From Bunker Hill, from Plymouth Rock, there comes a voice to-day,
  Calling Puritans and Pilgrims in every distant State,
  To rally for the safety of the Union, strong and great.
We send our solemn pledges forever to abide
By the principles of freedom for which our fathers died;
  That granite shaft of Bunker Hill shall crumble into dust
  Ere the sons of Pilgrim Fathers are recreant to their trust.

With this — and here in a lump we will report the applauses which frequently interrupted each of the speakers, Mr. Willey, Mr. King, and Mr. Swett — the speaking closed. It had altogether scarcely occupied more than half an hour, and then recommenced the festivities. The ankles and feet were eloquent henceforth, and all the poetry that followed was the "Poetry of motion." The house was then more crowded on account of the storm, since most of those who were there as late as nine o'clock determined to make a night of it.

At eleven o'clock, the heavenly bottles being corked up for a while, and nothing but the mud remaining to make the going terrible, the exercises of the evening were suddenly brought to a conclusion, and the crowd dispersed. Probably not one of the hundred who were there will forget for years that Forefathers' Day comes just before Christmas, in the very center of the rainy season, just after the very shortest day of winter, and that churches, school-houses, freedon of thought and of speech, are elements as essential to the picture of the settlers of New England as its colors are to a description of the rainbow.

Near the close of the year I was taken down with a sudden attack of typhoid fever, during which I suffered a relapse which left me for a week evenly balanced between life and death; but wise medical treatment by Dr. Warren, together with careful nursing, turned the scales in favor of life. In overhauling my papers to refresh my memory of events, I came across the following note, written during my sickness, while I was hardly able to hold a pen:

MY DEAR PUPILS:— December 13, 1861.

I have been thinking all day of school, and the tears have gushed into my eyes many times to think that I cannot be with you to-day.

Since I last met you, I have suffered severely; and during the long, painful watches of the weary nights, I have often thought of the cheerful, familiar, pleasant faces which greeted me at school. I do not know that I shall ever meet you again as teacher, and so feel still sadder that I cannot meet you to-day face to face. God bless each and every one of you. I hardly knew how much I had become attached to you all.

I cannot write any more. Good-by. Your principal,
JOHN SWETT.

The annual examination of teachers was held while I was delirious with typhoid fever, but the board of education granted me a reprieve for three months, though an attempt was made to declare my position vacant and elect another teacher in my place. Of this attempt, made in secret session of the board, I knew nothing until told of it a year later. After my recovery, I passed a rigid examination and was declared "fit to teach a common school for one year," unless the certificate "was sooner revoked by the board of education." This severe experience fixed in my mind a firm determination to get out of school-teaching as soon as I could see any other way of earning a living.

MY MARRIAGE

To me the most important event of the year was my marriage, May 8, 1862, to Mary Louise Tracy, in the Methodist Church on Powell Street, San Francisco, by the

Reverend M. C. Briggs, pastor of the church of which she was a member. My wife was the daughter of Judge Frederick Palmer Tracy,[1] a prominent lawyer and political leader in San Francisco.

[1] Frederick P. Tracy, born at Windham, Connecticut, in 1815, was educated in the common schools, and bred to work in his father's machine shop. At seventeen years of age he joined the Methodist Church and soon felt called to become a lay preacher. In 1837 he was ordained an elder and was stationed at Newbury, Mass., and later at Lynn. In 1840 he established a newspaper called *The People's Advocate.* In 1844 he was pastor of a church at Williamsburg, Mass., where two years later his health broke down. One of his parishioners advanced him the means to take a trip to Europe, in 1846–47.

At the end of two years he returned, and edited for a time *The Cayuga New Era*, in the state of New York. In 1849 he joined the Argonauts and settled in San Francisco, where he was elected *Inez de Paz*, an office resembling that of Justice of the Peace, but with more extended duties. In 1851 he engaged in the practice of law and became city and county attorney. In 1854 he made a visit to Connecticut and brought back with him his family, consisting of his wife and four children, — Mary Louise, William Frederick, Grace Amelia, and Thomas Garnier.

Judge Tracy in early life had been a consistent opponent of the extension of slavery, and he took an active part in organization of the Republican party in California during the Fremont campaign, when he was candidate for elector on the Republican presidential ticket in 1856. As an effective political speaker, he had few equals and no superiors in the Republican party in California. He was a delegate to the Republican National Convention that nominated Abraham Lincoln in 1860. He was appointed on the committee on resolutions, and was selected to make the rough draft of the party platform for that campaign. While engaged in stumping the state of New York, worn out by exposure and fatigue, he died suddenly during the campaign, from the effect of a severe cold. His body was brought back to California for burial in Lone Mountain Cemetery, and his resting place is marked by a granite shaft erected by the contributions of his numerous personal and political friends.

When Judge Tracy was making the tour of Europe he became interested in tracing up the pedigree of the Tracy family in France and England, and on his return began a genealogy of the descendants of Lieutenant Thomas Tracy of Connecticut, from whom he was a lineal descendant. For ten years his leisure evenings were devoted to the work, and the manuscript of a thousand pages in his now clear handwriting remains in the hands of his family. This

Our acquaintance began in 1857, when she entered the Rincon School at seventeen years of age as an assistant teacher in the primary department. Her early school education was obtained in common school and academy in Connecticut where she was born in 1839. Her school education was supplemented by the watchful care of her father, from whom she inherited a taste for literature. Our acquaintance grew into a firm friendship, which ripened into an engagement of marriage in 1860. But the sudden death of her father postponed our marriage for two years. Our union was a happy one, cemented by strong friendship, which ended in a deep and abiding love. Though I had not been fortunate up to this time in securing wealth in California, I now won a prize worth more to me than all the gold mines in the state. After a life of mingled success and failure, of joy and sorrow, we are growing old together, surrounded by children and grandchildren, with no shadow on the sunlight of our fervent love which for nearly half a century has known neither variableness nor shadow of turning.

manuscript shows the descent of the Tracy family from Sire de Tracie, a Norman baron who served as an officer in the army under William, Duke of Normandy, when he invaded England.

One of his two sons, Thomas Garnier, was a cadet in West Point, at the breaking out of the Civil War. He withdrew to take a commission as Lieutenant in a New York City regiment and served with credit during the war.

CHAPTER VIII

MY FIRST POLITICAL CAMPAIGN

During the first decade of political history in California, the Democratic party, in general, carried the election of state officers. In 1859 the vote for governor stood as follows: Milton S. Latham, Lecompton democrat, 62,000; John Curry, anti-Lecompton democrat, 31,000; Leland Stanford, republican, 10,000. Two years later (1861) the vote for governor stood: Stanford, 56,000; McConnell, Lecompton democrat, 33,000; John Conness, anti-Lecompton, or Douglas democrat, 31,000. Though Stanford was elected by a plurality, his vote was 8000 less than the combined votes of the two opposing democratic wings, now hopelessly divided on the question of extending slavery into the territories.

Under the pressure of civil war, prominent leaders among the republicans and the Douglas democrats proposed a fusion of the two parties, which was carried into effect by a call for a Union party convention, to meet in Sacramento in June, 1862.

One day, a personal friend, the Reverend John Elliot Benton, a Congregational minister who took a lively interest in politics and public schools, met me on the street in San Francisco and said: "Swett, you ought to become a candidate for the office of state superintendent of public instruction before the Union Party Convention that is to meet next month in Sacramento. You are well known all over the state as a successful teacher, and you have enthusiasm enough to make a good record for yourself and do good service for the schools. The state school superintendent is the only state officer to be elected in the coming election. The new Union party is sure to win. The main contest will be for the election of a United States senator in 1863."

The idea of running for public office had never before entered my mind, and I told him I would take time to think about it. I was devoted to my profession, but I had long been chafing under the humiliation of annual reëxaminations for certificates valid for only one year. If elected state superintendent, I thought I could secure legislation which in time might give some kind of a professional standing for teachers. On the other hand, up to this time no schoolmaster had ever dared to aspire for a state office. The politicians in convention had always nominated political "workers" for office. Even among county school superintendents there were few professional teachers. As an exception James Denman had been elected city school superintendent in San Francisco. It seemed like a rash act to risk my position as teacher for a temporary office.

Politically I had been a republican from the organization of that party (1856), though I had taken no active part in ward politics except in endeavoring to secure good men elected as members of the board of education in San Francisco. But I had many reasons for supposing that I should receive the support of the San Francisco delegation in the convention.

On arriving at Sacramento, however, I found that Frank Soulé of San Francisco had also entered the field as a candidate. Mr. Soulé was a pioneer resident of San

Francisco, well known as a writer, a journalist, and a former member of the legislature.

One of my strongest friends was James Laidly, who came to me shortly before the vote was taken, saying: "Swett, I am for you, but Soulé is a political friend and I don't want to vote against him, so I am going outside when the vote is taken." I had become fully satisfied that Mr. Soulé would receive the nomination, but it was too late for me to withdraw.

My name was placed in nomination by the Reverend John E. Benton of Sacramento, seconded by William Sherman of San Francisco, and J. J. Owen of Santa Clara. Frank Soulé was nominated by Mr. Fitch, of El Dorado; George W. Reed was nominated by Mr. James McM. Shafter, a lawyer and politician of San Francisco, who, in the course of his remarks, said that his candidate had one advantage over Mr. Swett, — that of having had a "classical education." It was then moved that the several candidates be invited to take the stand and address the convention. This unusual action was entirely unexpected, and, as I was called out first, without a moment to collect my thoughts, my speech was entirely offhand. But Shafter's fling about my lack of classical education roused my indignation, and my rather forcible remarks won my nomination in the face of what had seemed to be certain defeat. The hard-fisted miners from the mountain towns rallied to my support. The other candidates were called out, the ballot was taken, and the result was as follows: "Swett, 126; Soulé, 96; Reed, 37." Before the announcement of the vote was made by the chairman, Mr. Reed was withdrawn, various transfers of delegates took place, and the final vote stood: "Swett, 139; Soulé, 105; Reed, 7."

The following is the stenographic report of my offhand speech:

MR. PRESIDENT, AND GENTLEMEN OF THE CONVENTION:—In making my appearance before you to-day, I rise for the first time in my life to speak to a political convention, and appear for the first time in my life as a candidate for any office in the gift of the people. I am proud that I seek an office so intimately connected with the profession to which ten years of my life have been devoted in arduous labor in the public schoolroom. I am indebted for the commencement of my education to a public school in the Old Granite State; and whatever I am, I owe to the school system of New England. It was my misfortune that, after fitting for college in New England academies, circumstances prevented me from entering; but I have endeavored all my life to make up this deficiency by patient and persevering study, and I claim that though not a college graduate, I am not an uneducated man.

In defining my political position, I am a Union man. I always have been one. I should be recreant to my ancestors if I were not, for my grandfather was a good Union man who shouldered his musket in the Revolutionary War; and his bones would rise before me if every fiber in my body were not for the Union.

Now it has been said in this convention that the nomination of state superintendent is a trifling matter. Gentlemen have said: "Nominate your superintendent and let the schoolmasters go home." Gentlemen, you *need* them at home. You never will make California union to the backbone until you have a school system so thorough that all the people shall be brought into the schools and thoroughly Americanized. Gentlemen, you are taking an important step towards making this a "Union State," in the event of any crisis that may arise in the future.

Cast your eye over the map of our country to-day, and show me a section of States from which men shed their blood most freely in battle for the defense of the Union, and I will show you that such States have also expended the most money for public schools. . . . Why, gentlemen, the men at Concord and Lexington who poured out their lifeblood on the 19th of April, 1775, were graduates of the American common schools. The men of a later day who shed the first blood of this civil war answered, on the 19th of April, 1861, to the tap of the drum, from the schoolhouses of Massachusetts.

Gentlemen, why is it that these armies of volunteers are invincible when gathered in the field? It is the fact that, behind the guns, there is the intelligence of the public schools, playing around those loyal bayonets like flashes of lightning, making them as invincible as the sword of the Archangel Michael. (Applause.)

The public must be awakened, and the teachers must be encouraged. I claim to represent, in some degree, the teachers of this State. If you give me this nomination I shall take it as a compliment, not to me personally, but to the working teachers who perform regular duties in the schoolroom. (Applause.) If you confer upon me this nomination, I do not consider that you will give me any additional honor. I believe that the place which I occupy now is as honorable as that of superintendent of public instruction. If you give me the nomination, I shall thank you for it; and if not, I shall go back without a shadow of regret to my duties in the schoolroom, where I may do something toward Americanizing the children of this State and inspiring them with a love of liberty and a regard for the rights of men. (Applause.)

The Lecompton wing of the Democratic party nominated for state superintendent Rev. O. P. Fitzgerald, a clergyman of the Methodist Episcopal Church South. A wing of the Douglas Democrats that refused to follow John Conness into the Union party nominated for the same office Jonathan D. Stevenson, colonel of a New York regiment of volunteers sent out to California during the war with Mexico.

It so happened that the superintendent of public instruction was the only state officer to be elected in 1862, though members of the legislature and county officers were included in the election. The vote for state school superintendent, therefore, would be taken as an index of the relative strength of the three political parties. For this reason party spirit ran high, and the campaign was waged with intense bitterness. The public-school question was discussed at public meetings as it never had been before in California. The press teemed with editorials on schools and taxation.

The state central committee ordered me to stump the state, and then left me to take care of myself and pay my own expenses. Learning that John Conness was about to start out on a stumping tour in behalf of the legislative ticket of the Union party, I asked him to take me under his wing. He welcomed me cordially, and, as he was a veteran politician, a stanch Union man, and an earnest supporter of public schools, his aid was invaluable to a political tyro like myself. In this stumping tour I was allowed ten or fifteen minutes for making a few educational remarks as a kind of introduction to the main political speech by Mr. Conness. Though unused to public speaking, I got through the campaign creditably, because I made no attempts at oratory but confined my remarks mainly to the needs of the public schools. We filled engagements to speak in Sacramento, Marysville, Columbia, Sonora, Stockton, and many other places of minor importance. In this way I became personally acquainted with many of the leading Union men of the state.

I soon became accustomed to the misrepresentation and abuse of the opposition press. As I was a member of the Unitarian Church in San Francisco, I was held up as an "agnostic" and an "infidel." It was charged also that I was an abolitionist, and a believer in "amalgamation."

Thousands of illustrated handbills, after the style of the famous coffin handbills in the days of Andrew Jackson, were scattered broadcast over the state. These leaflets of campaign literature pictured a Yankee schoolmaster teaching a mixed class of whites and blacks standing in line, with a little negro boy at the head of the class. These attacks, however, had little effect on the vote on election day, which stood as follows: Swett, 51,238; Stevenson, 21,215; Fitzgerald, 15,514.

The Union party had a good working majority of members elected to the legislature, and at the following session

John Conness was elected United States Senator. Senator Conness, born in Ireland but educated in a New York City public school, proved to be one of the stanchest supporters of the administration of Abraham Lincoln during the stormy period of the Civil War. He was also eminently successful in securing important and much-needed legislation for the state which he represented so honorably and ably.

After the election I remained in school until I took office, December, 1862; but before retiring I delivered an address before the City Teachers' Association on the subject of "Public Schools and the Commonwealth," from which I quote the following paragraphs in order to show the spirit which moved me as I was about to enter on my responsible duties:

> Let me call your attention to the fact that this war of secession shows conclusively that our public schools have been not only the sources of intelligence and learning, but also the great nurseries of patriotism and devotion to constitutional liberty.
>
> Our American system of common schools was born in the old commonwealth of Massachusetts, where it early became an axiom of political economy that the only safeguard of republican institutions lies in the general education of all citizens of the state; for in a representative government public opinion constructs and modifies constitutions, and breathes vitality into all laws by which the people are governed. The common schools inherited democracy from a tough Puritan ancestry, and a stubborn love of liberty from the same source. The schoolhouses took up their line of march westward with the hardy pioneers; they spread over broad prairies and became camps of instruction; they poured through the passes of the Rocky Mountains, carrying in their train the blessings of liberty and law, and now they stand intrenched on the shores of the Pacific, conquerors of a continent and guardians of the Golden Gate. General intelligence, industry, prosperity, happiness, — all are the products of the common schools; but their crowning achievement is that they have educated an army of half a million of men who have volunteered to sustain the national flag with the bayonet.
>
> I have taught school long enough in San Francisco to see the boys of my first classes grow up into young men. Some of them are in the army, some

are in the foundries and machine shops and will soon be at work on an iron-clad monitor for the defense of our harbor; I find them in the stores, offices, and countingrooms; all over the state, wherever I go, I find some familiar faces to welcome me; and all these young men are Union to the backbone. The money which San Francisco has invested in schools and schoolhouses is paying more than two per cent a mouth. In the stress of civil war we begin to feel the real worth of free institutions, of sound statesmen, of honest men, and of a stable government. In no way can our patriotism take a more practical form than that of organizing and perfecting our common-school system.

Our state is one of the richest in its natural resources, favored in climate and situation above most other states; but what are lands, and seas, and skies, and mines of silver, and mountains of gold, without society, without culture and art, without morality and religion, and without free labor and free institutions? The Confederates say, "Cotton is king;" some say, "Gold is king;" but we say that free labor is a king mightier than both together. The real wealth of California lies not so much in gold mines as in the hard-fisted men that work them. Intelligent free laborers are working out the problem of civilization from ocean to ocean; educated fighting men are consolidating our government on the battle fields, and the common schools, free as air, vital as electricity, vivifying as the sunlight, are silently molding the life of the nation. In this great national crisis let us consecrate ourselves anew to our work in educating the boys and girls that shall preserve this government from future disunion and secession. . . .

It is my purpose to canvass the state, not by haranguing political gatherings, but by visiting schools, by encouraging teachers, and by talking of free public schools supported by liberal taxation, in every hall or schoolhouse where a dozen men and women will assemble to hear me. If the state refuses to pay my traveling expenses, I shall be ready to pack my blankets as I did in the mines on the Feather River, trudging along on foot and foraging on the line of march.

CHAPTER IX

OFFICIAL WORK AND PERSONAL REMINISCENCES

On the first Monday in December, 1862, I began my official duties as state superintendent. My predecessor, Mr. Andrew J. Moulder, had been allowed to hold his office room in San Francisco because that city was then the public-school center, and I secured a similar privilege. Only thirty-two years of age, I found myself the youngest of the state officials, among whom were Leland Stanford, governor, and Frank M. Pixley, attorney-general. Though inexperienced in political affairs, I was grimly in earnest about extending a free public-school system throughout the state of California. I set about my work, bearing in mind a saying of Horace Mann: "Be ashamed to die before you have won some victory for humanity."

The term for which I had been elected was fixed by the state constitution for three years, but in the election of 1862 an amendment to the constitution was submitted to popular vote and was adopted, which provided that the judges of the supreme court and the state superintendent of schools should be elected at a special judicial election to be held thirty days after the general election. The purpose of this amendment was to take these offices "out of partisan politics." Thus I was confronted at the outset with an official term cut short to one year, with no certainty that I should either be renominated or reëlected. If I hoped to accomplish anything, concentrated effort was needed at once.

Before making any outline of my official work, it seems essential that I should here briefly outline the successive stages of school legislation in California before my administration, in order to make the historical view complete.

The Beginnings of California School Laws

The foundation of the public-school system of California was laid in the constitutional convention held in September, 1849, before California was admitted into the Union as a state.

Article IX of the Constitution provided for the election by the people of a superintendent of public instruction, to hold office for three years, the salary to be fixed by the legislature.

Section II provided that the proceeds of all lands granted to the state by act of Congress for the support of schools, and the 500,000 acres of public lands granted to the new states for the purpose of internal improvements, should constitute a perpetual fund to be inviolably appropriated to the support of common schools.

Section III required the legislature to provide for a system of common schools by which a school should be kept up in each school district for at least three months of each school year.

Section IV provided that the legislature should take measures for the protection, improvement, or other disposition of such lands as have been, or may hereafter be, reserved or granted by the United States, or any person or persons, to the state for the use of a university.

The first state legislature held after the adoption of the state constitution (1849–50) enacted no law whatever to carry into effect the constitutional provisions relating to education. At the second legislative session (1850–51), a very primitive school law was enacted providing for the subdivision of counties into school districts; for a district board of school trustees, three in number, elected annually for the term of one year, by direct popular vote of school-district electors. These boards were given power to build schoolhouses, but they had no power to levy a tax for building purposes. They could examine teachers and issue certificates "valid for one year;" appoint teachers for the "term of one year," and pay their salaries when the money should come from the mythical state school fund. The school trustees were required to report directly to the state school superintendent at the end of each school year. Though as a matter of fact there was no "state school fund" in existence, this school law provided for the distribution of the interest on said fund to the counties according to the number of school-census children and, also, to "sectarian and denominational schools, orphan asylums, and almshouse schools." Over this latter provision there was a running legislative warfare which was not ended until 1861. This abortive school law made no provision whatever for district, county, or state school taxes, but left the schools dependent on rate bills, tuition fees, and subscriptions, until the appearance of the dazzling "state school fund" to be derived from the future sales of congressional land grants.

The next succeeding legislature (1852–53) amended the school law by authorizing counties to levy a school tax "not to exceed three cents on a hundred dollars." It also made the county treasurers *ex-officio* county school superintendents for the purpose of apportioning the beggarly pittance thus obtained. It furthermore provided that citizens should have power to raise by tax whatever amount of money was necessary for school purposes; that counties could levy a school tax not to exceed five cents on a hundred dollars; and that religious and sectarian schools should receive a *pro rata* share of the "school fund." In 1852–53 the total number of public schools in the state was twenty, with an enrollment of 3314 pupils; in 1853–54 there were 111 schools, with an average attendance of 4635.

In 1854–55 there was no school legislation, but in 1855–56 the school law was revised and materially improved. This law provided for the election of county superintendents by popular vote and defined their duties; empowered incorporated cities to raise a school tax not exceeding twenty-five cents on a hundred dollars; provided by election or by appointment for city boards of education and city school superintendents, and authorized counties to levy a county school tax not to exceed ten cents on a hundred dollars. It also provided that no school should be entitled to receive public-school money unless it had been taught by teachers duly examined and approved by legal authority, and that no sectarian books should be used and no sectarian doctrines should be taught in any school under penalty of forfeiting the public funds.

The legislature of 1857 made no school amendments worth mentioning, but in 1858–59 an advance was made which enabled school districts, by a vote of the electors, to levy district taxes for the support of schools or for building schoolhouses, under the restriction that the district should maintain a school four months in the year. A special law was passed providing for the sale of the remainder of the five-hundred-thousand-acre land grant of

Congress, and of the seventy-two sections for a state university.

In 1860–61 the maximum rate for county school tax was raised from ten cents to twenty-five cents on a hundred dollars; the state superintendent was authorized to hold annually a state teachers' institute, to appoint a state board of examination with power to grant state certificates valid for two years. County superintendents were authorized to appoint county boards of examination with power to grant certificates valid for one year. These advances in school law were secured in the main by Andrew J. Moulder, a graduate of the University of Virginia, who was elected state superintendent in 1856, and reëlected for a second term in 1859.

Thus ended the evolution of school laws for the first decade of common-school history in California. It is evident from the preceding brief statement of school organization that the general plan resembled that of the state of New York rather than that of New England. Indeed, the great area and the sparse and scattered population rendered township organization impracticable in California. From the beginning there were two distinct lines of development; one was that of incorporated cities with their local schools provided for by special charters; the other, that of rural schools in which the county was the unit of control under direct state school law. In this protozoic period the people in the centers of population were in a stage of school development far in advance of general state legislation, while the rural district schools were kept up in a rude way for three or four months in the year by means of tuition fees or rate bills.

In 1860, at the end of the first decade of school history,

California reported a common-school enrollment of 26,993 pupils, with an average daily attendance of 14,750, in 593 public schools, taught by 831 teachers, and conducted at an expense of $474,000. The total amount expended for common schools during this decade was in round numbers $2,586,000.

Amendments to the School Law, 1862–63.

After a careful study of the state school law and the reports of my predecessors in office, it became clearly evident to me that no general improvement could be made in the public schools except by first securing a material increase in school revenues. My plan of action included three lines of attack on the legislature: first, a small state school tax; second, an increase in county school tax; third, effective means of levying and collecting school district taxes. At the opening of the legislature I proceeded to Sacramento and secured from the speaker of the assembly and the president of the senate the appointment of several strong men on the two committees on education.

In drafting the provisions for county and school district taxes, I was fortunate in securing the efficient aid of Daniel J. Thomas, a lawyer in Sacramento, who had been a member of the board of education in that city. He was an expert in drafting bills of all kinds for members of the legislature, and was a strong believer in public schools supported by taxation. Mr. Thomas put into exact legal form my rough draft of the sections relating to school taxes and the collection of rate bills. The school bill was then placed in the hands of the assembly committee on education and fully explained to them. All the sections were approved except the one for levying a state school tax, which was to the legislators a new proposition for which they feared their constituents were not ready. Accordingly I reluctantly withdrew it, but at once planned an appeal to the people in the form of a petition to be addressed to the legislature that would meet at the next session in 1863–64.

The school bill, as approved by the assembly committee on education, was passed by the lower house with no material amendment; but in the senate it met with strong opposition. By careful management and constant watchfulness, however, I finally secured the passage of the bill.

This amended school law provided:

For an effective method of levying and collecting school district taxes for building schoolhouses, or for the support of schools, and a legal method of collecting rate bills, also a slight increase in the maximum rate of county school tax.

For a state board of examination composed exclusively of professional teachers, authorized to issue, on written examinations, certificates of three grades, good for four, three, and two years respectively, these certificates to be renewable without reëxamination; also "educational diplomas" valid for six years, to teachers after three years' experience in teaching.

For county boards of examination consisting exclusively of professional teachers, authorized to hold examinations in writing and to issue certificates valid for two years, renewable without reëxamination.

For the appropriation of a sum not to exceed $150 for the expenses of each county teachers' institute, payable out of the county general fund; for the election of district school trustees for a term of three years instead of one year; for a school record book suitable for recording the daily attendance of pupils and for keeping other statistical records, such school registers to be printed by the state printer and supplied at the expense of the state; for empowering the state board of education to adopt a uniform series of common-school textbooks for use in primary and grammar grades in district schools, but not including the schools in incorporated cities and towns having special boards of education; and for the payment of the actual traveling expenses of the state superintendent, not to exceed one thousand dollars a year.

Office Work

After the adjournment of the legislature, I was occupied for a month in revising the official blanks required in the office, and in drafting forms for a state school register, for the various forms of teachers' certificates, and for official blanks for school officers. In this work the official blanks of the state of Illinois, kindly sent to me by Superintendent Newton Bateman, proved of very great value. The state school register, a modified form of that of Illinois, has remained in use for more than forty years without material change. My next official document was a special circular to school trustees, setting forth their duties under the new school law, and closing with the following appeal:

> As school trustees, you are the executive agents of the public-school department. On you must depend, in a great measure, the prosperity and usefulness of the schools. It cannot be supposed that you will neglect your business to visit schools, but you may reasonably be expected to employ good teachers, and pay them well; to purchase maps and charts with a small percentage of the county school money; to insist on the adoption of good schoolbooks, and to inform yourselves thoroughly concerning all your official duties.
>
> It may reasonably be expected that if your schoolhouse is meaner than half the barns in the district, you will call a district meeting, levy a tax, and build a new one. In a recent tour through three of the most fertile counties

of the state, and among the wealthiest, I did not find a single public schoolhouse which ought not to be returned by the county superintendent opposite this heading of his report: "Number of Schoolhouses which Disgrace the State." If you fail to carry the vote at the first meeting, try a second, and a third. *Schoolhouses must be built, and you are the agents whose duty it is to build them.* You can never make public schools the best schools until you provide neat, spacious, and comfortable buildings; and having built a house, the grounds should be ornamented with trees, and all the surroundings made attractive. And having erected a schoolhouse, and furnished it with modern school furniture, your next duty will be to secure a professionally trained teacher.

State Teachers' Institute

Office work having been completed, I began the preliminary skirmishing in a battle for a state school tax, by issuing a call for a state teachers' institute, to be held for five days, in San Francisco, May 4 to 9, 1863. This call contained a full program of exercises, and in addition an appeal to school trustees, teachers, and the people, in favor of increased taxation for the support of schools. Two thousand copies of this official circular of twenty-one pages were printed and circulated among school officials, teachers, and the people. One short quotation will show the drift of this appeal:

Raise the rates of county taxation for the support of common schools ought to be inscribed over the doors of every schoolhouse in California. When our gold mines are enriching the world; when our valleys are teeming with agricultural wealth; when commerce is pouring its treasure into our lap — shall we give less for the support of schools than the older states on the other side of the continent raise by direct taxation? What are lands, and seas, and gold, and silver, compared with men, trained and educated in the public schools to an intelligent comprehension of their rights and duties as citizens of the state and of the Union?

While other states are moving onward in a liberal support of schools, ought we, in California, entering on a new career of prosperity, — ought we to make the war an excuse for relaxing our efforts in behalf of popular education? As teachers, we are debtors to our profession; and our patriotism, in this great crisis of national affairs, ought to incite us to make an earnest endeavor to secure a system of free schools — a system essential to the existence of a free people, and to the permanence of a republican government.

In accordance with this call the teachers and school officers, to the number of five hundred registered members, assembled in Platt's Music Hall, then the largest in the city. In interest, in enthusiasm, in working power, and in results, this convention marked the beginning of a new educational era in California. The evening meetings were crowded by hundreds of citizens, and the proceedings were fully reported by the city press and scattered broadcast over the state.

Thomas Starr King

Among a large number of able addresses before the state institute the evening lecture by Thomas Starr King on the "Biglow Papers of James Russell Lowell" was the most brilliant.[1]

[1] A brief but pithy report of this address was published in the *Evening Bulletin*. This report, written by Dr. Franklin Tuthill, himself an able editorial writer on that paper, is too good to lie buried in the musty files of a daily paper, and I quote it in full:

" Platt's Hall was crowded to the extent of its capacity to hear the Reverend Mr. King's lecture before the Teachers' Institute last evening. Mr. King expressed his regret that, by order of his physician, he had been compelled to cease writing on a lecture specially adapted for an address before a meeting of teachers. The audience, which was chiefly one of strangers, did not share his regret, however, after he had got fairly started, for "Hosea Biglow," they insisted, was "good enough for them," as it was certainly the most entertaining of all the lectures with which Mr. King has favored us. It is about as hard to read Yankee as to read Choctaw. We are free to confess we instinctively shy from the dialect when printed, as boys do from Virgil in the original. But with King as an expounder, Biglow looms up and assumes proportions he never did assume before. King reads Yankee in right royal Penobscot way, as familiarly as though it were his native lan-

This was Mr. King's last address to the teachers of California. At this time he was engaged in delivering his patriotic lectures on "Washington" and "Daniel Webster" in all parts of the state. He entered heart and soul into the work of raising funds for the Sanitary Commission, and it was largely by his eloquent lectures that the people of California were moved to contribute, for hospital service, more than one and a half million dollars. I recall one occasion when he addressed, without notes, a crowded audience of the citizens of San Francisco in Platt's Hall. As he rose to the highest pitch of patriotic eloquence, men and women, time and again, cheered, and cheered, and continued to cheer. I have heard in my life many great orators, but I never listened to a grander appeal than this. Only one other speech have I ever heard which wrought up an audience to an equal frenzy of patriotic enthusiasm, and that was delivered in 1860, at the American Theater in San Francisco by Colonel E. D. Baker when he was on his way from Oregon to take his seat in the Senate of the United States, at the breaking out of the Civil War. The great theater was crowded to overflowing, and the orator made the most brilliant speech

guage and he had been accustomed to strain syllables through his nose from infancy. Birdofredum Sawin himself could not have read his odes so well as his expounder does. We have been inclined to lament that Lowell had not written the Biglow papers in the common English language. The wit was so enveloped and hidden in husks and so atrociously uncouth and uncomeatable, that it scarcely seemed worth the trouble of picking. As a general thing it is a very cheap kind of wit that lies chiefly in the misspelling or mispronunciation of the language. But last evening it was made very plain that only through his nose could Biglow have fitly trumpeted forth the truths that he favored us with. There is a peculiar adaptation of the language he employs to the thought it clothes. With Mr. King to read them, the 'Biglow Papers' would prove a joy forever, if not a thing of beauty."

of his life. In his peroration he uttered the following words, often quoted, but never old:

> Everywhere the great idea of personal liberty develops, increases, and fructifies. Here, under the American government, in the land of liberty, the chosen of all freemen, the home of the exile, such is not the case. Here, in a land of written constitutional liberty, it is reserved for us to teach the world that, under the American stars and stripes, slavery marches in solemn procession; that under the American flag, slavery is protected to the utmost verge of acquired property; that under the American banner, the name of freedom is to be faintly heard, the songs of freedom, faintly sung; that while Garibaldi, Victor Emanuel, every great and good man in the world, strives, struggles, fights, prays, suffers, and dies, sometimes on the scaffold, sometimes in the dungeon, often on the field of battle, rendered immortal by his blood and his valor, that while this triumphal procession marches on through the arches of freedom, we, in this land of all the world — shrink back trembling when freedom is but mentioned. . . .
>
> As for me, I dare not, I will not, be false to freedom. Where in youth my feet were planted, there my manhood and my age shall march. I will walk beneath her banner. I will glory in her strength. I have seen her, in history, struck down on a hundred chosen fields of battle. I have seen her friends fly from her; I have seen her foes gather around her; I have seen them bind her to the stake; I have seen them give her ashes to the winds, regathering them that they might scatter them yet more widely. But when they turned to exult, I have seen her again meet them face to face, clad in complete steel, and brandishing in her strong right hand a flaming sword, red with insufferable light! And I take courage. The genius of America will at last lead her sons to freedom.

Then the vast audience cheered and shouted with a wild enthusiasm equal to that which had greeted Starr King. Colonel Baker, not long after this, gave up his life on the battlefield of Ball's Bluff; and Starr King, two years later, worn out by his patriotic efforts in the pulpit and the lecture field, gave up his life in San Francisco, as much a martyr to the cause of Freedom as was Colonel Baker.

On the occasions I have mentioned it has always seemed to me that both King and Baker fully met the conditions of "true eloquence" so clearly set forth by Daniel Webster, himself one of the grandest of orators. I still retain a vivid picture of the occasions and the speakers, — King, slender, scholarly, and youthful, with a voice like the mellow tones of a great church organ; Baker, a born warrior, with "god-like action," and a voice that rang like a bugle call to battle.

Starr King passed away in 1864. He needs no eulogy, for his noble works constitute a monument which will endure as long as our state and nation shall be known in history. The public schools of our state lost a good friend and an able defender. In the midst of all his various labors, which seemed to radiate into every department of society, he found time to connect himself with the cause of popular education. Soon after his arrival in California, he delivered an address at the dedication of the San Francisco High School. He had partially prepared an address on "Public Schools" to be delivered at the State Teachers' Institute, but, being prevented from completing it by sudden illness, he gave his lecture on "James Russell Lowell." Mr. King was engaged to deliver a lecture before the State Educational Society on "Teaching as a Profession." Two weeks before his death he was also engaged to deliver the address to the graduating class of the State Normal School. He was the soul of the large Sunday school connected with the Church of the Pilgrims, and however exhausted by his Sabbath duties, he always had a little strength left to cheer the pupils by his presence. Teachers coming from the East with letters to Mr. King always found him ready to leave his work and introduce them to the officers of the school department. Many young men in this state will long remember how he extended to them a helping hand. His self-sacrificing spirit was marvelous. Those who knew him best loved him most.

Results of the State Institute

Apart from the professional stimulus given to teachers and the awakening of public opinion, the substantial and practical results of this teachers' convention may be summed up as follows: Action indorsing a state school tax; the formation of a state educational society; the establishment of an educational monthly journal; the recommendation of a uniform list of textbooks; the issuing of a large number of state diplomas and certificates on a written examination. A report of the proceedings, including many of the addresses, was printed by the state printer in a volume of two hundred pages, and two thousand four hundred copies were distributed among teachers, school officers, and citizens.

Argument for a State School Tax

In my institute address on the subject of "Duties of the State to Public Schools," I gave a brief outline of the evolution of common schools in New England in colonial times, traced the history of taxation for school purposes, argued at length the proposition that it is the duty of a republican government as an act of self-preservation to educate all classes of people, alluded to public education in European countries, and closed with an appeal in favor of a state tax for the partial support of free public schools. This address ran, in part, as follows:

When we stop to ponder on the vital relations which public schools hold to our national life; when we begin to perceive, amid the terrible realities of war, that the schools have been the nurseries of loyalty, and the lack of them the right arm of secession, there is a deep significance in this educational convention, because it concerns the future stability of the government, and the integrity, power, glory, and unity of the nation. Constitutions and laws may be bequeathed by one generation to its successors; but patriotism, intelligence, and morality die with each generation, and involve the necessity of continuous training and education. Public opinion, the sum of the intelligence of the citizens of the nation, slowly modifies all constitutions, and breathes vitality into all laws by which the people are governed. . . .

"The first object of a free people," says Daniel Webster, "is the preservation of their liberty." In a government where the people are not only in theory the source of all powers, but in actual practice are called upon to administer the laws, it is evident that some degree of education is indispensably necessary to enable citizens to discharge their duties, maintain and administer the laws, and to retain their constitutional rights. In a government like ours, either we must have officers unqualified for their duties, or we must provide a system of public instruction which shall furnish a supply of intelligent citizens capable of discharging their various official trusts with honesty and efficiency.

If left to their own unaided efforts, a majority of parents will fail, through want of means, properly to educate their children; another class, with means at command, will fail through lack of interest. All the children can be educated only by a system of free schools, supported by taxation, and controlled directly by the people. The early settlers of our country recognized this vital principle by providing by law for schools, and by making schools and taxation as inseparably connected as taxation and representation are bound together.[1]

Common Sense in Teaching

During the institute session I made a short address on methods of teaching in the one-room schools of country districts, of which Dr. Tuthill, of the *Bulletin*, made a condensed report as follows:

He was not talking of the course of instruction for graded schools but for the common schools, especially of the country, where the child that tarries longest within school walls gets scarcely over four years of training. In general terms, he held that nine-tenths of all that the arithmetics contain is worse than useless to the pupil; that the grammars, grown fat on all other grammars from Lindley Murray's down to the present time, are a nuisance

[1] A full report of this address will be found in Swett's "History of the Public School System of California."

and a bore when forced on little children; that the history which is crammed full of dates of unimportant events is not a fit textbook. He gave some amusing specimens of the facts, done up in abstractest style, with which the best educated children were stuffed centuries ago, and doubted very much if a century hence some of our much vaunted methods would not seem quite as absurd. He begged teachers not to let arithmetic become the nightmare of their schools; not to let their grammar be an incessant tearing to pieces of other men's sentences, but to let it teach them how to construct their own sentences. Let their arithmetic be, not a perpetual torment of explaining why the divisor is inverted in dividing one fraction by another, but the shortest process to make out a bill, calculate interest, and the like. The self-educated often shame the educated by the schools, because the first learn nothing that they do not need to use — hence, what they learn they learn well. Napoleon dispensed with baggage in his greatest campaigns, and his armies took only what they must use and could not do without. Teachers would do well to study his example. A great deal of what is taught in schools should properly be headed, "Things worth forgetting." We stuff our children with the names of a thousand dots that we call cities, and of a hundred rambling lines we call rivers, and then set them up as proficient in geography. Nature expels nine-tenths of it all from their memories as soon as they get out into the world. . . . Would that the bookmakers were forced to learn the text of one of their own books! Terrible as the penalty would be, they deserve nothing lighter for their sins. (Applause.)

Children should be trained to a free and easy use of the English language. Let them study it in such practical way that they will know how to write a letter correctly, and to distinguish an inaccuracy of language the moment it is uttered. But just how to do this is one of the most difficult things to say, though not so very difficult to do.

Mr. Swett in this common-sense style explained what and how much of physiology, of music, calisthenics, gymnastics, hygiene, and other branches should be taught. He urged the point that in all things the teacher should be practical — the youngest scholar as surely as the oldest appreciates what is practical to *him*. Mr. Swett was often applauded vigorously, and some stern mathematical faces were relaxed into smiles that still must have deemed all such sensible talk the rankest kind of heresy.

Petition for a State School Tax

During the institute, one of the county superintendents introduced a resolution, drafted by myself, requesting the state superintendent to prepare a petition for a state school tax of half a mill on the dollar to be printed and circulated in every school district in California for the signature of taxpayers and citizens, and then to be sent to the legislature, which was to assemble in the session of 1864–65. Accordingly I drafted the following brief but emphatic petition:

To the Honorable the Members of the Legislature of the State of California: Whereas, We believe that it is the duty of a representative government to maintain public schools as an act of self-preservation, and that the property of the state should be taxed to educate the children of the state; and whereas, the present school fund is wholly inadequate to sustain a system of free schools; we, the undersigned, qualified electors of the state of California, respectfully ask your honorable body to levy a special state tax of half a mill on the dollar, during the fiscal years 1864–65, the proceeds of the same to be disbursed in the same manner as the present state school fund.

A copy of this petition was sent, through the county superintendents, to the clerk of each board of school trustees, with the request to secure signers and return to the county superintendent, and by him to be placed in the hands of the legislative delegation from his county, for presentation to the state legislature.

The institute declared in favor of establishing an educational journal, and elected as editors myself and Samuel I. C. Swezey, nobody else being willing to serve. Mr. Swezey, a graduate of the New York State Normal School at Albany, was an attorney at law in San Francisco. The work of editing the journal was an added burden to my other labors, and Mr. Swezey's unpaid assistance was of great value. In the first number of this journal (August, 1863) the resident editors' department thus set forth the main objects of the *California Teacher:*

We propose to edit a journal devoted to the interests of teachers and to the establishment of a system of free public schools in the state of California.

We intend that its pages shall represent the spirit of the progressive teachers of the state. We intend to urge upon teachers the importance of a higher standard of professional skill, and the absolute necessity of combining their strength and talent in a state educational organization. We intend to urge upon school trustees the importance of employing first-class teachers, and the necessity of paying them higher salaries, believing that a good school taught for six months in the year is better than a poor school kept open for ten months. We intend to urge upon the people the pressing necessity of a state tax for the support of a system of free schools; and we have faith to believe that before this journal ceases to exist the last rate bill will have died out.

My First State School Report — 1863

The closing month of the school year was given up to the preparation of this report, which made a volume of 214 pages. The following are some of the main topics touched upon: Teachers' wages; errors in statistical reports of county superintendents; school trustees; uniform series of textbooks; state normal school; school district libraries; state college of agriculture and the mechanic arts; state school tax; the schools and the state; and the department of public instruction.

The vital part of this report related to the imperative need of a state school tax. A few extracts will, in part, show the manner in which this subject was presented:

If one state in the Union needs a system of free schools more than any other, that state is California. Her population is drawn from all nations. The next generation will be a composite one, made up of the heterogeneous atoms of all nationalities. Nothing can Americanize these chaotic elements and breathe into them the spirit of our institutions except the public schools.

As the first step towards the organization of a system of free schools, a special state school tax of half a mill on the dollar ought to be levied on the assessable property of the state. This would yield a revenue of at least $75,000, or about one dollar per census child — or two dollars per child on the number enrolled in the public schools. True, this would not make the schools free, neither would it continue them ten months in the year; but it would give a fresh stimulus to county and district taxation, and in four years would, I believe, give the state a system of free schools.

Public opinion in California is in advance of legislation. After traveling extensively in different parts of the state, addressing public assemblies, with every facility for careful observation, it is my opinion that the people would indorse this measure, were it submitted to a popular vote, by an overwhelming majority. . . .

A state tax of half a mill on the dollar was levied last year, and is to be levied annually, for carrying on the work of building the state capitol. Shall the work of building schoolhouses cease? By the time the capitol is finished, it will have cost more than the value of all the schoolhouses in the state. Is it not quite as essential that houses should be erected for educating a hundred thousand electors, as that a costly pile should be built for the accommodation of a hundred and fifty legislators?

A somewhat extended traveling tour through various parts of the state afforded me a good opportunity of "estimating the value" of many of the schoolhouses. Language would utterly fail me were I to attempt a description of these redwood libels on public schools; these uncouth *squatters* by the dusty roadsides; these unpainted, unfenced, unfurnished, unfinished, almost uninhabitable hovels — compared with which a miner's cabin of '49 would be eminently respectable in appearance. In a new state like ours it is not to be expected that either costly or elegant schoolhouses will be erected, except in a few cities, for many years to come. But in most parts of the state, in towns and villages where costly private residences are numerous, where large and commodious churches are built for every denomination, where courthouses and jails are imposing edifices, it might reasonably be expected that something better than a shanty should be found at the place where the children go to school.

In visiting several of the most prosperous agricultural counties, I do not remember having seen a schoolhouse with an inclosed yard, or one surrounded by shade trees or ornamented with a single shrub or flower. Many of these substitutes for schoolhouses were so wretched that no intelligent farmer would think them fit for housing his prize pigs. The stables of wealthy ranchmen in the vicinity were elegant edifices in comparison.

These schoolhouses were mostly built by subscription, and they stand by the wayside, like tattered beggars, imploring charitable donations. In many districts where the assessable property amounts to half a million dollars a tax for building a good schoolhouse would hardly be felt. Until the principle of district taxation for building schoolhouses is more fully recognized, the "number of schoolhouses which disgrace the state" will not be materially lessened.

In compliance with the law requiring the state superintendent to travel in the different counties in the state at least four months of each year, for the purpose of visiting schools, of lecturing before county institutes, and of addressing public assemblies on subjects pertaining to public schools, I have visited the counties of Alameda, Santa Clara, San Mateo, San Francisco, Contra Costa, El Dorado, Amador, Sacramento, Solano, Napa, and Sonoma, have traveled more than three thousand miles by stagecoach, have delivered thirty addresses on public schools, and have visited ninety-five country schools. . . . During the first six months of the year, prior to the beginning of the fifteenth fiscal year, my traveling expenses, amounting to three hundred dollars, were paid by myself, the old law, with a liberality like that of the "Pickwick Club," kindly allowing the superintendent to visit all the schools in the state and lecture in every schoolhouse, provided "*no expense was incurred to the state.*" . . .

I have endeavored to set forth in plain words the defects and the wants of our public-school system. It would have been pleasanter to find more to commend and less to censure; but unmerited laudation seldom effects needed reforms. In entering upon another official term of four years, I am able to comprehend in some measure the magnitude of the work to be done, and I assume the task in no spirit of self-confidence. I have an ambition to coöperate with the many earnest and devoted teachers in California who are striving to awaken public opinion to a truer estimate of the relation of free schools to the future permanence and prosperity of the commonwealth. The efforts of teachers and superintendents, however, will effect comparatively little, unless seconded by judicious legislation.

I appeal to every legislator, in considering the question of a state school tax, to bear in mind that his vote will influence the destinies of a hundred thousand children for good or for evil; that the best "franchise" which can be granted to the state is a generation of young men trained to an intelligent patriotism; and that true economy, anticipating the future, sometimes consists in liberal expenditure rather than in shortsighted retrenchment.

Official Incidents

As I close this account of my first year's work in office, there comes to mind an incident which will illustrate the manner in which I talked to the people when I went out on a visiting tour. At a meeting of the State Teachers' Association held in Pacific Grove, 1901, an elderly woman, somewhat bowed with years, accosted me with the remark that she was glad to meet me again. "Where did you ever meet me before?" I asked.

"One day when I was teaching in the town of Santa Clara," she said, "a stranger entered the little room into which my school children were crowded almost to suffocation. He said he wished to visit the school for a few minutes, but did not give his name, merely asking me to go on with my class. Very soon he asked me if I would allow him to speak to the children. After telling the pupils that they had a good teacher and that they were intelligent and well-behaved boys and girls, he paused a moment and then went on as follows: 'You and your teacher are too good for this miserable little shanty in which you are crowded so that some of you have no desks and some are sitting on the platform. I want you to pack up your books when school is dismissed, carry them home, and say to your parents that the state superintendent of public instruction, Mr. Swett, visited you to-day, and directed you to tell them that you have struck work, and are not going to school any more until you are provided with a better schoolhouse.' Then, when the children had gone, you turned to me and remarked that you thought that message would wake up the people. And it did wake them up. The trustees immediately secured a larger room, and in the course of the year we had a new schoolhouse. This happened long years ago, and I have never had a chance to speak to you and thank you until to-day for what you did for me and my school."

In the heavy pressure of my work I had entirely forgotten this school visit until the words of this teacher brought vividly to mind the impulsive way I had, at that time, of expressing my indignation against wretched schoolhouses and overcrowded schoolrooms.

On that same visiting tour I had occasion to speak of an overcrowded one-room schoolhouse in Oakland, which was then a small suburban village. The one school building that the town then owned had been built by Horace Carpentier at a cost of perhaps a thousand dollars, and as a reward for his benevolence the town council granted to him a "franchise" covering most of the water front of the future city of Oakland. In this school I found some of the children seated on boxes and others on the teacher's platform. I condemned the condition of the school in scorching terms, much to the indignation of some citizens of Oakland; but the people next year built a larger schoolhouse. Another lecture at Redwood City resulted in the immediate building of a spacious schoolhouse.

In my visiting tours I delivered no elaborately written addresses on education in the abstract, but whenever the people met me in rural schoolhouses or in public halls I talked to them in forcible Anglo-Saxon about their needs and their shortcomings, about the pressing necessity of raising the rates of county, town, and city school tax, and of the imperative need of a state school tax to supplement local taxes. I believe that in these plain, informal home talks I awakened a widespread public opinion which enabled me, two years later, to secure effective school legislation.

While on a short visit to the schools in Solano County, I dropped into a small district schoolhouse not far from the city of Vallejo, where I discovered a teacher managing his pupils in a way that excited my admiration. I found that his name was Frederick M. Campbell, and that he had been a teacher in the city of New York. A few weeks later, on a visit to Oakland, I met the Reverend I. H. Brayton, the managing head of a small preparatory school for fitting boys to enter the little College of California, then in its infancy.

Mr. Brayton said to me, "Mr. Swett, can you recommend to me a young, earnest, and popular teacher who will take charge of this school and build it up?"

"Yes," I said, "I know the very man you need, and I am willing to stake my life on his success. His name is Fred Campbell. Write to him at once to come down to see you; you will engage him the moment you set eyes on him."

Mr. Campbell filled the bill. His well-trained pupils constituted most of the first small freshman class in the College of California, in Oakland, which became, in 1869, one of the corner stones of the University of California. Subsequently he was elected state superintendent of public instruction and then superintendent of public schools in the city of Oakland. He has joined "the innumerable caravan," but he will long be remembered for his genial qualities and his good educational work.

I recall a pleasant incident about another young teacher, James K. Wilson, who came into my office in search of a school. He hailed from the state of Maine. At the outbreak of the Civil War he had enlisted as a volunteer, served out his term of enlistment, and then decided to go to California. He was in a discouraged mood. The few letters of introduction that he brought with him had not enabled him to find employment of any kind whatever. Liking his manner, I said to him, "There is plenty of room in California for young men like you; don't get disheartened." Before he left the office I gave him a letter of introduction to the head of a large private school for boys in Oakland, which he presented, and secured an immediate appointment. Not long after, he became principal of the Lincoln Grammar School in San Francisco; next, principal of the Boys' High School in the same city; and, finally, the president of a national bank. A few days ago he met me on the street and said, as he gripped my hand: "Swett, I am glad to see you. You gave me the first words of hope and encouragement I got in California, and I have always kept a warm place in my heart for you. Come into the bank and see me often."

There is no part of my official work that I now look back upon with so much pleasure as upon the efforts I made to find situations for teachers who, on arriving in California, found themselves stranded in a strange land. There were then no "teachers' agencies," and everybody was told "to go to the office of the state superintendent." They came singly and by scores. Remembering my own early experience, I was always ready to lend a helping hand. If their financial condition was desperate, I invited them to stay at my own home until I could find places for them; and sometimes I advanced them the money to pay their fare to remote country schools. It is hardly necessary to say, that in all cases this money was promptly returned as soon as the teachers received their first payment of wages.

After the close of the Civil War large numbers of young men who had served in the Union army, together with many who fought in the Confederate ranks, drifted out to California. The war was over, and I looked after both sides impartially. I recall vividly one day when General O. H. LaGrange dropped into my office and told me who he was and what he wanted. He had enlisted in the Union army as a private from a Western state, served through the war, coming out as a brigadier general. He had studied law and had come to this state with his wife and child. He could find no immediate opening in law, but he said he could teach school. He was a splendid specimen of robust manhood, and his soul was greater than his towering stature. I told him if there was a vacant school in California, he should have it.

In three days I sent him a note asking him to drop into my office. When he came I said "General, I have heard of a good school at San Leandro, the county seat of Alameda County, five or six miles from the city of Oakland. I'll go there with you. When will you be ready to march?" "I'm ready now," said he, and away we started on a victorious campaign against the school trustees. He succeeded so brilliantly that, six months later, he was nominated for the office of district attorney of Alameda County and was elected. Next he became superintendent of the United States Branch Mint in San Francisco; then a lawyer in New York City; next a member of the police commission in Roosevelt's time; and he passed his declining years in an honorable position as superintendent of the United States Soldiers' Home at Santa Monica, near the city of Los Angeles. When General LaGrange was appointed superintendent of the Branch Mint I called on him to inquire if there was any kind of subordinate place in the mint for a capable young man, the brother of a very dear friend of mine, and the son of one of the organizers of the Republican party in California. Without a moment's hesitation he said, "My dear friend, I'll *make* a place for him. I have felt under lifelong obligations to you for giving me my first foothold in California. I'll do anything for a friend of yours." He appointed the young man as his private secretary.

At different times I had several ex-Confederate soldier-teachers quartered in my own house, waiting to be assigned to duty. With one more incident I must close these pleasant memories. One day George Brown came into my office, and his accent showed that he was born in Scotland. He had taught school for a time in Kentucky, and now had arrived here, a stranger in search of a school. I liked his manner, and said to him, "I know of no vacant school just at present, but if you can stay in the city for a week or two I think I can place you." He remarked in a pathetic kind of a way that he had but little money and could not remain long. "Then come to my house and stay until I find a place for you." In a few weeks he was sent to a good school in Mariposa County, which he taught successfully as long as he chose to remain there. Next he came to San Francisco, where I secured him a place in an evening-school class until he could do better. He was soon promoted to a place in the day schools, as vice-principal, and then as principal of the Hayes Valley Grammar School, the school which is now known as the "John Swett Grammar School." After a long and successful career, he resigned his position. By his thrifty Scotch habits he had saved a moderate competence. When he died he left me a bequest of five hundred dollars in recognition of the helping hand I had extended to him.

CHAPTER X

MY SECOND TERM OF OFFICE, AND THE REVISED SCHOOL LAW OF CALIFORNIA

An amendment to the state constitution, adopted at the election in 1862, cut short my term of office from three years to one year. Without opposition, I was unanimously renominated by the Republican state convention in June, 1863. At the general state election in September the entire Republican state ticket was elected by a sweeping majority of twenty thousand. The legislature elect was also strongly Republican in both houses, including many members of devoted patriotism, marked ability, and abiding faith in public schools. John Conness was elected United States senator, by this legislature. At the special election in October, Judge Sprague was elected to the Supreme Court, and I was elected superintendent of public instruction.

Frederick F. Low, governor, born in Maine, and B. B. Redding, secretary of state, born in Nova Scotia, were strong believers in public schools, who backed up their faith by their works. One of their first acts, as members of the state board of examiners, was to approve the bills for rent of a hall and for other expenses of the State Teachers' Institute held in May, 1863, in San Francisco. These were reasonable bills which the state superintendent was authorized by special appropriation to incur, but which the preceding board of examiners during the last year of Governor Stanford's administration had declined to audit on the ground that the expenditure was extravagant and unnecessary.

The main purpose in the school bill submitted to the legislature of 1865-66 was to secure a state school tax of half a mill on the dollar, and also an increase of county and district taxes. During the entire session I was in close attendance on the legislature, watching the successive stages of the school bill I had prepared. During the first thirty days of the session, school-district petitions came dropping into the senate and the assembly at the rate of from ten to twenty a day, until they seemed innumerable. The first petition was headed by the name of John Conness, United States senator. The legislators gradually began to realize that their constituents were in earnest about the half-mill tax. The signature of taxpayers to these school-district petitions numbered at least ten thousand, and the petitions were presented, day by day, in senate and assembly. One day a leading member of the assembly said to me, "For God's sake, Swett, stop these endless petitions for a half-mill tax, and we will give you whatever you ask for."

With but little opposition the school bill was passed by the assembly, but in the senate a fierce attack was made upon it by Senators Horace Hawes and James McM. Shafter, both from San Francisco. Senator Shafter argued that, under this half-mill tax, San Francisco would receive back by apportionment only about one-half of the amount the city would contribute to the state school funds; but his speech only made certain the passage of the bill, because it solidified the votes of all the senators from interior counties, who saw that their constituents would be the gainers by it. The advocates of public schools stood by it and the bill was passed.

The senate, however, attached an amendment which

came near defeating the entire school bill. This was a provision giving school trustees power to admit negro, Mongolian, and Indian children into the public schools, which was passed by a vote of 25 to 5. The assembly, however, refused to concur with the amendment, and after a protracted debate, in which strong efforts were made to kill the bill, the senate receded, and thus, after a hard contest, this decisive measure of a state tax became a law. This school bill had the earnest support of Governor F. F. Low; Secretary of State B. B. Redding; and John Conness, United States senator. Among the most active supporters of the bill in the state senate were the Reverend John E. Benton of Sacramento, C. B. Porter of Contra Costa, and Senators Crane, Cunningham, and Foulke.

I confidently expected that the half-mill tax would prove an entering wedge for a higher rate, and my faith was well founded. At the next session of the legislature, two years later, the rate of state school tax was raised from five cents on each hundred dollars to eight cents; and a few years later, the state tax was fixed at a rate sufficient to raise a school revenue equal to seven dollars per capita for each school-census child, at which it still stands in 1910. In 1864–65 the state school tax yielded $55,000; in 1900, it yielded $1,700,000.

Another provision in the school bill, hardly less important than that of the state half-mill tax, was a section requiring each county to levy a county tax sufficient to raise at least two dollars per capita for each school-census child between four and eighteen years of age. This seemingly innocent and reasonable provision, which encountered no opposition in either house, really increased the school revenue by a sum greater than that derived from the state tax, raising the rate of county school tax in many of the southern counties from five cents on one hundred dollars, to *thirty* cents on each hundred dollars. Before this act there had been no minimum rate of county school tax fixed by law. Of maximum rates the statutes were full. The first maximum rate was three cents on one hundred dollars; the next, ten cents; the third, twenty cents; the next, twenty-five cents; the latest, twenty-five cents. During all this period there had been no minimum rate, so that county supervisors had not been required by law to levy any county school tax whatever.

The school bill of 1864–65 also made it the imperative duty of the school district trustees to levy a district school tax sufficient, when added to other school moneys, to maintain a free public school for five months in each year, provided the revenue from state and county moneys was not sufficient for that purpose.

Mainly by the efforts of Governor Low and B. B. Redding, secretary of state, a special act was passed at this session which provided for the gradual funding of the indebtedness of the state to the school fund, which at this time amounted to $475,000. The necessity of some such action was occasioned by the plain fact that as fast as school lands had been sold the legislature had appropriated the proceeds to pay current expenses.

My Biennial Report, 1864–65

My biennial report for the school years 1864 and 1865 was submitted to the governor, as required by law, November 1, 1865. The school year in this state begins on the first day of July of each year and ends on the 30th day of June, in order to correspond with the state fiscal year. This report, a volume of 422 pages, was a full exposition of the educational condition of the state. In addition to statistical tables, the following topics were treated at length: Average length of schools; teachers' wages; school law; amendments to school law; school libraries; school teachers; the land-grant college; state and county boards of examination; improvements in methods of teaching; course of study for ungraded country schools; common sense in teaching; physical training; moral training; the Bible in the public schools; school discipline; public schools and taxation.

Attached to this report was an historical sketch of the evolution of the public-school system of California. This condensed history of one hundred pages gave an outline of the successive school laws, abstracts of the reports of state superintendents, and full tables of school statistics. It was made up from the records of the school department, from the journals of the state legislature, and from newspaper files.

It seemed to me a fitting time to gather up for future reference the fragmentary records of the schools during their early struggles; to trace their progress step by step; and to hold in remembrance the names of the men who were the more immediate agents in organizing schools, and who laid, by wise legislation, the foundations of their present prosperity. No complete file of state school reports existed at that time except in the legislative journals. Therefore I gleaned from the confused material something like a connected history of school legislation, reports, and statistics.

The financial exhibit for 1865 showed an increase of 92 per cent in the amount of school moneys raised by direct taxation over the amount in 1864; the average length of schools had been increased nearly one month; the average amount of school revenue from all sources had reached $2.58 per census child; and more than half the public-school pupils were relieved from rate bills. But there was a vital and intangible aspect which no statistics could exhibit. The stronger hold which the schools had taken on public opinion; the greater skill, earnestness, and ability of teachers; the improvement in methods of instruction and classification; the greater interest and enthusiasm of pupils, consequent upon the introduction of better books; the greater interest of parents; the civilizing agency of well-conducted schools in cities and incorporated towns,— these could not be expressed in figures nor conveyed in the words of an official report.

Sixteen pages of this report were devoted to the recommendation of amendments to the school law and an explanation of their necessity. One of the most important provisions related to school libraries. The need of school libraries was self-evident. We were entering on a new era in our public-school system—that of free schools. The time had come for *acting*. This recommendation was adopted in the school bill for the legislative session of 1865 and was passed without objection. It has remained on the statute books for more than thirty years with little change. During the past decade — 1890 to 1900 — this library money was chiefly used to supply the schools with sets of supplementary reading matter.

The state legislature ordered 4600 copies of my report printed, of which number the superintendent was allowed two thousand for general distribution and for Eastern exchange. Copies were sent to one thousand teachers in California, to state and city superintendents in other states; to educational journals and to public libraries. The Eastern educational journals highly commended it, and many distinguished educators sent me letters of approval.[1]

I have treated at length of the school law of 1866 because it represents the culmination of my study of the school system of other states, of my official experience, and of my persistent efforts with preceding legislatures to secure school legislation as the foundation on which to build up a public

[1] Professor William Russell, of Massachusetts, wrote to me as follows:

"Your Biennial Report is one of the most valuable documents that has appeared of late years, on the great subject of popular education. It seems to me most happily adapted to the circumstances of the Pacific States. . . . I need hardly tell you how much your course in California is doing to win the warm sympathy and best wishes for your success of all the working corps of teachers in New England. Your noble report is full of inspiration to the heart of every earnest worker in whatever part of the great field of education."

The Pennsylvania *Journal of Education* said: "Would that every sister state were in possession of a general school law equally comprehensive in its provisions, as methodical in the arrangement of its sections, and to as great degree divested of all mere verbiage and unnecessary legal technicalities. In its style and general provisions this is a model school law, and under its working, ably administered, as we know it will be, the El Dorado of the Pacific will make such bold strides onward as may render it necessary for older states to look well to their laurels."

Henry Barnard's *American Journal of Education* (1866) devoted ten pages to a notice of the California school law and the biennial report of 1864–65, and closed with the statement: "There is nothing so liberal in the way of taxation in any other state in the world. Superintendent Swett has, in this noble contribution to the interests of national education, laid our whole country under lasting obligations; and it is a highly gratifying indication of its value, that California's younger sister, Nevada, has adopted, for the molding of her public-school system, that of her elder sister, as matured and perfected by the indefatigable exertions of one whose long professional experience and peculiar qualifications for his present office, give such force to all his suggestions, whether regarding methods of instruction or legislative measures for the diffusion of education."

school system in California. The quotations that I have dragged out of the oblivion of official school reports have seemed better to represent the spirit of my work than anything I could now write about it. As a recognition of my educational work the College of California this year gave me the honorary degree of A.M., and soon after I received from Dartmouth College a similar degree. I have never made use of either, but I fully appreciate both compliments.

In addition to the strain of official life, I was worried at this time by financial embarrassment. In 1859, while on a visit to the Buena Vista vineyard of Colonel Haraszthy in Sonoma Valley, captivated by the beauty of the country and the glowing visions of the future profits of the grape culture, I was induced to buy from him a forty-acre tract of land and enter into a contract with him to plant it and cultivate it for three years, payable from year to year. I had long been dreaming of a small place in the country to which I could retire when worn out by teaching, and here seemed to be my opportunity. It is enough to say that, when it came into bearing, the vineyard crop did not pay the expenses of cultivation. Then the Civil War came on and there was no market for grapes. But I held on to it with a death grip, until it not only absorbed all my earnings, but compelled me to hire money at a high rate of interest to carry it on. Finally, like most of the pioneers in viticulture, including Colonel Haraszthy himself, I became financially involved with two partners, and was forced to sell out for the face of the mortgage. This was a severe loss, and the scar long remained; but fortunately the pressure of official duties was so great that I had little time to mourn over it.

CHAPTER XI

MY FINAL BIENNIAL REPORT

My final state school report was a volume of three hundred pages, which included, in addition to the usual statistics, summaries, and comments on schools, a discussion of the following educational topics: The inspection of schools; school discipline; the self-reporting system; religious exercises in school; moral training; coeducation; national Lincoln monument subscription; State College of Agriculture and the Mechanic Arts; the American system of public instruction; a general summary of public-school progress in school law and methods of instruction, from 1862 to 1867. As an appendix the "Revised School Law" of 1866, covering fifty pages, was published in full.

The school year ending June 30, 1867, marked the transition period of California from "rate-bill" common schools to an American free-school system. For the first time in the history of the state, every public school was made entirely free for every child to enter. In the smaller districts, having less than one hundred children and less than $200,000 taxable property, *free* schools were maintained three months; in the larger districts, having more than one hundred children and $200,000 taxable property, *free* schools were kept open *five months*. More than twenty-one thousand pupils attended *free* schools during the entire school year of ten months. A system of *free schools*, supported by taxation, was at last an accomplished fact.

When I assumed the duties of office in 1863, I saw clearly

John Swett in 1866

that it was useless to expect to improve the character of the public schools to any considerable extent without a largely increased school revenue, derived from direct taxation on property. At the session of the legislature in 1863–64, I secured a state school tax of five cents on the hundred dollars, which gave an additional school revenue of $75,000 a year. A bill was also passed providing for the gradual funding of the indebtedness of the state to the "School Fund," then amounting to $600,000. At the next session, in 1864–65, a further school revenue was secured by providing that the minimum county school tax should be equal to two dollars per census child. This little clause gave an additional county school revenue of $75,000. In 1866–67, by the passage of the revised school law, the state school tax was raised to eight cents on the hundred dollars, and the minimum county tax was raised to three dollars per census child, both provisions together increasing the school revenue by at least $125,000 a year. I need not say that to secure an additional school revenue of $300,000 per annum, in the face of the high county, state, and national taxation, during a period of civil war, was no holiday task.

During each of three sessions of the legislature I had been a persistent member of the "Third House," arguing, soliciting, meeting committees, and patiently waiting, with a determination to secure for every child in California a right, guaranteed by law, to an education under a system of free schools based upon the proposition that the *property* of the state ought to be taxed to educate the *children* of the state.

It was evident that even after the revenue was provided, the schools would be to some extent a failure, unless protected from incompetent teachers by a thorough system of state examinations and certificates. The schools cannot rise higher than the teachers. The second leading object of my administration was to secure professional teachers, and to elevate the occupation of teaching.

In 1862 only 50 per cent of the census children were enrolled on the public school registers; in 1867 the percentage of enrollment was 66. In 1863 the average public-school attendance was 20,000; in 1867 it was 46,000. In 1862 the amount of state school money apportioned was $75,000; in 1867 it was $269,000. In 1862 the amount raised by county taxes was $146,000; in 1867, $303,000. In 1862 the total receipts from all sources of school revenue amounted to $497,000; in 1867, to $1,287,000. In 1862 the amount paid for teachers' salaries was $303,000; in 1867, $696,000. In 1862 the total expenditures for public schools amounted to an average percentage of thirty cents on each hundred dollars of the assessment roll of the state; in 1867 the expenditures amounted to fifty-eight cents on each hundred dollars, besides leaving a surplus on hand for the next year of $150,000.

The Revised School Law of 1866

This school law, entitled "An Act to provide for a system of common schools," was approved by Governor Frederick F. Low, March 24, 1866.

Early in the session of 1865–66 I submitted a series of school-law amendments to the senate committee on education. The amendments were so extensive that the committee referred the entire law to me for revision. At this time neither the committee of the senate nor the assembly had a clerk or secretary, and I acted in that capacity for both branches of the legislature. The school bill was adopted, with a few slight changes. The bill, as submitted by the committee, passed the senate with only a few unimportant amendments, and the assembly in the same manner.

The more important advances gained by this law may be briefly summed up as follows:

1. A state board of education of nine members, and a board of state normal-school trustees of eight members; authorizing the state board of education to adopt rules, regulations, and a course of study for district schools, and to adopt a uniform state series of textbooks for such schools.

2. Providing that the legislature should furnish the state superintendent with at least two thousand copies of each biennial report for distribution among school officers and libraries.

3. Providing for the payment of necessary expenses for county teachers' institutes out of the county school fund.

4. Requiring the district clerk to furnish the schools with pens, ink, stationery, and school incidentals, at the expense of the district.

5. Providing for the legal establishment of separate schools for children other than white children.

6. Limiting the school hours of children under eight years of age to four hours a day, exclusive of intermission.

7. Establishing a system of school libraries by the reservation of ten per cent of the state school apportionment.

8. Authorizing a state subscription for an educational journal, two copies for each school district, one for the district clerk, and one for the school library.

9. Life diplomas for teachers having ten years' experience; city boards of examination; recognition of the normal school diplomas of other states; all boards of examination,

whether state, city or county, to be composed of professional teachers only.

10. A state tax of eight cents on each hundred dollars of taxable property; a minimum county school tax of three dollars per census child; and a maximum tax of thirty-five cents on each hundred dollars.

11. Authorizing and requiring school trustees to levy a district-school tax sufficient to keep a free school five months in a year.[1]

Free Schools At Last

In my biennial report for 1866–67 I stated that in 1867, for the first time in the history of the state, *all* the public schools were kept free to *all* pupils for a period of from three

[1] On this school law Professor Benjamin Silliman, of Yale University, made the following comments in an address at the commencement exercises of the College of California in 1867:

"By the admirably digested law of 1866 the people of California, in their 'Act to provide for a system of common schools,' have laid the foundation and set up the framework of the best system of general common-school education for the whole people which exists in any state or country where the English language is spoken. If the compulsory system of Prussia is more mandatory, we should hesitate long before exchanging for it the free scope of our own. Your distinguished superintendent of public instruction has done for the future of California what it rarely falls to the lot of any one man to accomplish,— the molding and training of the youthful minds of this and succeeding generations in the elements of a sound education upon a broad and liberal basis,— rich in the best fruits of a long and successful experience drawn from all sources. The full measure of practical wisdom embodied in this organic Act can be seen in its best development only as time crowns it with the fruits of successful trial; it lays broad and deep the foundation of intelligence and virtue in the commonwealth. . . . The same wisdom that has framed a law so catholic and ample as the common-school system will not fail when applied to the development of the details of the state

to ten months in the year, according to the number of school-census children and the taxable property of the school districts. This fact marked an epoch in the school history of California. The deathblow had been given to rate bills.

The Bible Question

For many years there had been more or less discussion in the public press and at teachers' institutes about the reading of the Bible in public schools. The school law contained no provision for or against the reading of the Bible in school, and the matter was left to the local option of cities and school districts. In drafting the several school bills of my administration, I left this question as it had been left from the beginning in California, one of local option. But from time to time, for this reason, I was attacked by some denominational zealots and some designing politicians as an agnostic and an infidel. Therefore, in my second biennial report I defined my position by making the following statement:

> Concerning the use of the Bible in public schools, there is a wide diversity of opinion. By some it is held that the Bible should be placed in the hands of school children, and used as a daily reading book; by some, that it should be used by the teacher only for reading short select passages; and by others, that it should not be read at all. The fact that the state school law has never contained any statutory provision either prohibiting or requiring the reading of the Bible in school, would seem to indicate that legislators have had doubts as to the right of the state to compel its use without conflicting with the religious liberty of its citizens. The Jew sends his children to the public school; and he holds the reading of the New Testament to be an interference with religious liberty. The Catholic objects to the old English translation of the Scriptures, and the Protestant to the Douay version. Therefore the decision of this question has wisely been left to local boards and trustees, who are supposed to represent the more immediate wishes of the people whose children attend school. In the schools of this state teachers who desire to read select passages of the Scripture in school are seldom interfered with by

either school trustees or parents. Both teachers and trustees have had too much good sense to attempt to force the daily reading of the Bible, when it would offend the religious prejudices or convictions of any large class of parents whose children attend the public schools. Every formal resolution to make the Bible a textbook in the common school has been voted down in state teachers' institutes and conventions; yet many of the same teachers who so voted were accustomed to read the Bible in school every day. The present is an age of the largest and broadest personal liberty of religious opinion; the children of all classes are found in the common schools, and school officers and teachers should manifest a tender regard for the religious scruples of both Jew and Gentile, Protestant and Catholic, and hold the schools free from any violation of the great principles guaranteed by the national and state constitutions, that every man be left free to worship God as he pleases, and to teach his children his own religious faith. The great purpose of the common school is intellectual and moral culture, as a foundation. It is left for the home, the Sunday school, and the church to teach forms of religious faith and worship. If each does its work without interference with the other, the result will be harmonious. If the church attempts to make the public school a Sunday school, the result will be disastrous.

After an interval of nearly forty years, it is with some degree of satisfaction that I call attention to the fact that the Bible question still remains one of local option. Furthermore, in all the cities and the larger towns, without exception, public opinion has decided against Bible reading in school, and the custom is retained only in a few rural districts having a homogeneous people among whom there are no objectors to such reading.

My final state report closed with the following leave-taking:

My term of office is now drawing to a close. I have not found the office a sinecure; I have not eaten the bread of idleness or of ease; for the past four years my work has been the hardest of my life. Traveling and lecturing more than half the time, attending county institutes, editing the *California Teacher*, the official school journal, conducting state examinations, twice revising the school law, attending three sessions of the legislature to secure the passage of amendments, preparing rules and regulations and courses of study for the public schools, answering the extensive correspondence consequent upon so many radical changes in school laws, preparing state reports and historical sketches of education—my powers of endurance have been taxed to the utmost limit. I sought the office for the purpose of raising the standard of professional teaching and of organizing a state system of free schools. I am willing to leave the verdict to the future. If, when my present term of office expires, I fall back into the ranks as a private, I shall feel proud of my profession, for I hold none more honorable, and to it I expect to devote my life.

I love the state of my adoption; I am proud of her educational record. I hope to see California as distinguished for her common schools, her colleges, her institutions of learning, as she has been for the enterprise of her people and the mineral wealth of her mountains; for the solid wealth of any state consists in educated and industrious men and women. If the common schools are kept up to the full measure of their usefulness, her future glory will be, not so much in her mines, her scenery, or her climate, as in the intelligence, integrity, and patriotism of a people that shall make wealth a servant of science, art, literature, and religion.

State Teachers' Institute, 1867

The fourth State Teachers' Institute assembled in the Lincoln schoolhouse, San Francisco, September 19–24, 1865, and was held without any state appropriation. The most important purpose for which it was convened was the holding of an examination of applicants for state diplomas and certificates. Among the formal addresses were: "The State and the Schools," by the Reverend John Eliot Benton; "A Practical Education," by Professor Martin Kellogg; "Physiology and Hygiene," by Henry P. Carlton, of the State Normal School; "Moral Training," by the Reverend S. H. Willey, of the College of California. An evening ticket lecture on "Queer People and Queer Places," by J. Ross Brown, netted the sum of fifty-four dollars for the *State School Journal*. An evening lecture was given on "Natural Philosophy," by George W. Minns, of the State Normal School, and State Superintendent Swett gave a lengthy address on "The State School Law."

The fifth institute, which met in San Francisco, May 7–11, 1867, was attended by about five hundred teachers. Among the addresses and papers were the following, in part: "The Teacher's Motives," by the Reverend Charles G. Ames; "Self-improvement," by Dudley C. Stone; "Readiness," by the Reverend John E. Benton; "State Educational Progress," by State Superintendent Swett.

Before adjournment the convention adopted the following resolution by unanimous vote:

"Resolved, That we look upon the official career of our able and energetic state superintendent, the Hon. John Swett, with admiration. That by the greatness of the results he has accomplished, by the wisdom of the measures he has inaugurated, by the conspicuous fairness and impartiality of his dealings with all who have business with the office of Public Instruction, and by the genuine integrity of his character, he reflects honor upon the State that he serves so ably, and is eminently worthy of the continued confidence of the people of this State."

From my institute address, delivered at the opening of this meeting, I rescue from oblivion a few selections setting forth the educational advance made during the five years of my administration.

STATE EDUCATIONAL PROGRESS

Four years ago, many of you now before me were present at the largest and most enthusiastic gathering of teachers that had ever assembled in this state. I remember well the circumstances under which we met. The army of the Potomac had been driven back from the disastrous field of Chancellorsville; and wounded, bleeding, and exhausted, the nation seemed to be gathering its power for the final wager of battle which should determine its fate forever. . . .

The old flag of a new nation now floats over every foot of the old republic, and everywhere under its protecting folds every human being may claim the right of free labor, free speech, free thought, and free schools. . . .

Since the institute of 1863, our public schools have been quietly and peacefully revolutionized. In the grand events of national history, in the building of cities, the construction of roads, the settlement of land titles, and the excitement of life incident to a new state, the progress of schools is hardly noticed except by those who are most directly interested in them. Then, we had little to be proud of in our educational record; now, California will not suffer by comparison with the most progressive states in the Union.

Then, the total expenditure for schools amounted to a percentage on the assessment roll of the state of thirty cents on each one hundred dollars; now, it amounts to more than fifty cents on the one hundred dollars.

Then, the teacher had no system of professional examinations, no organization, and little professional pride. In fact, a man generally apologized for being forced to resort to teaching until he could find something else to do.

Then, the "schoolmasters" of San Francisco were examined every year by doctors, lawyers, dentists, contractors, and business men, to "see if they were fit to teach the common school" another year. There was no standard of qualification, except the caprice of "accidental boards." Throughout the state, examinations were oral, and in most cases they resulted in issuing, to everybody who applied, a certificate "to teach school one year."

Now, California teachers have gained the legal right to be examined exclusively by the members of their own profession, and we have just cause to be proud of the fact. It has already done much to make the occupation of teaching respectable. It has relieved good teachers from useless annoyance and humiliation; it has increased their self-respect, stimulated their ambition, and guarded the schools against quacks and pretenders.

It was my sanguine hope for many years that, in this new state, teaching might aspire to the dignity of a profession; that teachers might learn to combine their strength, respect themselves, command the respect of others, and honor their occupation. It has been and is my highest ambition to elevate the profession of teaching, for I well know that in no other way can the public schools be made the great educators of the state and the Nation. If the citizens of this state desire to have good schools, they must pay professionally trained teachers high salaries.

It is only by raising the standard of attainments that the occupation can become well paid and respected. Set the standard high, and high wages will follow; set the standard high, and good schools will be the result; set the standard high, and teachers will be content to remain in the schools.

Four years ago county institutes were held in only two or three counties in the state; now, the law requires one annual institute in every county having at least ten school districts, and further requires that teachers shall attend and that trustees shall allow their wages to continue during the time of attendance. In this particular it is the most progressive law on record.

Our revised school law has received the warmest approbation from many of the most distinguished educators of the United States. Honorable Newton Bateman, Professor William Russell, Henry Barnard, Wm. H. Wells, John D. Philbrick, John S. Hart, and many others, unite in the opinion that the school law of California is one of the best in the United States, and in some points decidedly in advance of any in the older states. Our reports are found in every large library and reading room in the United States; are in the hands of all the prominent educators of the East; are sent to the Departments of Instruction in Europe, and are still requested by letters which arrive with almost every steamer mail.

Fellow teachers, the work is in your hands. All the machinery of school law, all the money raised by school taxes, all the schoolhouses built, are of little avail if you fail in the final work of actually forming and molding mind and character. But your work is not, indeed, limited to the schoolroom alone. You must make your influence felt on society. Attend the county institutes, write essays, and engage in debates and discussions. Write for the local papers. Subscribe for and read carefully a few of the best school journals, and learn what is going on in the educational world. Instead of complaining about the lack of interest on the part of parents, visit every family in the district, and wake up the fathers and mothers from their lethargy. Hold frequent examinations and exhibitions for the purpose of bringing the people in direct contact with the school and its influences. Start a subscription to increase the school library. A little money directly from the pockets of the parents will lead to a better appreciation of the value of books. Harass the trustees until they purchase school apparatus, furnish new desks, or build a new schoolhouse, if one is needed. If a special tax is necessary, canvass the district for it with the zeal and earnestness of a professional politician. Visit other schools, read new works on education, and adopt new methods of instruction. If you wrap yourselves up in your own conceit, and imagine that nobody can tell you anything about "keeping school," you will never rank among the progressives.

If the teacher be a man among men, he will command respect; but if he confines himself to the schoolroom, if he deals only with books and boys, if he writes nothing, says nothing, and does nothing, society will be certain to estimate him by value received. The true teacher should be a thinker and doer. The scholarship required of the teacher is a peculiar one. There is a sham scholarship which prides itself on diplomas, flaunts Latinized phrases, and ignores plain Saxon. There are pedants who hide their shallowness under the veil of dullness. Like Wouter Van Twiller, the old Dutch Governor of New York, they gain credit for knowing a vast deal by saying nothing at all. But any teacher with his intellectual and spiritual faculties in good working condition can be a scholar, whether educated *in* the schools or *out* of them.

We are apt to consider immediate results rather than their remote causes; and hence the power of the public schools is seldom realized. Light, heat, and electricity build up the material life of the globe out of inorganic matter so slowly and silently that we hardly observe the workings of their subtle agencies. So the schools act upon society, and organize its life out of the atoms of undeveloped humanity attracted to the schoolrooms.

A few weeks since I visited one of the great quartz mills in the interior of the state. I descended the deep shaft where stalwart men were blasting and delving in solid rock. Above, the magnificent mill, with fifty stamps, like some gigantic monster, was crushing and tearing the white quartz with its iron teeth; and I saw the immediate result of all this work in the heavy bars of pure gold, all ready to be stamped with their commercial value and to enter into the great channels of trade. Then I entered a public school a few rods distant, where a hundred children were sitting, silently learning their lessons. I realized the relation of the mill and the mine to the material prosperity of the state; but the school, what did it yield?

I rode over the line of the Central Pacific Railroad from the springtime of Sacramento into the snowy winter of the Sierras, and I saw the beginning of the great commercial aorta of a continent. On its cuts and embankments and rails and locomotives more money had already been expended than has been paid for schools since the history of our state began. I could see the tangible results of the labor expended upon the road; but where should I look for the value received to balance the cost of the schools? After thundering down on its iron rails from the mountain summit, I stepped into the Sacramento High School, and thought to myself: What are these boys and girls doing, compared with the men who are paving the great highway of a nation?

I go out into the streets of this great city; I hear everywhere the hum of industry; I see great blocks of buildings going up under the hands of busy mechanics; I see the smoke of the machine shops and foundries, where skillful artisans are constructing the marvelous productions of inventive genius; I see the clipper ships discharging their cargoes; drays are thundering over the pavements; the banks are open, and keen-sighted capitalists are on "Change"; and when I go to visit some little schoolroom, where a quiet woman is teaching reading and spelling, the school seems to be something distinct from the busy life outside. . . .

But when I pause to remember that the steam engine was once but a dim idea in the brain of a boy; that intelligence is the motive power of trade and commerce; that the great city, with its banks and warehouses and princely residences, has been built up by skilled labor; that in the construction and navigation of the ocean steamer so many of the principles of art and science must be applied — I see in the public school, with its busy brains, an engine mightier than one of steam; and the narrow aisles of the schoolroom broaden into the wide and thronged streets of the great city. I know that the school-boys will soon become workers; that one will command the steamship, and another will become the engineer; one will be a director of the Central Pacific Railroad, and another will ride over it to take his seat in the Senate of the United States; one will own the quartz mill, another will build the machinery, and still another will invent some improved method of working its ores; one will be the merchant who shall direct the channels of trade; one will be the president of the bank, and another shall frame laws for the protection of all these varied interests — and the teacher, whose occupation seemed so disconnected from the progress of human affairs, becomes a worker on mind which shall hold the mastery over material things.

Political Affairs

At the meeting of the Republican Union Convention in June, 1867, my renomination was conceded to be certain, but, as events turned out, it was not secured without a sharp contest. The nomination for Governor hung in even scale between John Bidwell and George C. Gorham, and in order to obtain the votes needed to secure the nomination of Mr. Gorham, the political managers, in making up the "slate," agreed to give the nomination of state superintendent to a candidate who was backed by the members of the Methodist Church North. But my friends, aided by the personal efforts of Governor Low, succeeded in breaking the slate. Under the lead of Honorable Ira G. Hoitt, who was some years afterwards elected state superintendent, twenty-one members out of the sixty-three from San Francisco broke free from boss dictation and voted for me; other delegates from smaller counties refused to be traded; and on the first ballot I received the nomination by a majority of forty votes. My speech to the convention just before the ballot was taken, as reported by the stenographer, ran in part as follows:

> MR. PRESIDENT AND GENTLEMEN OF THE UNION CONVENTION: Five years ago, when the Union party of this state was organized, I stood upon this platform as the nominee of that party for the office of superintendent of public instruction, the only state officer to be elected at the coming election. I then pledged myself to devote every energy of mind and body and soul to the public-school interests of this state and to hold myself true to the principles of the Union party. I shall hold myself true to the pledges I made five years ago. I come here backed by no combination or delegation. I present myself as an educational candidate for this office.
>
> If you deem that the experience of five years is of any value in administering the affairs of the department of public instruction, I ask the nomination at your hands. If you think any other man more worthy of it, give it to him, and I shall rest satisfied and content.

The nomination of George C. Gorham was regarded with disfavor by large numbers of Republicans who bolted the ticket and nominated an opposition candidate for governor. This action secured the election of Henry H. Haight, the Democratic nominee for governor, by a majority of eight thousand. The entire Republican ticket was also defeated, along with the candidate for governor. This result of the general election carried with it the defeat of the Republican nominees for judge of the supreme court and for state superintendent, at the special election one month later. The Democratic nominee for state superintendent was the Reverend O. P. Fitzgerald, of the Methodist Church South, who had been the nominee of the Breckenridge wing of the Democratic party in 1862. The educational and judicial campaign was one of great political and personal bitterness. Judge Curry was defeated by a majority of 3000 votes in favor of the Democratic nominee, and I lacked 1400 votes of an election. The personal efforts of teachers carried me 1600 votes ahead of the judicial ticket.

THE "CALIFORNIA TEACHER"

For four years Mr. Swezey and myself had borne the burden of editing the *California Teacher* without compensation, except during the final year of our editorial life, when there was a surplus of receipts over expenditures of about $250, which we divided equally. In the December issue, 1867, I find my valedictory as editor, from which I quote a few paragraphs:

My official connection with this department, and with the public schools of the state, closes with this month's issue of the *California Teacher*. I have been called upon to preside over the department of public instruction during the most trying period in the history of the nation, when the passions of men have been kept at fever-heat, and when the widely divergent extremes of popular feeling have admitted of neither compromise nor conciliation. It has been my endeavor during this period to keep the schools, as far as possible, free from partisan or sectarian control and influences. In the school law, drafted by my hands, there is no section which the bitterest partisan can truthfully characterize as "partisan," "political" or "sectarian." If speaking and acting for the Union during the war of secession was "partisan," then I plead guilty to the charge. . . . In my official acts I have known neither political parties nor religious sects. No teachers can justly charge me with any official discrimination against them on account of political opinions or religious belief. . . .

In my public acts and in my private life I have kept my character above reproach. I am willing to wait for the verdict of time to set me right. I am proud that, during my administration, a system of schools, free to all, has been organized; that teaching has been made a respectable occupation, partaking of the character of a profession, and that teachers have been paid something like reasonable wages. The work cannot be undone. The state will not go back of its progressive record.

CHAPTER XII

PRINCIPAL OF THE DENMAN GRAMMAR SCHOOL AND DEPUTY SUPERINTENDENT OF SCHOOLS

At the election in 1867, which proved so disastrous to the Republican party, Mr. James Denman, who at that time was the popular principal of the Denman Grammar School, was elected on the Democratic ticket to the office of city superintendent of schools in San Francisco. Fortunately I secured an appointment to the place made vacant by his election. The intense partisanship which had prevailed during the Civil War still existed to some extent, and the Democratic board of education hesitated about giving an important position to a defeated candidate of the Republican party. But many influential citizens urged my appointment, and thereby placed me under lifelong obligation for their earnest efforts in my behalf. At this time I was desperately in need of a position. By an unfortunate partnership investment in Sonoma vineyard land, all the careful savings of my life up to that time had been swept away, and financially I started anew without a dollar after my debts were paid, and with a wife and child to support.

The teachers in the Denman School received me with a warm welcome, and I cheerfully entered on my schoolroom duties. This school was in all respects a pleasant one. Under the school regulations at that time the principal was required to teach the highest grade class for two hours daily, taking entire charge of the class in arithmetic and grammar, which were considered the essential studies. The remainder of the principal's time was given to the general management of the school and the inspection of the lower-grade classes of assistant teachers. After five years of strenuous work in the state department of public instruction, my work in a grammar school for girls seemed like playing kindergarten. I now began a careful study of methods in teaching, by simplifying the instruction of the lower grades in arithmetic and by arranging work suited to the age and capacity of the pupils. For a time I took entire charge of written language lessons in the lower grades, and composition writing in the higher grades.

During the nine years that I had been principal of the Rincon School, the regulations had required principals to take entire charge of instruction in the highest-grade class, thus leaving them no time whatever for visiting other classes. But in the Denman School there was ample time for supervision and experimental work, as I was required by the regulations to teach a class only two hours a day. The school numbered seven hundred girls, divided into fourteen classes. My five years' work in the state office had enlarged my educational horizon. During that time I had made a study of city and state school reports, of school journals, and of the latest books on education. This extensive reading, combined with executive work, constituted an effective supplement to my previous academic and normal-school education, and though it never made up my loss of a college course, it helped to give me a fair equipment for my work as an educator.

On the 11th day of July, 1868, there was born into our family a son, whom we named William Russell Swett, after my revered teacher and friend, Professor William Russell.

He was a child of great promise, but when he was four months old a careless servant left open a window of his room on one rainy day, and he took a cold which ended in pneumonia. In a few days he passed away, though we did not consider him dangerously sick. Years afterwards a nurse that we employed confessed that she had thrown into the fire the medicine which our family physician had prescribed during her watch for a part of the night, and had then given to the child one of her own nostrums. We could not endure to live longer in the rented house in which our child died, and therefore bought a house on the installment plan, making a payment of $90 a month to the bank that held the mortgage. These monthly payments were made without default for a period of five years, ending in March, 1874. The burden was a heavy one, but with economy, prudence, and the wise home management of my wife, we carried it to the end, and appreciated our home the higher on account of the self-denial it had cost. My wife's mother had made her home with us for many years, and my own mother, after the death of her second husband, came to California and made her home with us. Notwithstanding my wife and myself each had a mother and a mother-in-law in the family, we lived in peace and harmony. At our home, 1419 Taylor Street, there was born, on November 22, 1869, our second son, Frank Tracy Swett, who grew through childhood under the watchful care of his mother and two grandmothers.

The Building up of the Lincoln Evening School

In 1868 I was elected as teacher of an evening school in the Lincoln building. In seeking this appointment I had a double purpose. One object was to eke out my salary of $1800 a year in the Denman School by the fifty dollars a month allowed for an evening school-teacher; the other was to build up a system of evening schools such as I thought the city needed. As early as 1856 Mr. Denman and myself had volunteered our services, without pay, if the board of education would open a city evening school. Accordingly, the school began in the basement rooms of St. Mary's Cathedral on California Street. At the end of a month we retired, and the board of education elected and paid three regular teachers. These classes dragged along for ten years without any marked increase.

The opening of my class was made known by a leading editorial in one of the daily papers and by a local paragraph in each of the other papers. As a result, on the first evening my classroom was crowded with more than a hundred pupils. Next day I asked the chairman of the committee on evening schools to assign me an assistant. In less than a month there were five classes, and before the end of the term there were eight classes, with a total of four hundred pupils. Then I was made principal and was relieved from teaching a class. Large numbers of young men over eighteen years of age flocked into the school, but under the regulations of the board of education a tuition fee of one dollar a month was required of such pupils. As I looked at them week after week, I had not the heart to collect this money. After three months had drifted away, Mr. John F. Meagher, chairman of the committee on evening schools, called at the school and asked me if I was collecting the tuition fee from the men over eighteen years of age. I replied, "No, Mr. Meagher, I am not, and I would rather resign my position than do so. Why, look at these men, Mr. Meagher; more than half of them came from Ireland, like yourself. They are working hard to earn a living and get on in the world. It is petty business for the city of San Francisco to collect from them a tuition fee of a dollar a month. Why not admit them free?" Like the warm-hearted Irishman that he was, he said at once: "You are right, Mr. Swett. Let them in free and say nothing more about it." And thus we two, Catholic and Puritan standing together, killed the rate bill in the evening schools. John F. Meagher passed away many years ago, but his name ought to be placed high on the roll of honor among the men who helped to build up the evening schools. In this connection I call to mind an incident that occurred soon after.

For several evenings I had noticed a man of middle age loitering on the sidewalk in front of the school building. When I asked him what he wanted he replied: "I want to learn to read. I was born in the backwoods and never had a chance to go to school. I have been hanging around here for a week, without daring to go in for fear the boys would laugh at me." I told him I would take care of that if he would come to school two days later. A new thought struck me. I gave notice through an item in each of the city papers that a class would be opened in the Lincoln building composed exclusively of adults who wished to learn to read. In a week there was a class of thirty men, and two weeks later another class was formed. Next I started a class in bookkeeping and assigned to it Joseph O'Connor, who had just come over from Ireland. His measure I took at once. I said to him: "There is the class. The pupils are of all sizes and all ages. Teach them as best you can in your own way." He managed his class so well that he was soon made vice-principal of a grammar school, and then principal. He became deputy superintendent under Superintendent Moulder, and finally principal of the Mission High School.

Next, William A. Robertson, a genial veteran of the Confederate army just arrived from Georgia, was sent to me as teacher of a new class. He managed his unruly boys as bravely as he had fought in Lee's army at Gettysburg. He was one of the hardest workers I ever knew, and his sense of humor made him a general favorite. We became the firmest of friends. He was soon promoted to one of the day schools, and finally was elected principal of the Hamilton Grammar School, in which position he remained until he answered to the roll-call of death, a few years ago. Then John C. Pelton, a pioneer teacher, stranded in fortune and broken in spirit, found a temporary place as teacher of a class. At a later period H. C. Kinne, a veteran teacher of country schools, drifted into the Lincoln Evening School, where he has remained for more than twenty years, doing missionary work among the men and boys that flock into his classroom.

A few months later a class in architectural drawing was opened, the board at my request giving the use of the room and the teacher charging a tuition fee of one dollar a month. In a short time this class was made free. Meanwhile the classes in the school were roughly graded by transferring pupils from one class to another. At the end of two years there were twelve evening classes in the Lincoln building, every suitable room being filled. The success of this evening school was owing to the fact that the discipline was strict, the classes were graded in a rough way, and tuition was free to adults. Every two weeks the older pupils were gathered in the large hall and addressed by members of the board, or other citizens interested in the school, and the proceedings reported in the papers. I appealed to the adult members of the classes to become my assistants in maintaining discipline among the boys. I remained principal of the school for three years and then resigned in consequence of being appointed deputy city superintendent of schools. As I look back upon my management of this school it seems to me to be one of my best pieces of educational work.

After I left the school it fell into the hands of Joseph O'Connor and was developed into a system of evening schools excelled by no other city in the United States. These schools have now become an integral part of the public-school system, continued for the same length of time as the day schools. The teachers are paid a salary of six hundred dollars a year and are permanent in their positions. The schools include commercial classes and high-school classes, in addition to the grammar grades.

As a striking illustration of the far-reaching influence of these evening schools, I mention one little incident. One day in 1895, as I was walking down Market Street, I met Judge Hunt, one of the most upright and most popular of Superior Court judges in the city, who has been repeatedly elected and reëlected regardless of political parties. He hailed me with, "Swett, do you know when I first saw you?"

"I hope it wasn't in your court as a criminal on trial," was my bantering reply.

"Do you remember, Mr. Swett, the evening school class of which you were the teacher in 1856, forty years ago? Well, I was a member of that class when I was a hard-working boy during the daytime. I owe my education to the start I got there. I have never forgotten what I owe to you and the evening school."

As a matter of comparative value, Judge Hunt has been worth more to the city of San Francisco than the cost of the whole system of evening schools for half a century.

An Old Rule is Abolished

In a previous chapter I alluded to the annual reëxamination of teachers which was required by boards of education during the first decade of the educational history of San Francisco. From 1851 to 1869 it had been the custom of boards of education to go into secret executive session at the end of each year, declare all positions of teachers vacant, and then proceed to elect teachers "for one year only." Not unfrequently good teachers were dropped out to make room for friends of new members of the board or for other teachers backed by powerful influences. When teachers so removed appealed to members of the board, the reply was, "There was nothing against you, only you did not get enough votes to elect you." One day in 1869 it occurred to me that it was time for somebody to make a protest against such "Star-chamber" proceedings. I went to the president of the board, stated the facts in the case, and secured a pledge of his support in electing teachers "during good behavior" instead of for one year, so that they might feel some reasonable security in their positions as long as their teaching was satisfactory. Joseph O'Connor, then a grammar-school principal, backed me in this effort, and John F. Meagher, member of the board of education, joined hands with both of us in this reform. We canvassed the board, but when the matter was brought up it failed to carry. We then invoked the aid of the press, and after a contest of six months, finally secured the desired reform. Of course, incompetent teachers could be dropped at any time, but most of the teachers remained reasonably secure. This action of the board was the first step towards the "teachers' tenure of office" law for San Francisco, secured by act of the legislature a few years later, for which teachers were largely indebted to Ira G. Hoitt, then a member of the assembly from San Francisco. Mr. Hoitt several years later was elected state superintendent of public instruction.

During the June vacation of 1869 I took advantage of the completion of the Central Pacific Railroad to make a four weeks' visit to New England. My stepfather, William Berry, had been bedridden for three years, afflicted with the worst type of inflammatory rheumatism, from which he suffered untold torments. My mother, worn with care and watching, had long been urging me to come home to see her. My stepfather died soon after my return to California, and in 1870 I went East with a teachers' excursion party, and brought my mother to California, where she lived in our family for twenty-six years.

Appointed Deputy Superintendent

At the autumn city election in 1869, Mr. J. H. Widber, a former member of the board of education, was elected city superintendent of schools on the "People's Party" ticket.

I accepted an appointment as deputy superintendent, on condition that the board of education should fix the salary at three thousand a year. I disliked to give up the Denman School, but a higher salary turned the scale in favor of acceptance, though the tenure of office was short and uncertain.

As Superintendent Widber had never been a teacher, he attended to business official duties and turned over some of the strictly educational details to me. I was occupied for two months in making a thorough and complete revision of the rules and regulations of the school department. I reduced these rules to plain English by cutting out a great deal of verbiage and rubbish. Then I was mainly occupied for some time with a revision of the course of study, which had become crowded with a mass of odds and ends that made it exceedingly cumbersome. The pruning knife was mercilessly applied. As usual, the conservatives set up complaints about "radical changes," but the teachers became satisfied when the course was fully understood.

The appointment of teachers had been for a long time a matter of personal patronage equally divided among the members of the board of education. Neither the superintendent nor his deputy had anything whatever to do with this reserved right of the school directors. The possession of a certificate constituted the only evidence of fitness to teach that was required by the board, and the nomination of a teacher by one school director was confirmed by the vote of all the others, with true senatorial courtesy.

In looking over my annual reports to the superintendent for the years 1872 and 1873, I find little worthy of note. These reports were mainly filled up with statistics and with sets of questions used in quarterly and annual written examinations. The preparation of such questions involved a great waste of time by the deputy superintendent, and still greater waste of time by pupils in writing the answers and by teachers in examining and crediting the papers. At that time all the city schools of the United States were running wild on the subject of written examinations. My protests were of no avail. The system was too strong to be broken up. I did succeed, however, in securing an order of the board of education authorizing an oral examination of each and every grammar-grade class in the school department. As it was utterly impossible for the deputy superintendent, alone, to conduct this examination, in addition to visiting the primary schools and doing his office work, Joseph Leggett, an experienced teacher and skillful examiner, was temporarily employed for three months as an examiner. From half a day to a day was devoted to the examinations of each class. Detailed reports in writing were made to the committee concerning the standing of each class in the more important studies, the general order and discipline of the class, and the apparent merits of the teacher.

During the months of April and May my own time was occupied in preparing the questions for the annual written examination. The time of Mr. Leggett was given to an oral examination of various classes in the two high schools, and to the preparation of full sets of questions for the annual written examination in those schools. In order to complete the oral examination of the grammar grades it was found necessary to employ an additional examiner for a month and a half, and H. P. Carlton was appointed for that purpose. The information thus obtained was so valuable, and the results were so satisfactory, that in June, at the close of the school year, Mr. Leggett was elected as a regular examining teacher at large. These oral examinations had a marked effect in encouraging both teachers and pupils. A good oral examiner is a traveling normal-school instructor, suggesting methods of teaching, and his salary is a trifling expense compared with the substantial educational benefits resulting from his services in the school department.

William Swinton

I first met Professor William Swinton soon after he had been elected (1871) to the chair of History and English Literature in the new State University of California, then holding its sessions in the city of Oakland. Mr. Swinton had won a high literary reputation as a war correspondent of the New York *Times*, and as author of an historical volume on the "Campaigns of the Army of the Potomac." When I met him he was engaged in writing his "Condensed History of the United States" for use in grammar schools, and he showed me some of the proof sheets. After this book was brought out I suggested to him that it ought to be accompanied by a primary history for the lower grades. He accordingly wrote a delightful story of our country, which was received with great favor. Shortly after, "Swinton's Word Analysis" appeared. His publishers then requested him to prepare a book introductory to word analysis which should be mainly a spelling book. Professor Swinton asked me to make a beginning of this book, remarking that he knew very little about teaching spelling, and that he would pay me whatever the work was worth.

I thought the matter over, made a beginning of twenty pages and submitted it to him, at the same time suggesting a plan for the remainder of the book. He then insisted that I should go on with the book to completion, and said that he would revise it if necessary. Accordingly, my leisure hours for a full year were given to this work, which Mr. Swinton took on to New York, where he passed his summer vacation. The only material change he made in the original manuscript was in cutting out a few lessons in spelling and substituting short lessons in defining. This book, entitled "Swinton's Word Book of Written and Oral Spelling," proved a success from the beginning. As Swinton had no money to pay for my work, he generously gave me a half interest in the copyright. A year or two later I wrote for him a book for primary grades, called "Swinton's Word Primer," which was published exactly as I prepared it. These two books, with "Swinton's Word Analysis," in which I had no hand, made up what was known as "Swinton's Word Book Series." This series, after an interval of a quarter of a century, is still in extensive use.

A year or two later, Harper and Brothers published "Swinton's Progressive Grammar" to which I contributed some exercises in composition work. This book was too hastily written to be of any permanent value. It was soon followed, however, by "Swinton's Language Lessons," which Mr. Swinton began at my suggestion. For two or three years I had urged on him the desirability of combining composition exercises with the principles of grammar, and he finally became convinced of the possibility of doing so. I furnished Mr. Swinton with the practical language exercises taken from actual work done in the Denman Grammar School, of which I was principal. The writing of the book was done entirely by Mr. Swinton, and I had no financial interest in it whatever, my contribution of plan and practical exercises being given as a labor of love. This book had an unprecedented run of popularity. It broke the long reign of Lindley Murray's method of teaching elementary grammar. Mr. Swinton next prepared for Ivison, Blakeman, Taylor and Company a two-book geography series — a comprehensive geography for the higher grammar grades and an elementary book for beginners. On these two books I was a collaborator, at times, for two years. This series included some excellent features, but the "Comprehensive" was too large, and neither of the books went into extensive use. In 1875 Professor Swinton asked a leave of absence for the purpose of bringing out his geography, but the board of regents declined to give it, and he resigned his position and moved to New York City. After this I met him but once, and then only for a day, though I afterwards did some geographical work for him. He was a rapid writer, who could toil at his desk twelve hours a day when in the mood for hard work. He had a happy way of putting things in clear and attractive form, and was quick to receive suggestions from teachers.

Meeting of the National Educational Association, Boston, 1872

On the 20th of July, 1871, there was born into our family a promising child that we named Walter Harper Swett. He was a very winning child and we loved him with passionate devotion. When eleven months old he had a hard time in teething. Our family physician being away, we called in a doctor who knew very little about treating a sick child. For a long and weary month every hour of the day that I could spare from my official duty, and every hour that I could snatch from sleep at night, was passed in watching over him. For thirty days and thirty nights of alternating hope and despair, as the disease ebbed and flowed, I saw the little life so dear to us drifting slowly and helplessly away from us. He died on the first anniversary of his birthday, and left on us the shadow of the deepest grief we had ever known.

Some months before our bereavement I had received and accepted an invitation from Dr. Emerson E. White, president of the National Educational Association, to read a paper at the Boston meeting on the examination and certification of teachers. I had only begun the outline of my address at the time my child became dangerously ill, and after his death I was so utterly prostrated that I felt unable to write. But my noble-hearted wife, herself prostrated by our loss, insisted on my going, saying that I needed an entire change of surroundings. So I started on my trip to the East and jotted down my address on the way. My traveling companion was William Swinton, at that time professor of History and Rhetoric in the State University of California.

The meeting of the National Educational Association at Boston, August, 1872, was a small one, the registered attendance being only 292 members. President White's address was able; Newton Bateman's was eloquent; the Reverend A. D. Mayo's paper on "Methods of Moral Instruction in the Common Schools" was full of enlightened common sense; and William T. Harris, of St. Louis, was a leader in discussions. The city authorities gave an informal evening reception to members in Faneuil Hall. Among the educators whom I met, I recall the names of Henry Barnard, S. S. Greene, Bronson Alcott, Elizabeth Peabody, John Hancock, C. C. Rounds, General John Eaton, B. F. Tweed, Wm. F. Phelps, J. P. Wickersham, and B. G. Northrop. My address at the general session created a ripple of interest because it was the voice of an outside barbarian, from the wilderness of California, calling for reform. It was, in fact, the earliest formal protest made in the United States by a public school-teacher before an organized body of teachers, against the existing manner of examining and certifying teachers and in favor of some kind of educational civil service.

It was thirty-eight years ago that I wrote this address, and now, as I run over the printed pages, I am surprised at my audacity, before an audience assembled at the hub of New England conservatism, in delivering an address made up of a mixture of historical facts, bantering humor, sarcasm, and righteous indignation. But I am not ready to take back a word of it. Within the last decade there has been a great quickening of professional spirit, but there still remains a pressing need of further reform. Therefore I proceed to reiterate educational heresy by quoting some paragraphs from my Boston address.

It may reasonably be expected, when a man accepts an invitation to prepare a paper for this association, and travels three thousands miles to read it, paying full fare each way, that he will condense his thoughts into the fewest possible words. The subject assigned to me is one that I have had to deal with for many years, and concerning it I have definite and decided opinions. For eight years I was principal of a grammar school in San Francisco, and — I am ashamed to own it, and would not tell it were it not necessary to illustrate what I intend to present — I had the cowardice, like other teachers with me, to submit, without protest, to eight annual reëxaminations to secure a certificate "valid for one year," in order to determine my fitness to teach the same school for each succeeding school year. Nor was this the end of humiliation and insult. After getting a "brand-new" certificate at the end of each year, before I could enter school again I had to be reëlected by the votes of the members of the city board of education, because my term of office was limited by law to one year. . . .

This annual reëlection of teachers was handed down to us from the primitive New England town meeting. Right here in Boston, in most New England cities, villages, and towns, and in most other parts of our country, this system is still kept up by law or by custom. A teacher holds his office for only one year, and then he is at the mercy of the whim of any school trustee, school director, or prudential committeeman that may have some spite to wreak or some relative to put into school. Much as I honor the profession of teaching, I am not in love with a legal system that tends to take all the manliness out of a man and all independence from a woman. . . .

Finally, when after eight years of continuous service in one school I was forced into a long and difficult written examination before I had fairly recovered from a typhoid fever that brought me to the verge of the grave, I made a vow to break up and root out the annual reëxamination farce and the annual reëlection tradition. I secured a nomination and an election to the only office then open to a teacher, that of state superintendent of public instruction. My official position enabled me to revise the state school law and secure needed reforms. During five years of strenuous effort I lobbied state legislatures, secured a state tax for the partial support of free schools; secured life diplomas for professional teachers and the renewal of the short-term certificates of lower grade without reëxamination; placed the examination of teachers exclusively in the hands of experienced teachers; gained a legal recognition of the normal school diplomas of other states, as well as a recognition of the life or permanent certificates of other states; and ridiculed out of existence the annual reëlection of experienced teachers in San Francisco.

You will now understand why I entertain strong convictions on the manner of examining and certificating teachers. My educational views have changed somewhat since I taught school near the city of Boston. New conditions have brought new issues. While I fully recognize how much the American public schools owe to the early common schools of New England, I take satisfaction in hurling a few educational brickbats against certain laws, usages, and customs that stand opposed to progress. . . .

One weak point in our school system is found in the short terms of office for school trustees and members of city boards of education. Annual elections were suited to the primitive New England towns and school districts, but when applied to large cities and to the vast expanse of Western states, they have proved demoralizing in results. When one set of officials succeeds another as often as the seasons change, there can be no systematic improvement. Each new set of officials is mainly bent on "reforming" the work of its predecessors. In many parts of our country, boards of education elected by one political party feel under no obligation to retain in place the teachers elected by the opposite party. There has been a great deal of talk about reform in civil-service appointments, but the country stands in greater need of reform in the manner of making *educational* appointments. . . .

If the teachers of New England are willing to submit to this condition of things, let them fold their arms with all due meekness, leaving the work of reform to the outside barbarians of the West. But until there is a reform in these two weak points of our school system, it seems to me there can be no marked and permanent improvement in our public schools as a whole. There will be individual schools that, under superior teachers, will attain a high degree of excellence; but the general average of the schools cannot be raised much higher than it is, because the system neither encourages independent thought nor tolerates progress. . . .

In addition to a state board of examination empowered to issue life diplomas on examination, or on certain specified credentials from normal schools or universities, it is desirable that there should be an efficient system of county or city boards of examination authorized by law to issue local certificates. These boards should be mainly composed of professional teachers. Thus, by combining state, city, and town examinations, together with interstate recognition of professional certificates, something might be done to raise the standard of professional teaching.

It may be urged against any plan of competitive examinations that "percentages" represent only scholarship, but fail to gauge the power to discipline, the tact to manage, and the skill to teach. This may be true to some extent; but it is also true that there is a fair standard of scholarly attainment below which no men or women should be allowed to make a trial of teaching.

It is often urged that a college diploma ought to be taken as a valid certificate. It *was* so taken in former times, and is so taken now in many places. But a college-bred young man may or *may not* be qualified to teach a common school. I have known many young men coming to California with flying colors and fresh diplomas, who failed to secure a certificate to teach even the lowest grade school, on an examination in reading, spelling, arithmetic, grammar, geography, and the history of the United States, so elementary in character that, to a pupil of average attainments in the highest grade of an ordinary grammar school, it would have been merely play. They exhibited a most lamentable ignorance of the very elements required to be taught in every common school. They might have been brilliant in the dead languages, but they misspelled and mispronounced their mother tongue, and could not cipher accurately. . . .

In conclusion, I submit the following propositions for the consideration of teachers, educators, and legislators:

(*a*) A comprehensive system of state, city and county boards of examination which shall be composed mainly of professional teachers and educators.

(*b*) A graded series of teachers' certificates ranging from life diplomas to temporary certificates.

(*c*) Interstate recognition of teachers' certificates and normal school diplomas.

(*d*) Longer terms of office for state, city, and county superintendents and for school trustees and members of city boards of education.

(*e*) A war of independence to be waged against the formal annual reëlection of teachers.

My somewhat caustic attack on the annual reëxamination of teachers and their reëlection for the term of one year attracted no special attention at the time, so far as I knew, but ten or twelve years later Mr. Carrigan, a lawyer from Boston, called on me in San Francisco and told me that he heard my Boston address, and that it made a deep impression on him. He said that he was at that time a law student in the law office of Benjamin F. Butler, and was also principal of an evening school in Boston. He at once set about securing an amendment to the Massachusetts state law which limited the teachers' tenure of office to one year. He put his bill before the state legislature for five years in succession, and finally secured a provision making it optional with city boards of education to elect teachers for a term of four years. I never saw Mr. Carrigan again, for on his way home he died in a Pullman sleeping car, probably from suffocation, though he was reported as having "died from apoplexy."

In 1877, five years after the Boston meeting, I attempted to stir up Eastern educators by a series of articles in the New England *Journal of Education*, of which I was the contributing editor for the Pacific Coast at the time when Thomas W. Bicknell was the manager and the Reverend A. D. Mayo was the leading editorial writer. By referring to a voluminous scrapbook, I find that in the issue of the *Journal*, March 1, 1877, there is a leading article, bearing my signature, on "Professional Certificates for Teachers," from which I quote a paragraph as follows:

There is a small army of teachers moving slowly westward across the continent; is it essential to the common school system that each teacher when he crosses a state line must halt to be examined to see if he is "fit to teach a common school for one year?" Is it necessary to the perpetuity of free institutions to keep up a system of passports worse than European? Is there no relief for teachers from annual reëxaminations and annual reëlections but in the grave? The legislatures of some of the states are now in session. One single educator of nerve can move a whole legislature if he knows where to look for its brains.

This was followed up by other articles, such as "The Art of Teaching;" "The Profession of Teaching;" "The Science of Teaching;" "The Next Step;" "Things Essential;" "Ungraded Schools," etc.[1]

After my short vacation of six weeks was over, I resumed my duties as deputy superintendent of schools in San Francisco for another year, at the end of which time, by a turn in the wheel of politics, I found myself adrift once more.

In 1873 Superintendent Widber was renominated by the Republican party, and James Denman became the nominee of the Democratic party. In the campaign that followed, an act of the legislature of 1872–73 was brought to light, which provided that a person to be eligible for the office of city or county superintendent must be a professional

[1] As a kind of supplement to all the preceding professional talk, I take great delight in stating that in 1902 the state of Massachusetts made by law a provision for the granting of state certificates by the state board of education. I have recently learned that a few of the leading educators and teachers of my native state have just held a meeting at Concord, the capital, to take measures to secure, at the coming session of the legislature, a law similar to that of Massachusetts. I rejoice greatly, and stretch out across the continent the right hand of glad fellowship to those twentieth-century teachers in New Hampshire. At the same time I am reluctantly compelled to admit that in all parts of California, except San Francisco, which has a special tenure-of-office law, school trustees are prohibited by law from electing teachers for a term exceeding one year.

teacher and the holder of a teacher's certificate. It was therefore contended that Mr. Widber would be ineligible if elected. The law was clearly unconstitutional and was soon repealed, but it proved to be the main cause of Mr. Widber's defeat.

As it was not in accordance with the unwritten code of political ethics that a Democratic superintendent should continue a Republican deputy in position, I retired from office, and was succeeded by my personal friend, Joseph Leggett, who had been a coworker with me in conducting oral examinations of the city schools. No better appointment could have been made, for Mr. Leggett combined democracy with enlightened common sense, energy, and scholarship. At a succeeding election Mr. Leggett was elected as a member of the board of education, in which position he served with credit to himself and with benefit to the schools.

As for myself, I was elected principal of the Denman School, to which I returned with delight. The position of deputy had not proved a bed of roses. The endless preparation of sets of questions for written examinations, in which I had little faith, had grown distasteful to me, and I welcomed the pleasanter work of teaching. In this school I found ample time for reading and study, and I made good use of it. There was also an opportunity to make experiments in methods of teaching in both primary and grammar grades. I was entirely content with my position, and expected to remain in it until disabled by old age or turned out by some change in the political make-up of the board of education.

In May, 1876, Ellis H. Holmes, after a long and successful career as principal of the Girls' High School, found himself able to retire from school and live upon his income. Accordingly, he sent in his resignation. Superintendent Denman, after an able administration of two years, was renominated on the Democratic ticket, but was defeated by the Republican nominee, Henry N. Bolander. Several of my personal friends on the board of education desired my promotion to the high school, and several of Mr. Denman's friends wished to return him to the Denman School. Rather reluctantly I consented to the arrangement, with the condition that a post-graduate course of one year should be added to the regular high-school three years' course, for the double purpose of fitting graduates to enter the recently established State University of California or to become elementary teachers.

CHAPTER XIII

PRINCIPAL OF THE GIRLS' HIGH SCHOOL AND NORMAL CLASS OF SAN FRANCISCO

THE Girls' High School, at the time I took charge of it in July, 1876, numbered about four hundred pupils in charge of twelve regular teachers, with a course of study limited, like other high schools in California at that time, to three years. From the time of its establishment in 1864 it had remained exclusively an English high school except for two years.

In 1871–72, when I was deputy superintendent, on my recommendation the board of education adopted the following rule: "Whenever there shall be a sufficient number of pupils desiring instruction in the ancient languages to form a class of at least fifteen pupils, a classical course shall be established in the Girls' High School for the purpose of fitting students to enter the college of letters in the University of California." Under this rule a small class maintained a lingering existence for two years, when the discouraged teacher of Latin and Greek resigned and the class was discontinued.

In 1876 George Tait was a leading member of the city board of education. He had formerly been a grammar-school principal, then city superintendent of schools for four years, next for two years principal of the State Normal School in San Francisco previous to its removal to San José. It was through his influence in the San Francisco board of education that I secured an indirect extension of the course of study in the Girls' High School to four years instead of the previous limitation of three years.

The resolution adopted by the board provided for the establishment of a post-graduate class to consist of high-school graduates who wished to fit for admission to the University of California, with a normal department for graduates that wished to fit themselves for teaching in elementary schools.

There were found forty graduates who desired to become teachers, but not a single one who desired to enter the university. Consequently only the normal class was organized. Mrs. Mary W. Kincaid, then head assistant in the South Cosmopolitan Grammar School, was appointed teacher of this class. Educated in a young ladies' seminary, she was herself without normal training, but she soon developed into a superior teacher.

What time I could spare from my regular high-school duties was given to instruction in methods of teaching. In the course of a few years the number of applicants for admission increased to a hundred, and Professor George W. Minns was invited from Boston to act as an assistant. Mr. Minns was one of the earlier teachers in the English High School for boys and girls in San Francisco (1856) and was afterwards for several years principal of the first State Normal School during a part of the time that the school was located in San Francisco. He was a graduate of Harvard University and a man of rare scholarship.

A teacher of German was elected to the high school in 1877, and as he was employed only a part of his time, I was allowed by the board to organize a class in Latin under his instruction. There were no pupils who desired to take Greek. In most respects the course otherwise continued in the line of the traditions of the school, — an English high school.

The course of study was not all that could be desired, but it had some good features, and in the main was adapted to the needs of the pupils; for the high school is essentially an outgrowth of the grammar school. Its course of study and its mental status are largely determined by the training given in the lower departments of the school system. At that time the fact that more than one half of all the pupils who entered the Girls' High School intended to become teachers was also to be taken into consideration in the curriculum.

Without going into details, the leading purpose of the school was to graduate girls with the ability to read and spell well; a fair knowledge of English grammar; some knowledge of the meaning and use of words, of etymology and of synonyms; a fair knowledge of algebra and geometry; some knowledge of physical and political geography; a general outline of the history of the world; some knowledge of what to read in English literature, and how to read it; the ability to express their thoughts in correct English, gained by actual practice in composition, rather than by study of technical textbooks on rhetoric; an elementary knowledge of physics, botany, and zoölogy; some knowledge of physiology and of the laws of health; some training in vocal culture and vocal music; a course, for those who desired it, of Latin, French, or German.

The main purpose of the school was, not to fit young women for the State University, but to give them a substantial general secondary education. Yet the school afforded the means of fitting for the university if students desired to go there. The average number from the school who entered the university was three or four a year, or less than two per cent of the graduates. It was found impossible to secure enough pupils to make up a "university class," not because the girls were not encouraged to enter such a class, but because few parents were financially able to send their girls through the university.

I soon found that my ideal of a high school with a normal department could not be realized, but I did what I could under existing conditions. Under any financial stringency the high schools were the first to suffer. From time to time special teachers of music, drawing, French, German, and Latin were dismissed as a measure of economy.

As the school increased in numbers, the classes were crowded up to fifty pupils to a teacher. When the normal class increased to eighty pupils, it was found impossible to crowd them into a room containing only fifty-six desks. But there was only one room available in the school building, and we were compelled to divide the class into two sections of forty each, one section being distributed among the primary schools of the city for practice work while the other was under instruction.

The school soon outgrew the Bush Street building, and three branch classes were opened in a rented building, on Market Street nearly a mile away, and later two or three classes were located in the old high-school building on Powell Street near Clay.

The distribution of the pupils in three buildings a mile apart was a great disadvantage to the school. Aside from the loss of time by principal and special teachers in traveling a daily round of three miles, no number of scattered classes could constitute a *school* in the full sense of the term. There was a pressing need for a centrally located building capable of accommodating one thousand pupils, but there was no money to be obtained for that purpose. Meanwhile, with every change in the board of education there was more or less tinkering on the course of study. At one time a commercial member of the board insisted on forcing the study of commercial bookkeeping into the school, making it immediately compulsory on every class from the lowest to the highest, including the normal class. When the term of this school director expired, bookkeeping was discontinued.

I think it was in 1882, during the summer vacation, that a secret movement was made to abolish the normal department, which then had grown to three classes numbering one hundred and fifty students. I discovered the plot and immediately went to the president of the board, Mr. Stubbs, of the Central Pacific Railroad. I said, "Mr. Stubbs, I hear the board intend to abolish the normal department of the high school; is my information correct?"

He answered "Yes, it is. There are too many teachers already."

"Mr. Stubbs, you are a business man, and I want to make you a business proposition. Limit the normal department to one class of fifty students, selecting from the graduates of the high school those who stand highest in scholarship. The city can afford the cost of one teacher for the normal class."

"That's a fair business proposition. I'll accept it," said he. The business was settled in less than five minutes, and the class was saved. Meanwhile all my efforts to secure a larger building ended in failure.

The Kindergarten Movement in San Francisco

Felix Adler of New York City made a visit to San Francisco in 1878 and began a movement which ended in the establishment of the Silver Street Kindergarten school under the management of Miss Kate Douglas Smith, who afterwards, as Mrs. Kate Douglas Wiggin, became widely known as an author. Soon after this school was opened I visited it, and, on request of the principal, detailed two student teachers, partly as assistants and partly as students of kindergarten methods. Then I called the attention of Mrs. Sarah B. Cooper to the school. As she was a born philanthropist, she became deeply interested in the work, and proposed to start another class in what was known as the "Barbary Coast," — the old "Five Points" of San Francisco. She soon secured by subscription the money to pay the rent of a building and also to pay a teacher. I went with her to explore the region and select a suitable location. When the school opened I detailed as assistants two student teachers, one of whom was my own daughter, Emily Tracy Swett. Next I organized a class of children between five and six years of age, in a vacant room, kept the school running for three months under the entire charge of pupils from the normal class, and finally, with Mrs. Cooper's assistance, succeeded in 1880 in making it a free public school under the name of the "Experimental Class." One year later a second class was opened in connection with Mrs. Cooper's kindergarten school on Union Street.

Mrs. Cooper entered on the free kindergarten work with her whole soul. She was a woman of marked literary ability. For many years she earned enough with her pen to aid in the support of her family and in the education of her sister's children in Memphis, Tennessee. She had no money to contribute to the kindergarten cause, but she gave what was needed more than money,— the wealth of her clear intellect, her winning manner, and her devoted Christian philanthropy. It was through her influence that

Mrs. Leland Stanford became interested in the work and finally endowed three kindergarten schools with one hundred thousand dollars for their support. Mrs. Phoebe Hearst was induced by Mrs. Cooper's persuasive power to endow another kindergarten school. A large number of citizens subscribed five dollars a month, each, for the support of other classes. The Golden Gate Kindergarten Association was organized, and in ten years there were forty-six kindergarten classes supported entirely by endowments and subscriptions. Mrs. Cooper's annual reports were distributed and read wherever the English language is spoken.

After the death of Mrs. Cooper's husband, she still continued her management of the kindergarten schools, her daughter Hattie meanwhile supporting the family by giving music lessons. Mrs. Cooper steadily refused to receive a dollar for services, though persistently urged by the officers of the association to accept a salary. Once when I urged her to yield to the wishes of the association, she replied, "This is the Lord's work, and I feel it would not be blessed if I received pay for it." She held frequent consultations with me about any new undertakings, and probably there is no person living who knows more fully than myself the extent of her labors, and the wealth of philanthropic devotion and Christian self-sacrifice that she brought to the work of training, reforming, and educating the children of the poor in San Francisco. Her sad and sudden death cast a gloom over the city in which her great work was accomplished.

Incidental Educational Work

In 1875 I proposed to H. H. Bancroft and Company of San Francisco, that if the firm would publish a brief history of the California school system, I would furnish the manuscript without compensation and without copyright. My reason for this was that I thought there ought to be some book of reference in which should be gathered the fragmentary bits of school history at that time scattered in forgotten or destroyed reports. The firm accepted the proposition and issued the prospectus of such a book. The replies to this circular were not reassuring and the firm declined the risk of publication. As most of the volume was ready for the printer, I then decided to publish it at my own expense, as a personal contribution to the public-school history of the state. An edition of one thousand copies was printed at a cost of $900. Sales were made to the amount of $400, four hundred copies I gave away, and a few copies still remain as an addition to my own library. This book is no longer for sale, but special students may find copies of it in the State University library. This history was made up of brief abstracts of the reports of state superintendents; of the successive steps in school legislation; of sketches of state teachers' institutes; of full tables of statistics; and of several educational addresses that seemed to be worth publishing.

It was a part of my school duties to give occasional talks to the normal class on methods of instruction, as a supplement to their textbook study of Russell's "Normal Training." Then I fell into the habit of summarizing these informal talks into condensed written statements, some of which were dictated to students and taken down in their notebooks. At length, when the one class had increased to three classes, it occurred to me to put these condensed directions into book form for more convenient use. Accordingly I supplemented these notes with working models in arithmetic, geography, grammar, and composition, which

I had used when principal of a grammar school, and submitted the manuscript to Mr. Emerson, of the schoolbook department of Harper and Brothers. The book was accepted by the house and published in 1880. Four thousand copies were sold in less than a year, and for ten succeeding years the sales were about a thousand copies annually. The press notices of "Methods of Teaching" were highly complimentary to this unpretentious volume.[1]

I may add that "Methods of Teaching" was warmly welcomed in some of the Southern states by the young men and young women that were teaching in the newly established common schools. These teachers had been fairly educated in academies, but had received no normal school instruction in detailed methods suited to public schools. From time to time I received many letters from them, stating that the writers, though strangers to me, could not resist the impulse to thank me for the inspiration my book

[1] The New England *Journal of Education* (Boston) said of it in a leading editorial: "This book by John Swett reads like a catalogue of educational maxims which have survived in a twenty years' war of schoolmasters and children in the most vigorous of new American states. Every paragraph has a fist in it. With the broadest outlook over modern theories of instruction, the author does not attempt to give us either a philosophy or a theory; but in a series of forcible and concise chapters, illustrated by working models and illuminated by numerous apt quotations from the leading school authorities of the modern world, he comes to the aid of every teacher in the land. The most inexperienced teacher in a plantation school in South Carolina and the most famous master in New York will find on every page a direction so full of common sense, so appreciative of childhood, so respectful of broad culture, so pregnant with patriotism, that the most natural thing to be done will be to dash off a hasty vote of thanks to the author. We commend this volume to all teachers in all sorts of schools. But especially would we urge the young teachers in the common schools of the South and the more isolated schools of the North where the means of normal training are not at hand, to buy this book and read it till the intense and powerful spirit of its author moves to a new insight and consecration to work."

had given them in their daily work under discouraging conditions.

I call to mind an evening visit at my home in San Francisco, made by two accomplished ladies from Selma, Georgia, introducing themselves as teachers on a vacation trip to California, who had learned how to teach from a book written by John Swett whom they desired to thank personally for having lent them a helping hand.

At the recent charter-day exercises of the University of California (March, 1906), I had the great pleasure of listening to an eloquent address by the well-known speaker, educator, and lecturer, Edwin A. Alderman, president of the University of Virginia. After the exercises were over, when President Wheeler introduced me to President Alderman, the latter exclaimed as he cordially grasped my hand: "Mr. Swett, I am glad to meet you. I have known you for many years through your book on 'Methods of Teaching' which I used when I was learning how to teach. You are an old friend."

The New Constitution

At the annual meeting of the State Teachers' Association in Sacramento, June, 1878, I submitted for approval, to the small number of members in attendance, three sections relating to education which I intended to bring before the convention that had been elected to revise the state constitution. One of these sections provided that county superintendents should be elected for the term of *four* years instead of two years. This was approved by the State Association, though nobody except myself believed that this extension of the term of office could be secured. It was afterwards adopted by the constitutional convention without objection. Another section which I submitted read as follows: "The public school system shall include primary and grammar schools, and such high schools, evening schools, normal schools, and technical schools as may be established by the legislature or by municipal or district authority." The State Association approved this section, but added an unfortunate amendment, which subsequently led to trouble in organizing high schools. This *proviso* read as follows: "*but the entire revenue derived from the state school fund and the state school tax shall be applied exclusively to the support of primary and grammar schools.*" This amendment was offered by an able high-school teacher, not for the purpose of discrimination against high schools, but to help along, as he supposed, the adoption of the original section, the opinion prevailing that otherwise the convention would reject it. The section was afterwards adopted by the constitutional convention without opposition, but the original section without the *proviso* would have been passed in the same manner.

It was owing to the timidity of the teachers themselves in asking for what they really wanted, not to any hostility to high schools in the constitutional convention, that high schools and technical schools were not included in the state apportionment of school moneys. Another section which I drafted was approved by the association and afterwards by the constitutional convention without material change. This section reads as follows:

Sec. 8. No public money shall ever be appropriated for the support of any sectarian or denominational school or any school not under the exclusive control of the officers of the public schools; nor shall any sectarian or denominational doctrine be taught, or instruction thereon be permitted, directly or indirectly, in any of the common schools of this state.

These sections were placed in the hands of a county superintendent who was a member elect of the constitutional convention, and by him placed before the committee on education, together with the resolution of approval by the State Teachers' Association.

My Acquaintance with John Muir

In the winter of 1874 I first met John Muir in the city of Oakland, where I found him engaged in writing an article about his studies on glacial action in the Sierra Nevada mountain range. We at once established a close friendship, which has continued unbroken for more than a third of a century. Soon after our first meeting I persuaded him to come to San Francisco and occupy a vacant room in my house. He was to become a member of my household for three months without charge, and in return he was to go with me during the next summer vacation as a guide into the Yosemite Valley and the surrounding mountain region, in company with J. B. McChesney, the veteran principal of the Oakland High School, and William Keith, who was then beginning his successful career as a landscape painter.

At that time Mr. Muir was engaged in writing for the *Overland Monthly* a series of articles on mountain sculpture. After long and urgent persuasion on my part, he consented to prepare for *Harper's Magazine* an illustrated article on California mountain scenery. Mr. Keith, who like Mr. Muir was born in Scotland, dropped into Mr. Muir's room two or three evenings a week and lent his aid in selecting illustrations from sketches taken from Muir's notebooks. The editor of *Harper's Magazine* accepted his first article and asked for other papers. Those long evening meetings in Muir's study room are among the pleasant recollections of my life.

In June following we made our visit to the Yosemite Valley, secured our outfit of saddle horses and equipments for camp life, and started out on a four weeks' trip into the high Sierras above the valley. We did our own cooking and had no guide except Mr. Muir. We camped near the "soda springs" in the Tuolumne meadows; crossed through the Mono Pass down Bloody Canyon to the dead sea of Mono Lake; thence struck southward along the range for forty miles, and then climbed upward into the mountains and encamped for several days in a glacial meadow nine thousand feet above sea level, in the loveliest little mountain nook that my eyes ever beheld. Thence we ascended various mountain peaks, returning at night to camp. On our return trip we visited the Lyell glacier. Under the instruction of Mr. Muir, every day was crowded with the richest and rarest of lessons.

During the following winter Mr. Muir again made his home in my family. It was this intimate friendship that led me in 1881 to purchase a tract of land adjoining his home in Alhambra Valley, near Martinez, and begin upon it the planting of an orchard and vineyard to make a country home when it should become possible for me to retire from school life. It was during this time that my youngest daughter Helen, then about three years old, became a special pet in Mr. Muir's study. My son, Frank Tracy Swett, then six years old, was also a frequent and welcome visitor to Mr. Muir's room.

Mr. Muir's articles in *Harper's Magazine* were followed a year later by a series of papers in *Scribner's Magazine*, and later still, another series of articles appeared in the *Cen-*

tury Magazine. His first book, "The Mountains of California," was published by the Century Company (1892); his second book, "Our National Parks," appeared in 1902, published by Houghton, Mifflin and Company. Both of these books are invaluable to all lovers of mountain and forest scenery and to teachers interested in nature study. As a keen observer and poetic interpreter of nature, as an enthusiastic explorer in California, Alaska, and the Rocky Mountain regions, John Muir stands without a rival. He combines strict scientific accuracy with poetic expression in a manner that lends a singular charm to his writings.

Henry George

My acquaintance with Henry George began at the time he was publishing a daily evening paper in San Francisco, and continued during the period that he was engaged in writing "Progress and Poverty." He was a genial friend, and I often dropped into his home on Sunday evenings. When he brought out in San Francisco, at his own expense, the first edition of his now famous book, I subscribed for ten copies of it, and when I paid him he said in a pathetic tone, "Swett, this is the first money I have ever received for my book." His receipt ran as follows:

San Francisco, May 23, 1879.

Received of John Swett twenty-five dollars ($25), in payment for ten copies of the book "Progress and Poverty." Henry George.

When the books were delivered I kept one copy, and presented the others to personal friends.

During the setting up of his book, Mr. George had asked me to run over the proof sheets to detect any ungrammatical constructions. He said, "All I know about English grammar was picked up in a printing office, and I may have made mistakes." But I found his English so good that it needed no correction by a schoolmaster. His political economy and his land-tax views we never discussed.

I can well understand how the idea grew in his mind that "the rich are growing richer, and the poor are growing poorer." His book was written during what is known in San Francisco as the "sand-lot period," when times were very hard and there was much real poverty. The city was crowded with men from all parts of the state, seeking for work but unable to find it. Mass meetings were held on the sand lots near the city hall. Dennis Kearney was the leader and chief spokesman of the agitators. It really seemed as if the foundations of society were breaking up. A part of George's book took its tone from these hard times. I told him that under existing conditions in San Francisco there was no room for him, and urged him, again and again, to go to New York, where his talent would be better recognized. Other friends gave him similar advice, and to New York he went, there to win success as a reformer, a lecturer, and an author of books on political economy and land-value taxation.

Personal Matters

My uneventful life as a school principal was made up of the routine work common to all teachers. During this period, as a relief from the monotony of school life, I was more or less engaged in some kind of literary work which occupied my leisure time. In 1880 I prepared a book entitled "School Elocution," designed for use in high schools and normal schools, which was published by A. L. Bancroft and Company and afterwards transferred by that firm to Harper and Brothers. This book had a fair sale for several years, but it never went into extensive use. It was perhaps unfortunate in its title; besides, it did not treat of dramatic elocutionary training for platform readings. It was really a high-grade reading book designed to develop the ability to read with effect good standard selections of prose and poetry. Next I prepared the third and the fourth books of a series of readers for the Bancroft Company.

In 1879 there was born to us in our home on Taylor Street the last of our family of six children, John French Swett. In 1881 my eldest child, Emily Tracy Swett, was graduated from the normal class of the Girls' High School. In the volunteer kindergarten work, in one of Mrs. Cooper's schools, she showed a marked talent for teaching. For two years I tried hard to secure a position for her in a primary class at fifty dollars a month, but without success. Members of the board of education told me that they would like to give her a place, but the political pressure was so strong that they had no power to make appointments on merit. Finally she obtained a position as teacher of French in a private seminary. Next she became a teacher of music, and then gave up teaching, established a literary bureau, and organized the Pacific Coast Women's Press Association. After the year 1880, indeed, it was seldom that any graduate of the normal class, however talented, was able to secure a position in the city schools. The city government had drifted into the control of political "bosses," and teachers were appointed mainly through political or personal favoritism. The best graduates of the city normal class went out into the remote district schools of the state, in which they performed missionary work. I did, however, secure, in 1884, from a strong partisan board, a standing rule that each year the one graduate of the normal class who attained the highest standing should receive for a reward an appointment as teacher in a primary school.

The National Educational Association

The year 1888 was a notable one in the educational annals of San Francisco on account of the meeting of the National Educational Association held in that city, July 17–22. The convention was very large, and the Eastern educators were greeted with enthusiasm and royally entertained. Aaron Gove presided with grace and dignity. Among the well-known educators from other states were William T. Harris, of Massachusetts; Louis Soldan, of St. Louis; J. M. Greenwood, of Missouri; John W. Cook, of Illinois; Jerome Allen, of New York; John Hancock, of Ohio; E. C. Hewett, of Illinois; W. E. Sheldon, of Boston; James H. Baker, of Colorado; J. L. Pickard, of Chicago, and others too numerous to mention. I had been invited to prepare a paper on "The Relation of the State to Schoolbooks and Appliances." As this topic is still a vexed one, and as yet an undecided question, I give here some brief extracts from my paper on that occasion.

After a study of the school laws and school systems of the several states in the Union, it is evident that school laws have followed the general law of evolution, beginning with simple functions and becoming more complex and differentiated with the general development of society in population, wealth, and civilization. The general tendency has been to enlarge the powers of both state and local laws and regulations.

In the beginning, the state required by law that a public school should be kept in every school district for three months in the year, provided for the formation of school districts and the election of school trustees, but left all other powers, such as the voting of school taxes, the building of schoolhouses, and the control of schools in general, to school districts, to counties, or to cities.

The general principle may be roughly stated as follows: The scope of state law in relation to schools has been whatever the people have chosen to make it in order to meet the evident needs of the schools in different stages of development.

As to school appliances I can speak from personal experience. When I began to go to school, fifty years ago, in a New Hampshire village, there was a summer school of three months taught by a woman, and a winter school of three months taught by a man. The summer school was generally supplemented by a tuition or private school for a month or more. Out of this New England custom of supplementing the free school by tuition fees, there grew up the rate-bill system, which prevailed in most states for a long time, and which still maintains a lingering existence. In California the rate bill was abolished by law in 1868, the same year that the state of New York got rid of the incubus that had weighed upon her rural schools for more than a century.

Fifty years ago pupils, except in some incorporated cities, bought their own pens, ink, paper, pencils, slates, books, and all other school appliances. The school apparatus consisted of a piece of chalk and one small blackboard, six feet by three. This was the condition of things in California only a few years ago. In 1863, when revising the school law, I incorporated a provision requiring school trustees and boards of education to supply to pupils, free, all minor school appliances, such as pens, ink, paper, pencils, crayons, wash-basins, etc., and nobody, so far as I know, grumbled about it. This law also provided that free textbooks should be supplied to pupils whose parents presented evidence of inability to buy them. The history of other States shows the same general tendency toward free minor supplies.

The original unit for the adoption of textbooks was the school district, or the chartered city. This was succeeded in course of time by town adoption in the New England states, and by county adoption in the Southern and Western states. Finally, a few states and territories have tried the experiment of a uniform State Series, adopted by a state board of education. Take California as an illustration.

From the organization of schools in 1850 up to 1863, cities having local boards of education were authorized to adopt textbooks, and so were the local rural school districts; but in these districts it generally happened that there was a heterogeneous mixture of such books as the pupils happened to have on hand. As a result of this evil the rural teachers were clamoring for state uniformity. So in 1863, when I came into the office of state superintendent, I drew up a bill, which became a law, providing, except in incorporated cities, for the adoption of a uniform state series of textbooks. But this law applied to only about one-third of the school children — that is, to those in the small rural districts. But in 1868 the incorporated cities were placed under the jurisdiction of the state board of education and trouble began immediately.

So great was the popular dissatisfaction that, when the State Constitution was revised in 1879, it contained a provision for county adoption by county boards. Again, in consequence of popular clamor about changes in textbooks, an amendment to the constitution was adopted in 1884, providing for a uniform state series to be edited by the state board of education, printed by the state printer, and sold at cost price. This action lies outside of what has generally been considered the proper scope of state law.

As to free textbooks, until within a few years they were seldom supplied at public expense, but there are two notable exceptions. The schools of New York City have been supplied with free books since 1806, the year in which public schools were fully organized in that city. The reasons urged in 1806 hold good to the present day. They were: (1) to guard against invidious distinction among pupils on account of indigence; (2) To facilitate uniform and prompt supplies; (3) To guard against extravagance. In Philadelphia, free books have been supplied since 1818, the date of the organization of free schools in that city. It remained for Massachusetts, the cradle of free schools in their infancy, to make, in 1884, the most notable advance among the states. A law was then enacted requiring free books throughout the state, the books to be adopted and purchased by local boards of education.

The verdict of the people is that this measure is wise, beneficent, and economical. Other states are now following the example of Massachusetts. There is no mistaking the tendency of this evolution. It is natural that the views of teachers and educators should be biased in favor of the laws and customs of the state in which they reside; but an impartial survey of our whole country shows that the evolution of school law is, with a few sporadic exceptions, toward free supplies, free textbooks, and toward city, town, or county uniformity.

Affairs in the Girls' High School

Meanwhile, the Girls' High School moved along with varied fortunes. It was in 1885, I think, that seventy-five pupils from the highest grade of the grammar schools failed to pass the annual written examination for admission to the two city high schools. The board of education passed an order that they should all be promoted on trial. The Girls' High School thus received a class of forty-five girls entirely unfitted for high-school work. After a trial of three months we reported them as "failures," but the board insisted that they should remain in the school. At the end of the year they failed to be promoted, and the parents, as well as most of the members of the board, laid the blame on the teachers and the principal.

Furthermore, the teacher of a class in general history and Latin, Henry E. Senger, made some remarks on a topic in medieval history which offended some Catholic parents; whereupon he was disciplined by the board and the school superintendent with a suspension for one month. I endeavored to save him from this sentence, but without avail. He resigned, and secured a position in the University of California as assistant professor in German. The high school was left without a Latin teacher, and the board neglected to appoint another to the vacancy. In 1888, during the summer vacation, when I was absent from the city, the board of education adopted a new course of study without any consultation with the teachers or the principal, materially changing the organization of the school. Long afterwards I learned that it was hoped that this action would secure my resignation.

At this time the political condition of San Francisco was deplorable. Christopher Buckley, known as "the blind boss," had secured absolute control of the city government. Mr. Buckley had been trained to politics in the city of New York, and he set up in San Francisco a local "Tammany Hall." The president of the board of education, Buckley's lieutenant, died several years ago, and I need not mention his name nor characterize his acts. There was a reign of terror in the school department. During the school year 1887–88 I worked hard to bring order out of chaos in the high school, but the whole political power was against me. The political "boss" of the board of education first demanded the resignation of George W. Minns, the veteran high-school and normal-school teacher, on the ground that he was "too old to teach school." Deeply grieved, Mr. Minns resigned from the Girls' High School and returned to Boston. For the same reason one of the oldest and ablest teachers in the school, Mrs. Dorcas Clark, was requested to resign, and she retired to grieve over her great wrong. Another veteran teacher was given a leave of absence, and she did not again return to the school. The remaining teachers were alarmed and dissatisfied, but they did the best they could under trying conditions.

When the term closed in May, 1889, I knew that my turn would come next. During the vacation the "boss" of the board requested my resignation, which I sent in without any explanation. I had too much pride to submit to further humiliation and insult. I did not intend to be publicly tried and dismissed by a packed jury under the control of a political boss. I have never regretted my action. The main complaint urged against me was that I was too old, and I had to plead guilty to the fact that I was fifty-nine years of age. It was a pet idea of the "boss" of the board that no man or woman was fit to teach school after forty years of age. At the next succeeding election the boss of the board disappeared forever from public office. As for myself, though I retired under a cloud of misrepresentations and petty persecutions, I received my vindication at the hands of the citizens of San Francisco in the general election a year and a half later, at which I was elected city superintendent of schools by the overwhelming majority of two-thirds of the entire vote cast.

During the time that I was principal of the high school, from 1876 to 1889, thirteen years, the total number of graduates was 1312, or an average of 101 a year. From the normal class during the same period, the number of graduates was 844, or an average of 65 a year. My reputation as a teacher is safe in the memories of these graduates.

My successor was Mrs. Mary W. Kincaid, instead of the man who had been "slated" for the position by the boss of the board. Soon after, the high school building was burned to the ground, and the school was quartered in a primary school building. After two or three years, Mrs. Kincaid found the position intolerable, and resigned. The normal class maintained a lingering existence for several years, and was then disconnected from the high school, and made a "City Normal School," in the old Powell Street building, the home of the pioneer high school in California. Miss Laura T. Fowler was made principal, and Mrs. M. E. Fitzgerald, one of the early graduates of the Girls' High School and normal class, was made assistant.

This school continued to flourish until, in 1898, when a hostile city board of education suddenly abolished it on the ground that it was no longer needed, and was an unnecessary expense to the city. But a committee of indignant citizens went to the state legislature in 1899 and secured the passage of a bill to reëstablish it, as a state normal school. The board of state normal school trustees appointed as president Frederic Burke, under whose energetic management the school has become noted for its attention to the art of teaching, rather than to academic scholarship or metaphysical psychology.

At a recent meeting of the California Teachers' Association, July, 1905, I shook glad hands with scores of the earlier graduates of the normal class who are now occupying honorable positions as teachers in many parts of California. One is vice-principal of the John Swett Grammar School in San Francisco; another is principal of a large grammar school in San Francisco; another is principal of a large primary school; and still another, vice-principal of the Mission High School in the same city. Large numbers of those graduates became pioneers in remote rural schools in different parts of the state, and very few of them have made a failure. Several hundred of them are doing good service as successful grade teachers in the elementary schools of San Francisco, Oakland, and Alameda.[1]

[1] As I was standing on the platform at Hearst Hall in Berkeley, receiving the congratulations of my friends after the presentation, by the teachers, to the State University of a portrait of myself, and its acceptance by President Wheeler in behalf of the Board of Regents of the University of California, an incident occurred which deeply moved my feelings. A pleasant-faced teacher approached me and said: "Mr. Swett, I came down to this meeting from a remote county in the hope that I might meet you here. Perhaps you will recall me when I tell you that I am the young woman from Canada that called at your office in the Girls' High School in 1886, and asked you if it would be possible for me to be admitted into the Normal School. After questioning me about where I had been educated, you told me that under the rules of the board you could not admit me; but you added, that if I was in earnest about becoming a teacher, perhaps you could help me. Though not enrolled as a regular member of the class, I was given a seat and a set of books and all the privileges of the class. You advised me to remain until the end of the term and then you thought that I could probably pass a county examination and secure a country school. I secured both, and have been teaching ever since. I have won a reputation as a successful teacher. And I want to say to you that there has never been a day since I began to teach, that, as I entered my schoolroom, I did not think of you and your kindness in lending me a hand when I needed help."

My own heart was swelling with gratitude to my fellow teachers for the honor they had done me that day, and with this story of one of my former pupils, I felt my eyes "cloud up for rain."

CHAPTER XIV

ELECTION AS CITY SUPERINTENDENT OF PUBLIC SCHOOLS IN SAN FRANCISCO

AFTER my resignation I retired at once to Hill Girt farm near Martinez, and busied myself with the management of an orchard and a vineyard. The sudden change from school life to farm work was something of a wrench for the first six months, but at the end of that time I found myself in fair health and good spirits. At the end of a year there were signs of a revolution in city politics, and it became probable that Christopher Buckley and his satellites, together with the board of education, would be driven out of power. The city superintendent of schools had received the nomination of the Republican party for state superintendent of public instruction, leaving the city office open for a new candidate. My friends in the city, indignant at the treatment to which I had been subjected, began to urge me to become a candidate. I held out for some time against this movement, but finally gave way to the pressure and allowed the use of my name as a candidate, with the condition that no personal effort on my part was to be required in securing the nomination. When the Republican convention assembled I received the nomination by acclamation. At the election following, I received two-thirds of the entire vote cast, having the highest vote of any candidate on the ticket.

Thus the people of San Francisco triumphantly vindicated my reputation by a very emphatic vote of approval.

Until that campaign I never realized how many friends I had, nor how true they were. The *Examiner*, the leading Democratic paper, came out editorially in my support. My former pupils in the high school, the Denman Grammar School, and the Rincon School, canvassed the city by scores and hundreds, calling at the offices of merchants and business men to solicit votes for me.

One day as I was passing along Market Street, a group of three men hailed me, and one of them called out:

"Hold on a minute, Mr. Swett; we want to speak to you. Do you know why we Irishmen think so much of you?"

"Indeed I don't," I replied; "I didn't suppose that you knew me at all."

"But we know all about you. Our children went to school to you when you were in the Rincon School, years ago, and we know that you always treated a poor man's boy just as well as you did a rich man's son. We are all Democrats, and you are on the Republican ticket, but we are going to vote for you, sure."

I thanked them for one of the highest compliments that I had ever received and replied, "When I was a hard-working boy, many years ago on a New Hampshire farm, I was as good an Andrew Jackson Democrat as the best of you." Then another of these warm-hearted men laughingly broke out with, "It's true, Mr. Swett, you haven't any handle to your name, before it nor after it, but you always get there just the same."

A few minutes later I met Mr. Donelly whose four daughters were under my care in the Denman Grammar School, and in the Girls' High School. He gripped my hand till it ached, saying: "I'm glad to see you, Mr. Swett. I owe you a great deal for your kindness to my girls. You know

I am a poor man, but I have a hundred dollars laid by, and if you need it to help pay your election expenses, you are welcome to the use of it until you can pay it back when you are elected."

I thanked him warmly, but told him that I did not need any help, and that my election assessment of seven hundred dollars made by the county committee, was already paid in full with my own money, and beyond that I did not intend to spend a dollar. As I write this page in the year 1907, a daughter of this generous-hearted Irishman is vice-principal of the Mission High School, of which the principal is Joseph O'Connor, whom I had the pleasure of introducing to a class in bookkeeping in the Lincoln evening school.

On the first Monday in January, 1891, I entered on the duties of my office. For the first two months I was engaged in revising and codifying the rules and regulations of the board, and in learning the routine work. Then I began a visiting tour to every school and class in the department, and at the end of three months I knew something about the educational condition of the schools from personal inspection. Next I called a series of meetings of the teachers, by grades, for the purpose of discussing the course of study and of proposing some changes for the coming school year. For three months I went to my office at seven o'clock in the morning and worked on the details of a new course of study until nine o'clock, the hour for opening the office doors, thus securing two hours a day of uninterrupted thought. To this work, also, I devoted every day of the six weeks of summer vacation, in order to have the course ready for the opening of school in July.

This revised course of study was by no means an ideal

one, but it was adapted to the prevailing conditions. The state textbooks required by law were entirely unsuited to the needs of graded schools. Unfortunately a majority of the grade teachers taught mainly by means of memorized lessons, marked out by certain prescribed pages of the textbooks. This division of work by pages was in the main left undisturbed. But the outlines in textbooks were supplemented by many pages of suggestions which involved modern psychological and pedagogical principles. The whole course consisted of a volume of two hundred pages, and the size of it at first alarmed many conservative teachers who imagined that it was harder because it was longer than the old course. The chief merit of this manual was that it allowed greater freedom to progressive teachers, simplified the work in arithmetic and grammar, and provided for supplementary reading matter.

In visiting the schools I found many things to commend. The essentials to be learned by children in the five primary grades are reading, writing, spelling, arithmetic, and enough of language to write a letter correctly. All these things were well done in the classes that I visited. In all the schools the children were quick at figures; and in some schools they were accurate. The main criticism made on the teaching of arithmetic in the primary grades was the general tendency to make use of long, complex, and tiresome operations with very large numbers, instead of simple, short, business drill on ordinary business forms of reckoning. But this was not so much the fault of the teachers as it was of the textbooks, and of interminable written examinations which tended to worry and puzzle children instead of instructing them.

In respect to supplementary reading I found the city

schools ten years behind the times in comparison with many of the rural district schools of California. My report to the board of education on this matter reads as follows:

"I beg leave to call your attention to the state school law in relation to school libraries. The revised school law of 1866, which, slightly amended, has remained in force ever since, provides that 10 per cent of the state apportionment of school money to each district, not to exceed $50, shall be set apart as a school library fund, to be expended exclusively in buying books for school libraries. In incorporated cities the amount so reserved is $50 for every 1000 census children. This law has been strictly observed throughout the state except in San Francisco, where, for ten years, through ignorance or defiance of law, the library money has been diverted to other purposes. I recommend the board to comply with the law."

By custom as well as by law, the superintendent had nothing whatever to do with the appointment of teachers. He was allowed a seat in the board, but had no vote. He was given no power to decide anything, not even to send out a substitute teacher for a single day. He could not suspend or reinstate a pupil. He was required by law to make monthly reports to the board, to sign warrants, and to visit schools. He was expected to revise the course of study from time to time and report it to the board for adoption. Though nominally he was the executive officer of the board, all the executive work was really divided up among the several committees.

By unwritten law, for many years the patronage of appointing teachers had been mathematically divided among the board members, each director in alphabetical order being allowed to appoint a teacher when his turn came round. The worst of such a plan was that the members themselves were not free agents in making appointments, but were compelled to yield to the demands of partisan "bosses," or political leaders, or ward politicians. During my term of office, I can recall but one instance in which my opinion of the fitness of a teacher for appointment was asked by a school director. One director, a personal friend, once showed me his memorandum list of over one hundred applicants for a position, each one backed by strong influences. Under this system the best men in the board, along with the weakest, were compelled to yield. One director, nominated by myself to fill a vacancy, in less than a month after his appointment by the board, showed me a letter from a United States senator from California, earnestly demanding the appointment of a young lady to the position of a primary teacher. Another boasted of the fact that he had appointed three teachers by the request of a notable millionaire. At another period, some years previous to this, there were several political "school brokers" who engaged to secure appointments for the sum of three hundred dollars each. These brokers pocketed the money, and secured appointments by political or personal pull.

My second annual report, 1892–93, was a document of two hundred pages which treated of various topics, among which were the following: School visits; revised course of study; individuality in teachers; physical training; home study; average daily attendance per class; names of schools; the Golden Gate free kindergartens; historical sketches of city high schools and the evening schools; overwork in the high schools; historical notes of early school history in San Francisco; the Kate Kennedy case; election of teachers; and the manner of electing school directors.

I find by reference to this report that, during the year, I visited each of the 74 schools and 775 classes in the city at least once. During these short visits of from ten to twenty minutes I was able to give a few drill exercises in arithmetic for testing accuracy and quickness; to inquire about writing or drawing; and, in the higher grades, to question pupils about the kind of books they were reading at home.

The order in the schools was, with very few exceptions, good. The yards were under strict supervision. Pupils filed into and out of the building with military precision, to the beat of a drum. The yard drill in free gymnastics was generally good, and in many cases excellent. The calisthenic drill in the classrooms was faithfully carried out. There were a few schools in which the discipline, it seemed to me, was carried to extremes. It is possible to have a discipline that represses activity and cheerfulness. A class in which a smile never dawns on the face of either teacher or pupil is over-disciplined. The hum of a beehive in open sunlight is preferable to the oppressive darkness and silence of an Egyptian temple. The best government prevails where the pleasant countenance of a cheerful teacher rises on the children at nine o'clock in the morning and beams upon them all day long. A Gatling-gun discharge of deportment checks by the teacher all day long, a continuous nagging of dull pupils, a multiplication of petty rules until a boy cannot wink his eye without a reprimand, everlasting faultfinding, never-ending scolding, depressing threats of failure to be promoted — these are not the best aids to cheerful obedience or to mental or moral development.

I found that teachers, in general, had made a good beginning on the new course of study. In nature study the work was encouraging. Pupils had begun to open their eyes to the world around them. The windows of the schoolrooms were full of sprouting peas, beans, and corn. Drawings had been made of the successive stages of plant growth.

School cabinets had been begun and the children were eager to contribute specimens. Nearly every room had its glass jar of young tadpoles, and pupils were delighted with watching the metamorphosis of polliwogs into frogs. In the grammar grades the time given to arithmetic had been materially reduced, and methods had been simplified. In some schools intelligent work has been done in the study of grammar as applied to speaking and writing English. Under rational methods in drawing, so interested had the pupils become that in many classes they asked their teacher to allow them to remain after school to draw. The introduction of new and interesting reading books had greatly stimulated a taste for reading. Some of the schools were supplied with sets of primary histories of the United States, which were used as supplementary readers in the fourth, fifth, and sixth grades. Statistics show that one-half of the pupils leave school before completing the fifth grade. If such children learn anything about the history of our own country, that knowledge must be gained by supplementary reading in the lower grades.

The leading aim in the new course was to make it flexible enough to allow the exercise of some individuality by both principals and teachers. In essentials there must be a general uniformity of studies, but a dead level of Chinese uniformity in details is the greatest of educational evils. Enthusiasm is the secret of success in teaching. Without some degree of freedom there can be neither enthusiasm nor earnestness.

The vital part of my report for 1893 related to the method of electing teachers and to the office of "head inspector." It was an attack on certain abuses of power that had grown up by degrees in the department, and I realized in making it that I should excite fierce antagonisms, which would in all probability defeat my renomination for the office of superintendent. The following extracts from this report will exhibit one of the evils that I attacked:

The weakest point in our school system is the method of electing teachers. . . . It is an outgrowth of the "spoils system" in politics. It is contrary to all principles of civil reform. The number of new teachers to be elected is about thirty-six each year, or three appointments to each director. As places become vacant during the year, each director, in regular order, makes one appointment, and by mutual understanding this appointment is absolute, the only condition required being that the nominee must be the holder of a legal certificate. The names of appointees are handed to the chairman of the committee on classification, who makes the nominations in open board; consequently no one knows what director is responsible for the appointment of a teacher. Under this system no selection of the best teachers out of a large number of applicants is possible. The election of a teacher becomes merely the personal opinion or personal favoritism of one man. Young women who are graduates of the high school and normal school are reduced to a dead level with young girls who leave the grammar school and in a few months cram to pass an examination for a certificate. The most talented and accomplished teachers coming here from other cities stand no chance of an appointment on merit. School directors are subjected to the political or personal "pull" of United States senators, of governors and ex-governors, city officials, supervisors, members of county committees, political clubs, and active politicians generally. The present plan of appointments has become so strongly intrenched that there is little hope of a change except by the adoption of a new charter and a change in the manner of securing a board of education.

It would be better if the board would agree to a rule requiring that all assistants in primary or grammar grades should be selected exclusively from the graduates of the City Normal School, the State Normal schools, the State University, or from experienced teachers elsewhere who have won a reputation. The annual average of salaries paid to the teachers of this city is higher than in most large cities. While educated, trained, and experienced teachers are worth every dollar they are paid, untrained, unskilled, and poorly educated teachers do not earn such salaries. There is no good reason why any school director should appoint an unskilled, untrained, and inexperienced teacher, when twenty professionally trained teachers are waiting for positions, and as many more experienced teachers that have won a reputation stand ready to fill a vacancy. It is sometimes urged that, as school directors receive no salary for their services, they have the right to the personal patronage of appointing their friends. But it seems to me that citizens who seek and secure such an office of honor have no moral right to prostitute their power to selfish and personal ends.

For one year I managed to run along smoothly with the board, and then trouble arose. Seven members, a majority of the board, then addressed me a communication requesting me to dismiss my deputy for reasons which I did not consider valid. As the deputy superintendent had discharged his duties faithfully and efficiently, I declined to remove him. The board then reduced his salary from $250 a month to $25, hoping that he would resign. After three months the board rescinded its action and restored the salary. At the end of another year there was an election of school directors, at which one half of the old board was reëlected, the other half being composed of new members. This board took the first steps in reform by consolidating classes in accordance with the recommendations made in my second annual report, and in effecting other changes for the better. After the classes were filled up to a reasonable number, there were found to be sixty-three superfluous teachers who were temporarily retired, but who were all reinstated as vacancies occurred during the year.

The Death of my Daughter Emily

In April, 1892, our eldest daughter, Mrs. Emily Tracy (Swett) Parkhurst, lingered three weeks after her confinement, and then drifted away from life, leaving behind her an infant daughter. This loss was a crushing blow to us, and it was fortunate perhaps that the pressure of official duties kept me hard at work and thus enabled me better to endure my loss. Mr. Parkhurst committed the motherless child to the loving care of my wife, and the little girl, Ruth Emilie Parkhurst, seems to us like one of our own children. At the time of her death Mrs. Parkhurst was twenty-nine years of age. She received her education in the public schools of San Francisco, and was graduated from the normal department of the Girls' High School in 1881. She early manifested a strong taste for literature. When sixteen years of age in the high school, she was one of seventy-five competitors for the prize of a gold watch and chain offered by the San Francisco *Chronicle* for the best Christmas story, and to her the prize was awarded. After her graduation from the normal school, unable to find employment in the city school department, she accepted a position as teacher of music and French in a private seminary at Eureka in the northern part of California. She was a pleasing writer of both prose and verse, and in her literary work was often employed by publishers to translate French and German articles and books. She was at one time employed as the private secretary of a publishing house, and in this capacity she developed executive ability of a high order. In 1889 she was married to John W. Parkhurst, an employee in the Bank of California, but she did not discontinue her literary work. For a year before her death she was assistant editor of the *Californian Illustrated Magazine*, from which I quote the following tribute to her memory:

The Pacific Coast world of letters has suffered a loss in the past month in the death of Emily Tracy (Swett) Parkhurst. Mrs. Parkhurst was connected with the *Californian* as an assistant editor, was a contibutor to its columns, and wrote its literary reviews. She was a woman of rare promise, possessed of great talent, which, combined with executive ability, made her a prominent figure in many assemblies. Her especial work was the formation of the Pacific Coast Women's Press Association. A few years ago she traveled through the state and made the personal acquaintance of all the Pacific Coast writers, her object being to advance the interests of women writers — bring them out and aid them in obtaining a field for their work. In this she was extremely successful. She gathered about her hundreds of contributors to the literary press of the day, and finally organized the Press Association, of which she became secretary. The work thus accomplished did much in encouraging women to make a fight for themselves, and by her means many are now self-supporting who, previous to the movement, realized little or nothing from their literary work. Mrs. Parkhurst combined rare executive ability with literary discernment and taste, and was a brilliant organizer. At the time of her death, she had plans laid out for work that would have appalled many. One was a thorough investigation of the possibility of woman's work in horticulture and agriculture in this state. This was not theory, as the plan included a system by which women could enter the lists with men in farming and marketing their products. Few women had so large an acquaintance; few will be missed by so great a number; and so a well-spent, bright life is ended, apparently cut short, yet leaving a rich heritage, a rare example to those who are left behind.

Educational Progress

A beginning of manual training was made in 1892 by organizing, in the commercial high school, classes in woodwork, architectural drawing, and freehand drawing. Two classes in cooking were established in grammar schools, and two in sewing. By resolution of the board, August 8, 1894, it was ordered that two additional classes in cooking should be established, and also three classes in manual training, for pupils in the higher grammar grades.

The most notable educational work of the board of education during the year was a movement towards civil-service rules in the appointment of teachers. The rules adopted provided for the appointment, annually, to the "substitute class" of the six graduates from the city normal school who stood highest in rank; for a competitive examination to determine the election of twelve additional teachers; and for further vacancies. That such appointments shall be made in the manner at present provided; but no one shall be appointed a teacher in the schools of this city who is not a graduate of some normal school, or other institution of learning of equal or higher rank, with a regular diploma therefrom, or who shall not have had at least one year's successful practice in teaching in primary and grammar schools, and holding first-grade certificates.

Political and Personal Reminiscences

When, in my school report for 1892, I attacked the personal and political system of electing teachers, I was well aware that I should antagonize the political bosses and the managers of ward politics. Consequently, when the time arrived in 1894 for the nomination of a school superintendent, I was not surprised to find some of the political managers of the Republican party bitterly opposed to me. Therefore, I made no effort to secure the nomination. However, on the urgent request of many friends, my name was proposed in the convention, but I had it withdrawn before the convention proceeded to make a nomination. I knew that the convention itself had no freedom of action in the matter, and that all the nominees were selected by the two political bosses in command of the party. In the following election, the Republican nominee was defeated by the candidate of the Democratic party, Andrew J. Moulder, my predecessor in the office of state superintendent. The politicians who defeated me were rebuked by the voice of the people.

Before retiring from office, I delivered a final address at a teachers' institute meeting, and introduced my coming successor to the city teachers. This address closed with the following paragraphs:

Outside of the routine executive work of the office, the main points to which I have directed my efforts during my term of office for nearly four years may be summed up as follows:

1. To secure in all the lower grades simple, thorough, and practical training in reading, writing, and spelling our mother tongue; a thorough training in the essentials of arithmetic, while rigidly excluding the non-essentials that have been crammed into the textbooks; practice in simple, natural, and attractive exercises in freehand drawing; a business style of penmanship.

2. The introduction into the schools of sets of supplementary readers, and sets of good literary extracts from American authors, to supplement the state readers; the introduction into all grammar grades of sets of primary histories of our country as supplementary reading.

3. The extension of the course in nature study or elementary science; moral training by means of talks on topics and the reading of extracts from the best books on this subject; training in politeness by means of talks on topics and of reading from special books on this subject.

4. Frequent meetings of grade teachers and a free discussion of methods; teachers' institute meetings, with lectures by the ablest educators that could be secured.

5. A course of study flexible enough to allow the exercise of some individuality in teaching, both to principals and class teachers.

6. The establishment of classes in cooking; and the beginning of manual-training classes in grammar schools.

As I am soon to retire from official connection with the schools at the expiration of my term of office, I wish here to return to the teachers in the school department my sincere thanks for their personal kindness and courtesy. Under the circumstances attending my election to office, four years ago, I should have been recreant to duty if I had not put my whole life into my official work. I may have made mistakes; I may not always have done the wisest thing under complicated conditions; but I have fearlessly done my duty as I understood it, without regard to personal consequences. I have stood by the teachers. I have defended many from unfair attacks. I have done my utmost to secure some method of appointing teachers better than that of personal favoritism or of political spoils.

In taking leave of the nine hundred teachers in this city, some of whom have been personal friends and coworkers for many years, and nearly one half of whom were my pupils in the Girls' High and Normal School, I do so with regret, as my retirement from office, in all probability, marks the end of my lifework in teaching and in school supervision.

I wish, also, on this occasion, to return my sincere thanks to the people of this city for their long-continued kindness to me, both in prosperity and in adversity. Forty years ago, I came here a young man, friendless and unknown. Here I have devoted my youth, my manhood, and my advancing years to the public schools.

As teacher, as state superintendent of public instruction, as city superintendent of public schools, I have put into my work all my enthusiasm and all my energy. I love the city of my adoption. I am proud of her schools. I have a profound faith that a good system of public schools is essential to the preservation of good government. The public schools must be made the nurseries of intelligent patriotism. They must be jealously guarded against attacks, and must be kept in line with the best of modern thought in education. I am thankful that it has been my privilege to aid in laying the foundation of the public-school system of this city and of California.

After my retirement from office the election of teachers soon fell back into the old channels of personal and political "pull," and for several years the entire city government grew from bad to worse, until finally the better class of citizens succeeded in securing a new charter, which changed materially all departments of local government. The new charter provided for a board of education, appointed by the mayor, and paid a salary of three thousand dollars a year, each; also, for four deputy superintendents at a salary of eighteen hundred dollars a year, each. Civil-service rules were applied to a certain extent to the appointment of teachers. I have the satisfaction of feeling that my attacks on educational abuses contributed materially to this reform.

CHAPTER XV

OUTLINES OF THE CALIFORNIA PUBLIC-SCHOOL SYSTEM AS A WHOLE IN THE FIRST DECADE OF THE TWENTIETH CENTURY

As these reminiscences began with a sketch of the common schools and academies in New England, where I was born, it seems fitting that one of the closing chapters should contain a brief summary of the educational situation in California, which has been my home for half a century.

At the beginning of this century all the omens are auspicious. California is now at the high tide of prosperity in agriculture, in mining, in commerce, in the mechanic arts, and in all other industrial pursuits. Our whole public-school system, from primary schools to the State University, is keeping even pace with our rapid increase in wealth, in population, in science, in art, and in literature.

The California public-school system now consists of a free State University open to both young men and young women; of six State Normal schools; of nearly two hundred high schools; and underlying all these, as a broad foundation, an efficient system of common schools, or, in modern terms, elementary schools.

The common schools of the state are under the executive control of the superintendent of public instruction. The state board of education is composed of *ex-officio* members as follows: the governor, the superintendent of public instruction, the president of the University of California, the president of each of the six State Normal schools, and the professor of pedagogy in the State University. This board is empowered to adopt rules and regulations not inconsistent with the state school law, and to prescribe by general rules the credentials upon which persons may be granted certificates to teach in high schools.

County boards of education consist of the county superintendent and four other members appointed by the county board of supervisors. A majority of each board must consist of experienced teachers holding certificates not lower than of grammar grade. These boards are empowered to hold annual examinations of applicants for grammar-school certificates, valid for the county, and to issue kindergarten-primary certificates and special certificates on credentials as prescribed by the state board.

City boards of education are elected by popular vote, except in the city and county of San Francisco. The powers of city boards vary with the different city charters, subject to the general provision of the state school law.

Each district board of school trustees consists of three members elected by popular vote at school district elections, for the term of three years, one member being elected each year. These boards are empowered to appoint teachers and fix their salaries; to appoint census marshals; to provide school supplies authorized by law; to keep the schoolhouses in repair, and to enforce the general provisions of the state school law.

One of the most beneficent of many good provisions in the California school law is that relating to school libraries, incorporated into the "revised school law" in 1866, and retained, with slight amendments, on the statute books up to the present time. The number of volumes in all the school libraries in California in 1904 was reported as 1,448,464. These books have been specially selected to suit the taste or the needs of young children. Thus, year by year, new books are added to the library. Every school in California, however small or however remote, has at least a few volumes of choice books used to cultivate in the pupils a taste for reading. The report of the state superintendent shows that for the school year ending June 30, 1904, a total of $138,439 was expended for school library books.

School Revenue

The school moneys, annually apportioned from the state treasury for the partial support of common schools, are derived from various sources. The securities held in trust by the state treasurer for the support of common schools consists of state funded debt bonds aggregating $1,726,500, together with bonds of various counties of the state, making a total of $4,847,650, the annual interest of which is applied to the support of schools. The amount derived from the state property tax of seven dollars per school-census child is about four millions of dollars.

The second source of revenue is the county school tax, the minimum rate of which is six dollars per school census child. This tax gives a school revenue of over three millions of dollars. Another source of revenue is the city or district tax, which amounts to half a million dollars. The grand total of all receipts for school purposes is about twelve millions of dollars.

It is said that Californians are given to boasting about their climate and their resources, but California teachers and educators make only the modest claim that their schools compare favorably with those of older, wealthier and more populous states that have a common school history running back, for more than two hundred years, into the colonial period of the thirteen original states of the Union. The city schools in California closely resemble those in other states. The rural schools have some points of superiority over the corresponding rural schools in some of the older states, owing to the fact that the California school law provides that the county superintendent shall apportion outright five hundred dollars for each teacher in each school district. All remaining moneys are apportioned to districts in proportion to the average daily attendance. This direct appropriation of five hundred dollars a year for each teacher in the small, weak, or newly formed school districts, to which may be added from one hundred to three hundred dollars by pro rata apportionment on average daily attendance, enables the small one-room rural schools to secure competent teachers, and continue school at least eight months in the year. The state, in turn, by means of a heavy state school tax, lends a helping hand to the weaker counties by compelling the cities, where wealth and population are concentrated, to aid the rural counties, which have a sparse population and a relatively smaller amount per capita of taxable property. This plan is regarded by Californians as dictated by enlightened common sense.

The High Schools

In the early days of California, before the establishment of high schools, secondary education was provided for by numerous private, parochial, and denominational schools, under the name of college schools, "seminaries," "boarding schools," and "academies," all of which were supported mainly by tuition fees. The first public high school opened its doors to both boys and girls, in San Francisco (1856), under the name of The Union Grammar School, given to it out of deference to the objection of certain city officials, who contended that a high school did not constitute a legal part of the common-school system. Nevertheless, it was an English high school, *sub rosa*, with a course of study which included algebra, geometry, ancient and modern history, literature, physics, and chemistry. Two years later, official opinion had become enlightened enough to allow the school to assume the full-blown name of the San Francisco English High School. A few years later a Latin School was established "to fit boys for college." The second high school in California was opened in Sacramento (1859), and at a later date high schools were begun in Marysville, Grass Valley, Nevada City, Oakland, Los Angeles, San José, and Vallejo, in the order named.

The opening of the State University of California (1870) stimulated the existing high schools. The upward pressure of the elementary schools, growing stronger and stronger, led to the passage of a state law (1891) whereby contiguous common-school districts could unite to form a union district and establish a union high school, and thereafter the number of high schools was rapidly increased. Authorized by an amendment to the constitution (1903), the state legislature levied an annual high-school tax of one and a half cents on each one hundred dollars of the state assessment roll, the proceeds to be distributed to aid in the local support of high schools. The first annual apportionment under this law amounted to $232,386.

The state law of California requires a high standard of qualification for high school teachers. The power of granting such certificates is vested exclusively in the state board of education, which issues certificates on credentials, the standard being a university diploma, together with a certificate of having pursued the required pedagogical course in the University of California. The diploma of certain other universities of equal rank with the state university, and having also pedagogical courses, are recognized as the basis of credentials on which teachers' certificates may be issued.

State Normal Schools of California

The first state normal school in California was opened in San Francisco, July 21, 1862, under an appropriation by the legislature of three thousand dollars for its support. This appropriation was secured by a volunteer committee consisting of Andrew J. Moulder, state superintendent of public instruction, George Tait, city superintendent of San Francisco, and myself, state superintendent elect. Dr. Hill, of Sonoma, a state senator, after long-continued persuasion, reluctantly consented to introduce our brief bill, which appropriated three thousand dollars, leaving the details of organization to the state board of education, then consisting of the governor, the surveyor general, and the state superintendent. The school, in charge of Ahira Holmes, a graduate of the Massachusetts State Normal School at Bridgewater, opened in San Francisco with six pupils, just the number with which the first Massachusetts State Normal School began. Its growth was slow, on account of the general indifference of the city school authorities and the hostility of a majority of public-school teachers. After my election to the office of state superintendent, the responsibility of looking after the school fell mainly on me for a period of five years. The city board of education reluctantly granted the school part of an old primary school building in the rear of the Lincoln Grammar School. A model or training school of two classes was soon opened, in charge of Miss Helen Clark from the Oswego Normal School. On account of the neglect and indifference of San Francisco, this pioneer normal school was removed to San José (1871), where a suitable building was erected by the state. The five later state normal schools were established in the following order of time: Los Angeles (1882), Chico (1889), San Diego (1898), San Francisco (1899), Santa Barbara (1909).

The standard of admission to these schools is the possession of a certificate of graduation from an accredited high school, or of an equivalent education; the normal course, mainly professional, is completed in two years. A diploma of graduation from a California state normal school entitles the holder to a life state certificate of the grammar grade.

The Free State University of California

Preceding the establishment of a state university in California, whatever there was in the way of the higher education was provided by various denominational colleges and college schools, such as the College of California at Oakland, the Santa Clara College at Santa Clara, and the St. Ignatius College in San Francisco, the University of the Pacific (Methodist) at Santa Clara, and a number of smaller college schools and seminaries.

The College of California, an institution designed by its founders "to furnish the means of a thorough and comprehensive education under the pervading influence and spirit of the Christian religion," began with a preparatory school at Oakland (1853) under the name of the Oakland

College School, in charge of the Reverend Henry Durant and the Reverend I. H. Brayton. In 1855 the College of California was incorporated, and in 1860 was organized by the appointment of a faculty, of which the Reverend S. H. Willey was Vice-President, the Reverend I. H. Brayton, Professor of Rhetoric, Belles Lettres, and the English Language, and Reverend Henry Durant, the Professor in Greek and Literature. In 1866 the number of students was thirty, and the number of professors, five. The total number of graduates up to 1866 was eight.

In 1868, legislative action having become imperative in order to secure the congressional land grant for an agricultural college, John W. Dwinelle, then a member of the state senate, introduced a bill which secured "a college of agriculture and the mechanic arts." Meanwhile, the College of California, slow of growth, feeble in numbers, and encumbered with debt, was struggling for a precarious existence. The friends and officers of this institution and a number of far-seeing men, among whom were ex-governor F. F. Low, John W. Dwinelle, and the Reverend Samuel H. Willey, planned and carried into effect a consolidation of the College of California with the new-born State University, by which the university board of regents assumed all debts of the college, and the college transferred to the university its students and its lands in Oakland and at Berkeley. It was a good bargain, both for the college and for the university.

The University of California opened its doors (September 23, 1869) in the old college building at Oakland, with an attendance of fifty students. Dr. John Le Conte, made acting president for a few months, was succeeded (1870) by the Reverend Henry Durant, who held the office until the election of Daniel C. Gilman (1872). In 1873 the university was transferred to its permanent site at Berkeley, contiguous to Oakland. The full list of its presidents runs as follows: Henry Durant ('69–70); Daniel C. Gilman ('72); John Le Conte ('75), acting president; William T. Reid ('81); Edward S. Holden ('85); Horace Davis ('88); Martin Kellogg ('93); Benjamin Ide Wheeler ('99 to date).

In the beginning, the endowment of the university was small. From the sale of two townships (46,080 acres), reserved by the celebrated ordinance of 1787 "to be given perpetually for the purpose of a seminary of learning to be applied to the intended object by the legislature of the state," there was due from the state school fund $84,000 ready money, about enough to pay the debts of the "College of California." The 150,000 acres of land granted by Congress in aid of a "college of agriculture and the mechanic arts" constituted a fund of about $750,000, the interest of which could be applied to the university. The state soon appropriated from the sales of tide lands $800,000 invested in bonds. For the rest, excepting a number of bequests for special purposes, the university has been supported by special appropriations by the legislature, and by an annual state tax of two cents on each one hundred dollars of the state assessment roll. Thus the university is in reality an integral part of the public-school system of the state.

For the first twenty years the growth of the State University was slow, but in 1884 the faculty, following the example of the University of Michigan, adopted the "accrediting system," by which high-school graduates are admitted to the university without examination. This action was followed by a rapid increase in attendance. The formation of "union high schools," under the act of 1891, added to the number of students. In numbers, in organization, and in strength, the University of California ranks high among the great universities in the United States. It is open, without tuition fees, to men and to women on equal terms. Its curriculum, which includes various groups of elective studies, is broad enough to meet most of the demands of modern social and industrial conditions.

The college of agriculture and the mechanic arts, reaching out in various directions includes horticulture, viticulture, wheat growing, dairying, stock raising, and other highly specialized pursuits of country life. The strongly organized pedagogical department, designated as the Department of Education, exerts a powerful influence upon the high schools and the teachers. The university has a flourishing college of mechanical engineering and mining, and a college of commerce. The college of letters is strong in history and literature, and in the ancient languages. The affiliated colleges of law and of medicine, located in San Francisco, constitute an important part of the university. The university "summer school" ranks high in numbers. The "university extension" lectures reach out to large numbers of people in various parts of the state.

California is fortunate in having another great institution of learning, the Stanford University, founded and endowed by Mr. and Mrs. Leland Stanford (1890). Though not under direct state control, it fulfills many of the functions of a state university. It is open to both men and women; it has no tuition fees; it has a pedagogical department for the training of teachers; it has the elective system in studies; it has had from its beginning David Starr Jordan for its president.

CHAPTER XVI

THE PROFESSIONAL SPIRIT OF CALIFORNIA TEACHERS AS EXHIBITED IN STATE AND COUNTY TEACHERS' INSTITUTES

THE professional spirit of the teachers of California has been developed largely through the agency of state conventions, state teachers' institutes, state normal schools, county institutes, and the California Teachers' Association. Teachers' meetings for mutual improvement began to be held in the city of San Francisco, and early in 1854 the first state teachers' convention, called by state superintendent Paul K. Hubbs, met in San Francisco, December 6–8, 1854. The attendance was small, and the most notable event of the session was the delivery of an eloquent address by Colonel Edward D. Baker, lawyer, soldier, and orator, who in his youthful days had taught a district school in Illinois.

The first California State Teachers' Institute assembled in San Francisco, May 27 to June 1, 1861, under a call by the state superintendent, Andrew J. Moulder, who had secured from the legislature a small appropriation for the payment of necessary expenses. The program was well arranged, the attendance large, and the proceedings were interesting and instructive.

The second state institute, which met in Sacramento, September, 1862, was called by Superintendent Moulder near the close of his second term of office. This meeting was small in numbers and the time was given up mainly to reports of committees and to discussion. The state board of examination, consisting of Superintendent Moulder and six county superintendents, held an oral examination of candidates for state certificates, which resulted in the granting of five grammar-school certificates, valid for two years, and twelve "mixed-school" certificates, valid for the same length of time.

The third, fourth, and fifth institutes have been mentioned in previous chapters of this book. After 1865, no state appropriations were made for state institutes, and consequently, they grew weak and weaker, until they died out in 1875, when the state board of education called a convention of teachers which met at San José and organized a state teachers' association.

This new organization maintained a lingering existence for a decade. Meanwhile the county teachers' institutes grew stronger under the state school law of 1863, which provided for an annual appropriation of at least $150 a year for each institute, made attendance compulsory, and required the school trustees to continue the salaries of teachers during institute week. Finally, two or more counties began to unite in joint institutes, and at length the county institutes began to affiliate with the state association, which grew large in numbers and strong in spirit. Next, the Southern California Teachers' Association came into existence, followed by a similar organization of the northern counties in the Sacramento Valley. The annual payment of a membership fee of one dollar has enabled all three of these teachers' associations to secure special lecturers from abroad and to publish a volume of proceedings. Within the last decade these associations have been reinforced by lecturers from the University of

California and from Stanford University, among whom are included Benjamin Ide Wheeler and David Starr Jordan.

At the meeting in San Francisco (1903), fifteen hundred members were in attendance. The meeting in San José (1904), numbering twelve hundred members, was a combination of four county institutes with the state association. The work of this meeting was carried on in many sections. Jacob Riis came from New York City to lecture on "The Battle with the Slums" and "The Making of an American." W. H. Mills, of California, lectured on "Our Prison Schools," and Governor George C. Pardee, on "School Money" and the "Salaries of Teachers." It was a hard-working session of four days.

At the Berkeley meeting, December 26–29, 1905, the professional spirit of California teachers appeared at its best. The county institutes of seventeen counties and the city institutes of five cities of San Francisco, Oakland, Stockton, Berkeley, and Alameda, were fused into the annual meeting of the California Teachers' Association under the wise and able leadership of President James A. Barr, city superintendent of the schools of Stockton. The State University buildings and grounds were thrown open to teachers. The organization of this great gathering was modeled after that of the National Educational Association. Two of the general sessions were held in the largest theater in San Francisco, to accommodate the thousand teachers of that city, and two were held in the large auditorium of the university at Berkeley. The section work filled every available lecture room in Berkeley. The proceedings were published in a volume of 545 pages.

It was one of my cherished illusions, half a century ago, that there might be, in the far-distant future, a time when teaching would be regarded as a profession, and that teachers might combine and grow strong. At this Berkeley meeting my wildest dreams were realized.[1]

At the annual meeting at San José, 1908, the association amended its constitution, elected L. E. Armstrong as secretary, and took over the Sierra *Educational News* as its official organ for the publication of proceedings.

The annual meeting, held in San Francisco, December 27–30, 1909, was a combination of the California Teachers' Association with the county institutes of San Francisco,

[1]It seems fitting in this connection to quote the words of one of the foremost of California teachers, himself an embodiment of professional spirit. They were written as a leading editorial in the *Western Journal of Education* by Dr. C. C. Van Liew, President of the Chico State Normal School.

"But the greatest achievement of the year was the work of President Barr in preparing for the Berkeley meeting of the State Teachers' Association. Such an awakening of the teaching force of the state as he has occasioned is bound to be historic; the year will long be known as the great year. . . .

"The unique success of the week, among departments, was unquestionably achieved by the Farmers' Institute. It is certainly significant that agricultural education appealed to a greater variety of people than any other line of educational work. The great attraction here was the address of Dr. A. C. True, director of experimental stations of the United States Department of Agriculture, and chairman of the committee on methods of teaching agriculture of the Association of American Colleges and Experimental Stations. . . .

"Not the least interesting on this program was the address of John Swett, whose direct questions, both to farmers and to teachers, were welcomed because they showed how simply some very effective things might be accomplished. . . .

"And in this state we have a schoolmaster whose service was one of devotion to all the good purposes of the teachers. It is a great thing to have achieved the right to retire from active service with a strong, clear record, and to remain the inspiration of fellow workers. The capsheaf of the Berkeley meeting was the John Swett evening in Hearst Hall. It was not the addresses there made, but the thing that was done, the presentation of Mrs. Richardson's fine portrait of John Swett to the University of California, by the teachers of California, that was significant. Let us not forget that."

Alameda, Sonoma, Contra Costa, and Marin. The program was wisely and thoughtfully prepared, and the great gathering of the clans represented the high-water mark of professional spirit. The general sessions filled to overflowing the great Dreamland Pavilion in which the meetings were held.

The "section" meetings included in their varied programs the following topics: kindergartens, elementary schools, high schools, nature study, drawing, music, short stories, manual arts, manual training, English, the classics, history, science, and mathematics. The addresses and discussions in these numerous sections, or "round tables," showed that, during the past decade, the teachers, both men and women, have been learning the value and power of educational "team work."

At the first general session President E. Morris Cox read his annual message, a lengthy document full of wise suggestions and thoughtful recommendations. In his easy, offhand manner, Dr. Luther H. Gulick, of New York, spoke on the subject of "What Play Means in Education." I have been in attendance at meetings of teachers in California ever since the first state convention in 1854, and I am free to say that I never heard a more delightful lecture than this talk by Dr. Gulick.

Allison Ware, from the faculty of the San Francisco State Normal School, next addressed the meeting in stirring words worthy of his high reputation as an institute lecturer.

Then Dr. George E. Vincent, from the University of Chicago, spoke on "The New Duty of the School." He is a popular platform orator who speaks at the rate of three hundred words a minute, and compels reporters to lay down their pencils in despair.

The social side of this great meeting was delightful. The women teachers of San Francisco gave a reception to the state teachers at the Palace Hotel. The Women's Club gave a reception at the Fairmont Hotel. The Schoolmasters' Club held its quarterly meeting. Various other clubs and organizations met in school gatherings. As the climax of this great meeting, at the annual election of officers, Dr. A. F. Lange of the University of California was chosen as president, and a central representative council was elected to look after school legislation in the state legislature. Though retired from active service, I hold myself as a volunteer private in the ranks, keeping step with the advance guard of educational reformers.

CHAPTER XVII

MY PILGRIMAGE TO NEW ENGLAND IN QUEST OF EARLY TOWN RECORDS RELATING TO THE BEGINNINGS OF COMMON SCHOOLS

In the summer and autumn of 1898 I enjoyed the longest and pleasantest vacation of my life. Starting East by way of the Canadian Pacific Railway, I caught glimpses of mountain scenery so wild and grand that I have longed ever since to repeat the trip. In Boston I met Dr. A. E. Winship, editor of the weekly national *Journal of Education*, and also a popular lecturer at teachers' institutes, personally known to more American teachers than is any other living educator in the United States; George H. Martin, the able secretary of the Massachusetts state board of education; Professor Paul H. Hanus of Harvard; Honorable John Conness, formerly United States Senator from California, residing near Boston; and Walter H. Page, at that time editor of the *Atlantic Monthly*, now editor of the *World's Work*.

Hearing that Dr. A. D. Mayo was passing the summer months in Boston, I hunted him up and secured a room in the large boarding house where, surrounded by his library, he was busily engaged in writing a history of the American system of public schools. We became friends at once. He was at work eight hours a day, but his evenings and Sundays he devoted to me. My days were occupied in making a study of Boston and in visits to the state library. For three weeks I lingered there, a willing pupil at the feet of

John Swett in 1900

the great master, who had been personally acquainted with many prominent educators such as Mann, Barnard, Harris, and White; with clergymen such as Emerson, Channing, Edward Everett Hale, and Theodore Parker; with writers such as Holmes, Whittier, Longfellow, and Lowell; with political speakers like Webster, Choate, Seward, and Abraham Lincoln; with lecturers like Wendell Phillips and Edward Everett. Himself a popular lecturer as well as a distinguished clergyman, he gave up the pulpit, and, impelled by a sense of patriotic duty, became for seventeen years an educational missionary in the states of the South devoting himself to his work with the zeal of Horace Mann, the genial earnestness of Starr King, and the outspoken boldness of Theodore Parker.

When I met him in Boston his missionary work was nearly over, and he was busily engaged in writing an additional chapter of his history of the common-school system of the United States. The chapters of this work published in the annual reports of the United States Commissioner of Education from 1894 to 1902, run as follows:

I. Colonial Common Schools. Report for 1894.

II. Education in the Northwest. Report for 1895.

III. School Systems in the North Atlantic States, 1830 to 1865. Report for 1896.

IV. Horace Mann and the Great Revival of 1830 to 1850. Report for 1897.

V. Common Schools in New York, New Jersey, and Pennsylvania. Report for 1898.

VI. Developments in the Western States, 1830 to 1860. Report for 1899.

VII. Establishment of the American Common School System in North Carolina, South Carolina, and Georgia, 1863. Report for 1900.

VIII. Schools in the Central States of the South, 1830 to 1860. Report for 1901.

Dr. Mayo died suddenly in the city of Washington, in April, 1907, leaving his great work unfinished.

When my evening school with Dr. Mayo was over, I turned to my native state and made my headquarters for a time at the hospitable home of my cousin, John C. French, in Manchester, the great business center of New Hampshire. Mr. French took an interest in the history of his native state, and I found in his library many volumes of town histories and other historical documents. Then we went together to our native town of Pittsfield, and I made my headquarters at his summer home, on the farm where I had worked as a "hired hand" in the spring and summer of 1848.

I rambled all over the little town, through old crossroads half overgrown with trees, and along the banks of the Suncook River where I had so often gone a-fishing when a boy, and where now there runs a branch of the Boston and Maine Railroad. Then I climbed to the summit of Catamount and studied the deep grooves on its bald granite crown which showed the marks left by the great ice sheet that covered all New England during the glacial period. I stood on the very spot where, forty-six years before, I had taken a farewell view of my native state as I was about to start for California. Day after day I lingered around that mountain, recalling slumbering memories of the past. I became impressed by the relatively large number of teachers and educators, born and bred on the hill farms of New Hampshire, who began their education in the common school, continued it in rural academies, and perhaps in Dartmouth College, and then started out to seek their fortunes in the larger and richer states of the West.

New Hampshire is a small state, having an area of about seven thousand square miles, subdivided into over three hundred small towns (townships) and into several thousand small farms. Its population in round numbers at the present time is only 400,000. According to the census taken by order of Congress in 1790, the population of New Hampshire was 141,985; of Massachusetts, 378,787.

The rough lean soil of the "Granite State" is hard to till. The winter climate is harsh and cold. The early settlers, before the development of manufactures of various kinds, had a hard struggle to earn a frugal living. The small farms could not be subdivided, and if there were several boys in the family, only one could remain on the home farm and the others were forced to push out into the world to earn a living. To all boys the common school opened the gates of opportunity to make a fair start in life.

In the early colonial days, New Hampshire, in comparison with other New England states, ranked relatively higher in population and influence than it does at the present time. Therefore I have gathered up the names of men who made their mark, at home or abroad, in the early history of the state. My original notes, jotted down on the spot, have been filled out, verified, and put into the form of a monograph study on the far-reaching influence of the American common school in New England, the spot of its origin.

A Few New Hampshire Boys

Standing on the summit of Catamount and turning my eyes southward, I looked down on Deerfield, the birthplace of John D. Philbrick, the distinguished educator who was so long superintendent of the Boston public schools. I remember him with gratitude for his encouragement of my work in California, for many valuable Boston educational reports, and for two delightful days passed with him in visiting the Boston schools.

Here was born Lorenzo D. Harvey, teacher and educator, who at an early age was taken out West by his father and mother. He grew up to become state superintendent of schools in Wisconsin, a distinguished lecturer on "Industrial Training in the Public Schools," and a manager of the Stout schools of Menominee.

Benjamin F. Butler, lawyer, soldier, and politician, was born in this town. His father, John Butler, served as a captain of dragoons under General Andrew Jackson at New Orleans. His mother was a descendant of the Cilleys, a New Hampshire family of Scotch-Irish blood. Captain Butler was engaged in trade with the West Indies, where he died in 1819, when Benjamin was one year old. His widow, a woman of great force of character, sent her two boys to the common schools in Deerfield as soon as they were old enough to go. Ambitious to give Ben a good education, she removed (1828) to the city of Lowell, Massachusetts, where she increased her scanty means by taking boarders, and managed to keep her son at school until he was fitted to enter Waterville College. After his college course he studied law, teaching school a part of his time to help pay his expenses.

Contiguous to Pittsfield on the south there lies the small town of Epsom, where I could see Sanborn Hill, on which was born General John B. Sanborn, whose ancestors dwelt in Old Hampton. He began his education in the common school, supplemented it by hard work on a hill farm, continued it at Pembroke Academy, in Dartmouth College, and in a law office. Then he went West to St. Paul, Minnesota. On Sanborn Hill there was also born Walter Sanborn, nephew of John B. Sanborn, who emigrated to Minnesota, and became judge of the United States Circuit Court. In Epsom was born Enoch Eastman, my much-loved teacher when I was a boy in a Pittsfield school. He went out West to practice law, and during the Civil War became lieutenant governor of Iowa. In Epsom was born Andrew McCleary, Scotch-Irish by descent, who served as major in Stark's regiment of New Hampshire militia. Major McCleary reached Cambridge just in season to join his regiment on the morning of the battle of Bunker Hill. While marching across Cambridge neck, which was raked by the fire of the British war vessels, he was struck dead by a cannon ball which carried away his head.

Facing northward I looked down on the town of Loudon, where was born Frank French, the artist, who delights to picture New Hampshire scenery though he makes his home in the city of New York. In Loudon was born Joseph C. Morrill, who emigrated to California with me, became a teacher in San Francisco, and then, during the Civil War, a captain in Colonel Connor's regiment of volunteers.

At my feet lay Pittsfield village and town. I could see the Drake-Swett homestead, which has passed into the hands of strangers; the Abraham French homestead, likewise occupied by strangers; the homestead of Colonel

Nathaniel Batchelder, from which the whole family emigrated to Illinois; the White homestead, from which the whole family removed to California; the Elliott homestead, from which two sons also went to California; the John Jenness homestead, which sent one son to California.

I looked down on the homestead where was born Nehemiah C. Berry, a farmer boy, educated in the common school, Pittsfield Academy, and Dartmouth College. He was principal of the Pittsfield Academy for one year, after which he studied law and established a law office in Boston. From the same homestead his brother, Jonathan Berry, married my cousin Harriet Berry, and moved to Illinois. On the slope of Catamount, in Dowborough, was born John H. Prescott, educated in common school and academy, who served as captain in the Civil War, studied law, and went to Kansas, where he became a leading judge. On the slope of Jenness hill, I could distinguish the Norris homestead, where was born Moses Norris, a leading lawyer in New Hampshire, and a senator of the United States.

High up on the slope of Catamount, as near to the summit as it was possible to clear a rocky farm, was built the stately old farmhouse of Major William Berry, one of the early settlers of the town. In that house he reared a sturdy family of eleven children, among whom was my stepfather and guardian, William Berry, Jr. Another of his sons, John Berry, built a fine house in Pittsfield village and kept a country store. John Berry's e dest boy, John M. Berry, educated in the common school, Pittsfield Academy, and Dartmouth College, studied law, went to Minnesota and became a judge of the State Supreme Court. Another of his sons enlisted as a private in the Civil War and served through the war.

A Sturdy Barrington Boy

Southeast from Pittsfield, ten or twelve miles over a hill road, there lies the town of Barrington, where was born (1815) a New Hampshire boy whose grit is worth recording. Up to fifteen years of age he worked hard on a rocky hill farm on which his father was vainly trying to pay off a mortgage of one hundred and fifty dollars. He went to the district school about two months in each winter. Then John Perry, Jr., spoke up and said: "Father, I want you to let me go to Boston, where I think I can earn some money to pay off the mortgage on the farm." Reluctantly his father consented, and off this daring boy started on foot for Boston, eighty miles away, with only twenty-five cents in his pocket and with no clothes except the homespun suit he wore on his back. It was in the month of March, and the roads were heavy with melting snow and ice, but he made fifteen miles the first day, and found lodging and supper in a farmhouse.

Next day, as he trudged along, footsore and weary, a farmer overtook him and said: "My boy, where are you going?"

"I am going to Boston to earn some money to pay off the mortgage on my father's farm."

"Well, you look about tuckered out. You get right into my wagon and ride home with me, and stay all night. To-morrow I'll see what I can do for you."

Next day the old farmer took him to see the minister, who wanted a steady boy to take care of his horse and to work in his garden. John Perry secured his first job for four months at eight dollars a month. Then the good old minister told him he had better go to school for four months, and to school he went, where "he finished up" all the school education he ever got. Finally he reached the Mecca of his pilgrimage two years after he started from home. On the streets of Boston, as he wandered around looking for something to do, he came across a broker who said that he wanted a messenger boy. He filled the bill so well that he was soon taken into partnership in the brokerage business. In less than five years he sent one hundred and fifty dollars to his father to pay off the mortgage on the old homestead. In 1836 he considered himself worth $25,000; but the great financial panic of 1837 swept away his stocks, bonds, and possessions. Nothing daunted, he resumed business, with no capital except a good reputation, and was again successful.

I first saw this persistent New Hampshire boy in the city of San Francisco (1855), when he was a member of the board of assistant aldermen, and I was a young public-school teacher. In 1906, just half a century later, he was in active business as a broker, and could be seen bustling about the streets and banks with the elastic step of a young man, notwithstanding his advanced age. He was for many years the most picturesque business man in San Francisco, distinguished for honor, honesty, integrity, and by a character above reproach. I met him one evening at a meeting of the members of the Mercantile Library and said to him: "John Perry, Jr., tell me where you discovered the fountain of perpetual youth?" His reply was, "On a rocky little farm in the town of Barrington." "Why, that town," said I, "is only ten miles distant from the rocky little farm in Pittsfield on which I was born. Let us shake hands again;" and then he told me in substance the story which I have here given. A group of members gathered around us as we talked, and a white-haired boy, seventy-five years old, broke out with, "Take me into your circle; I, too, was born on a rocky little farm in the Old Granite State. New Hampshire is a good state to emigrate from."

Thirty days after the earthquake and fire in 1906, John Perry, Jr., was attending to his regular business as a broker, but his step was less elastic. A year later he died, in June, 1907, at ninety-two years of age.

The Hampton Seacoast Region

Far away to the southeast, where on a clear day, with a good glass, the glimmer of the Atlantic can be seen from the summit of Catamount, lies the seaside town of old Hampton, in which, or near which, lived my paternal and maternal ancestors. In Hampton Falls was born Franklin B. Sanborn, author, journalist, and one of the Concord School of Philosophers. In Hampton was born Aaron Gove, a lineal descendant, in the seventh generation, of Edward Gove, one of the early settlers. At three years of age he entered the district school, which, like its prototype in 1649, kept its doors open "to all children of the towne both mayle and femaile." In that school he remained four years, until he was transferred to Hampton Academy. Like thousands of other New England boys, he went "out West," where he became the able and clear-headed superintendent of public schools in the city of Denver, Colorado, for a period of twenty-five years. In North Hampton was born Henry Deerborn, physician, soldier, and congressman, who was captain in Colonel John Stark's regiment at Bunker Hill, and an officer in Arnold's expedition through the Maine wilderness against Quebec.

In this section of New Hampshire lies Bedford, the birthplace of Colonel Francis W. Parker, the evangelist of advanced ideas about elementary teaching, who preached the educational gospel of training young children how to observe and how to think. Born and bred on a farm, educated in common school and academy, he became a teacher, a soldier in the Civil War, an educator, a lecturer, a school superintendent, and principal of the Chicago Normal School. This town claims as a native son Zachariah Chandler, United States senator from Michigan during the Civil War, notable as one of the uncompromising leaders of the Republican party.

In this same region, in the town of Epping, there was born and bred on a rocky farm a boy named David P. Page, whose name is known to all American teachers as the author of Page's "Theory and Practice of Teaching." He was the first principal of the first state normal school in the state of New York. He died early in life, a martyr to overwork in building up the Albany Normal School. In Epping was born another farmer boy named Benjamin F. Prescott, whose father sent him to the common school, then to Pembroke Academy, and next to Dartmouth College. He became a journalist, a lawyer, a farmer, and governor of his native state. In Lee was born Ira G. Hoitt, another farmer boy, who fitted for college at Phillips-Exeter Academy, worked his way through Dartmouth College, and then went West to become a public-school teacher in San Francisco, and state superintendent of schools in California.

The historic town of Exeter, famous for the Phillips-Exeter Academy, claims, by birthright, the sculptor, Daniel Chester French. Exeter claims Dudley Leavitt, schoolmaster, editor, and almanac maker, known as "Old Master Leavitt," whose almanacs were long found hanging by a string in most of the farmhouses in New England. Lewis Cass was born in Exeter and educated in Phillips-Exeter Academy. His father, an army officer, was ordered out West when his son was seventeen years old, and Lewis became an adopted son of Michigan, where he studied law, made his way in the world, became secretary of war under Andrew Jackson, and held other official positions. He was the defeated Democratic candidate for President of the United States in 1848.

In Nottingham, a few miles from Exeter, was born Bradbury L. Cilley, the eldest of the nine children of Joseph L. Cilley. He fitted for college in Phillips-Exeter Academy and was graduated from Harvard. Soon after his graduation he was elected professor of Greek and Latin in Phillips-Exeter Academy, in which position he remained for forty years, honored and beloved by his pupils. It was a relative of this great teacher, Mrs. Martha (Cilley) Berry, a resident of Pittsfield, that lent me a complete file of the New York *Knickerbocker Magazine*, for which favor I am grateful to this day.

Of the Cilley family, the first Joseph Cilley, a soldier and lawyer, was one of the early settlers in Nottingham (1728), whose education was limited to farm life, the common school, and home study of law. He served during the Revolutionary War as colonel of a New Hampshire regiment, and was engaged in the battles of Monmouth, Saratoga, and the storming of Stony Point under Wayne.

In the town of South Newmarket was born John W. Lane, who attended the common school until he was apprenticed to learn the trade of house carpenter. His apprenticeship over, he earned money to pay for his attendance at several academies. Slowly but surely he fitted himself for college, and finally was graduated from Amherst. He taught school, studied theology at Andover, and became a Congregational minister. At eighty-five years of age he is the efficient pastor of a small church at North Hadley, Massachusetts. He studied elocution under Professor William Russell, and for many years trained students in elocution at Amherst College.

In Westmoreland was born Thomas Sherwin, teacher and schoolbook author, who was head master of the Boston high school for boys for thirty-one years (1838–69).

In Durham was born James F. Joy, whose father was agent of the Pittsfield cotton factory when I was a boy. James was sent to the common school, to Pittsfield Academy, and to Dartmouth College. He taught school, studied law, went West, and in Michigan became a millionaire and the legal adviser of the Michigan Central Railway.

In 1774 Durham was the home of John Sullivan, son of "Schoolmaster Sullivan," and Alexander Scammel was a law student in Sullivan's office. Both of these young patriots were destined to become notable leaders in the war for independence.

On the 13th day of December, 1774, Paul Revere, riding posthaste from Boston, brought letters to the Committee of Safety at Portsmouth stating that General Gage was on the point of sending, by sea, a detachment of British troops to reinforce the small garrison at Fort William and Mary that commanded Portsmouth Harbor. Revere also brought a strong appeal for powder. The militia of Portsmouth mustered under arms, and on December 14th proceeded to the fort, only two miles distant, overpowered and disarmed the feeble garrison without bloodshed, broke open the magazine, carried off one hundred barrels of powder and placed them in the care of the Committee of Safety at Portsmouth. On December 15th, as soon as the news reached Durham, Captain John Sullivan and Alexander Scammell immediately summoned an armed force of about twenty men and at night dropped down Oyster River to Portsmouth, took a few more men on board their "Gondola," proceeded to the fort, and took off fifteen four-pounders, one nine-pounder, all the small arms, and a quantity of cannon balls, all of which they placed in the hands of the Committee of Safety.[1]

Four months after these stirring events, the "minute men" of Massachusetts met a detachment of British troops at Concord and Lexington and drove them back to Boston. When the news of these battles reached John Stark at work in his sawmill at Londonderry, he instantly mounted his horse, spread the tidings to his townsmen, telling them to take every ounce of their ammunition with them and to follow him to the camp at Cambridge. It is said that every able-bodied man, except two, responded to his call.

On the morning of the eventful day of the battle of Bunker Hill, Colonel John Stark's regiment, the largest and best equipped in camp, was ordered to reinforce the militia occupying the redoubt thrown up on Breeds Hill. Stark's sharp military eye took in the situation at a glance. He marched his men to a gap in the American line between the redoubt and Mystic River only partly filled by a small Connecticut regiment under Colonel Knowlton. There,

[1] According to the official reports the captured powder was distributed as follows: Exeter, twenty-nine barrels; Kingston, twelve barrels; Epping and Nottingham, eight barrels each; Brentwood, six barrels; and Londonderry, the home of Colonel John Stark, one barrel. See *Manchester Historic Association Collection*, Vol. 1, Part 1, 1896.

behind a stone wall and a rail fence which his men filled with new-mown hay, he formed his line of battle.

When the Welsh Fusileers, one of Gage's picked regiments, made a flank attack on the American line, they were almost annihilated by the deadly fire of Stark's men, most of whom were expert marksmen trained to the use of both rifle and musket. In this battle none of the Americans were equipped with bayonets, and when the British made the final charge which carried the redoubt, the Americans, having exhausted their ammunition, fought only with clubbed muskets. Thanks to the foresight of Stark, his men had a reserve of powder and bullets, and they formed the rear guard of the retreating militia, protecting them from the bayonets of the pursuing enemy.

The ancient seaport town of Portsmouth claims as her native sons James T. Fields, publisher and author; Thomas Bailey Aldrich, poet and author; John Wentworth, the last royal governor of New Hampshire; John Langdon, congressman, soldier, governor, and United States senator; Woodbury Langdon, lawyer, jurist, and judge of the Supreme Court of New Hampshire; and Dr. John Lord, clergyman, author, and lecturer on history.

The Mount Monadnock Region

Into the southwestern corner of New Hampshire there is crowded the small town of Hinsdale, the birthplace of Charles A. Dana, the great journalist of the New York *Sun*, and of Elisha Benjamin Andrews, the distinguished educator and university president, formerly of Brown and afterwards of Nebraska University. There are many interesting towns grouped around Mount Monadnock, the most striking landmark of this region.

In the rural town of Amherst the traveler can find the worn-out farm on which was born Horace Greeley, the founder of the New York *Tribune.* In the district school of his native town, this boy of Scotch-Irish blood picked up all the school education that he ever got; but, like Benjamin Franklin, he finished off his education in a printing office into which he was driven by his father's poverty.

Isaac Hill, though born in Massachusetts, was an adopted New Hampshire boy. At fourteen years of age he entered the office of the *Farmers' Cabinet,* a weekly paper at Amherst, N. H., as an apprentice to learn the art of type-setting. He had been born to poverty, but like Horace Greeley, had picked up a limited knowledge of reading, writing, and arithmetic by attending the common schools. While serving his seven years of apprenticeship, he continued his education by reading all the books that he could get hold of. At twenty-one years of age he left Amherst with a capital of one dollar in his pocket, and assumed charge of the *American Patriot,* a weekly paper, at Concord, the state capital. He soon became the owner of this sheet, and changed its name to the New Hampshire *Patriot,* the paper that I read with lively interest when a boy. It is needless to state that he made his journal intensely democratic and aggressive in tone.

Hill made so brilliant a campaign in favor of President Jackson that he was appointed to the second comptrollership of the treasury, which carried with it a salary of three thousand dollars and the gift of ten clerkships. The senate refused to confirm Hill's appointment. Then Levi Woodbury, senator from New Hampshire, resigned for the purpose of making a vacancy, which the New Hampshire legislature filled by the election of Isaac Hill to the vacant seat. Levi

Woodbury was held in reserve for appointment in Jackson's Cabinet. Isaac Hill was not only an incisive editorial writer and a clear-headed politician, but he was also a successful business man. He kept a bookstore, published books, and managed a good farm.

It was in this part of the valley of the Merrimac that in 1719 about a hundred families of Scotch-Irish Presbyterians from Londonderry, Ireland, made a settlement which they named in memory of their home over sea. By trade they were mostly spinners and weavers of linen, and in their new homes they set up their looms and spinning wheels and began raising flax, thus introducing into New Hampshire a new form o domestic industry. In this town was born John Stark, Scotch-Irish by descent, who gained his education in a district school and grew up to become the ablest military commander in his native state during the Revolutionary War. Here was born Samuel Bell, of Scotch-Irish descent, lawyer, governor, legislator, and United States senator from New Hampshire. His brother, John Bell, was elected governor in 1830. In Londonderry was born a farmer boy of Scotch-Irish stock, Samuel Harvey Taylor, a famous teacher, who was principal of Phillips-Exeter Academy from 1837 to 1871. He died in his classroom.

Peterborough, in this same section, is the birthplace of Jeremiah Smith, Scotch-Irish by descent, one of New Hampshire's most distinguished lawyers and jurists. Here too was born General James Miller, who won honor in the battle of Lundy's Lane in the year of 1812. This is the town that by vote in town meeting, in 1833, laid the foundation of a free public library supported by town tax, the first in New Hampshire, and one of the first of its kind in the United States.

In the town of Winchester, bordering on Massachusetts, was born Leonard Wood, army surgeon, colonel of the "Rough Riders," and major-general of the United States Army. In Francestown was born Levi Woodbury, lawyer, jurist, congressman, and United States senator.

The Mount Kearsarge Region

When I was a boy, the mountain peak that most attracted my longing eyes was Mount Kearsarge, rising blue in the western horizon on the verge of the fertile valley of the Merrimac River. On the foot-slopes of this lone granite peak lies the rural town of Sutton, the birthplace of John Eaton, of whose record New Hampshire has good reason to be proud.

He was the eldest of a family of nine children. At four years of age he entered the little district school. He was bred, as a boy, to hard work on his father's farm in spring and summer, and to earnest study at school in winter. But while he worked on the farm he also read and studied by himself. Then he went to Thetford Academy and began the study of Latin. At sixteen years of age he taught his first school in New Hampshire. Next he worked his way through Dartmouth College, graduating in 1854 with only three cents left in his pocket. He secured the principalship of a grammar school in Cleveland, Ohio, where he taught for two years.

His success secured for him an appointment as superintendent of public schools in the city of Toledo, Ohio. Next he entered Andover Theological Seminary and was ordained for the ministry, but, instead of preaching, he enlisted in the Union Army and was commissioned chaplain in the Twenty-seventh Ohio Volunteer Infantry. He was made colonel of the Ninth Regiment of United States Colored Infantry, and on recommendation of General Grant, was commissioned brevet brigadier general of volunteers.

During the war, as fast as the Union lines were extended southward, General Eaton established schools for colored freedmen. In 1867 he was elected superintendent of public instruction for the state of Tennessee. The crowning work of his life was done after his appointment by President Grant as United States Commissioner of Education in 1871.

John Pillsbury, one of the early settlers on a farm in this hill town of Sutton, was the father of four typical New Hampshire boys, born and bred on a farm and educated in the common schools. One of these boys, John Seargent Pillsbury, born in 1827, after leaving school at sixteen years of age, began his business career as a clerk in his brother's store, then emigrated to Minnesota, settled at Minneapolis, entered into the hardware business, acquired a fortune, and was elected governor for three successive terms. His brother, George Alfred Pillsbury, at an early age became clerk to a Boston merchant, next a purchasing agent of the Boston and Concord Railroad, bank president, member of the legislature, and, finally, followed his brother to Minneapolis and entered into the milling business of C. A. Pillsbury and Company, composed of his brother, Governor John S. Pillsbury, with his brother's sons, C. A. Pillsbury and Fred C. Pillsbury. The flour mills of this company became the most extensive in the United States, turning out at one time seven thousand barrels of flour a day.

The youngest brother of this family, Benjamin F. Pillsbury, born in 1831, remained in his native town for forty-seven years and then emigrated to Minnesota, engaged in the lumber business, purchased timber lands, and became a millionaire.

The first-born son, Simon Wadleigh Pillsbury (1812), was the only one of this family that received anything more than a common-school education. Simon was sent to Dartmouth College, from which he graduated with high honor as a mathematician, but overstudy broke down his health, and he died at the beginning of his career.

Near Mount Kearsarge, in the valley of the Merrimac River, lies the homestead of Captain Ebenezer Webster, in the town of Salisbury, where was born the greatest of the sons of New Hampshire, teacher, lawyer, orator, and statesman, Daniel Webster. Here too was born Ezekiel Webster, elder brother of Daniel. He was educated in the common school, Boscawen Academy, and Dartmouth College, and was a successful lawyer.

The towns of this central part of the valley of the Merrimac sent forth a remarkable set of men that won their way into historical records. In Hillsborough was born Franklin Pierce, a farmer boy who became a lawyer, governor of his native state, senator, and president of the United States. In Boscawen were born General John A. Dix, adopted by New York and made governor and United States senator; William Pitt Fessenden, adopted by the state of Maine and sent to the senate of the United States; Charles Carleton Coffin, farmer boy, war correspondent during the Civil War, historian, and journalist; and Moody Currier, journalist and governor of his native state.

In Warner was born General Walter Harriman, teacher, veteran of the Civil War, and governor of New Hampshire. Concord claims William E. Chandler, lawyer, and United States senator; Joseph C. Abbott, soldier, lawyer, journalist, and senator; and Frank W. Rollins, lawyer, banker, and governor.

The town of Acworth claims as a native son Hiram Orcutt, a typical farmer boy, with slender means but with indomitable energy, who worked his way through common school, academy, and college, and then during forty years held various educational positions as a professional teacher.

In Pembroke was born Thomas W. Knox, who was newspaper correspondent and author of numerous books of travel for boys; in Dunbarton, Carroll D. Wright, soldier, labor commissioner, university lecturer, statistician, and president of Clark College.

Croydon, in the valley of the Connecticut, is the native town of the Reverend Samuel Read Hall, the pioneer teacher of the first private normal school in New England, and the author of "Lectures on School Keeping," the first handbook for teachers published in the United States in the English language. His biography may be found in Barnard's "American Teachers and Educators."

Newport is the birthplace of Austin Corbin, railroad president and millionaire, who, beginning with the small hill farm on which he passed his boyhood, enlarged it by degrees into the "Corbin Game Preserve," which now includes several thousand acres of woodland and pasture, eleven miles in length by four miles in its greatest width. It is stocked with herds of buffalo, elk, deer, and other wild animals.

In Cornish was born Salmon P. Chase, who emigrated to Ohio, where his first public position was that of school examiner in Cincinnati. He became a political leader, secretary of the treasury, and chief justice of the Supreme Court of the United States. Center Harbor is the birthplace of James H. Smart, educator, author, and college president, who was three times elected state superintendent of public instruction in Indiana.

Rochester, bordering on Maine, claims as a native son John P. Hale, who began his education in the common school, continued it in Phillips-Exeter Academy and Bowdoin College, studied law, was elected to the state legislature, and then to the senate of the United States, where for two years he was the first open and avowed opponent of the extension of slavery in the territories.

In Farmington, contiguous to Rochester, was born to poverty Henry Wilson, of Scotch-Irish descent. At ten years of age he was "bound out" to a farmer, for whom he worked until he was twenty-one years of age. He was allowed to attend the common school only one month each year, but meanwhile he borrowed and read many books. When his long term of service expired, he went to Natick, Massachusetts, to learn the shoemaker's trade. As soon as he had earned money enough to pay his way, he entered Stratford Academy, and began teaching in the winter terms of the common school. Next, he was elected to the state legislature of Massachusetts (1850) and five years later was elected United States senator to succeed Edward Everett. In 1872 he was elected vice-president of the United States.

My Native Town

On my way down from the summit of Catamount I lingered in the little graveyard where a plain headstone marks the grave of my great-grandfather on the maternal side, — Elder David Knowlton. Far below me lay the fields where I had once raked hay, and the pasture from which when a "barefoot boy" I drove home the cows. Next I rambled through Pittsfield village and made a visit to the one-room brick schoolhouse in which I sat as a school-boy. The building was in good repair, but its doors were closed for the summer vacation. When I looked for the old academy, I found in its place a well-planned high-school building, and, a few blocks distant, a modern brick grammar-school building in which were centralized all the grammar-grade pupils in the town. A few of the old district school-houses in parts of the town remote from the village were still in use for primary-grade pupils.

On the green fronting the old academy grounds there stood a beautiful monument on a granite pedestal with this inscription: "To all her sons who enlisted to defend and perpetuate the Union, Pittsfield dedicates this monument." Pittsfield has good reasons to be proud of its war record. In 1861 the population of the town did not exceed two thousand, and the assessment roll of taxable property amounted in round numbers to $636,000 Yet this little rural town raised and expended for war purposes, from 1861 to 1865, the sum of $152,000 — about one-fourth of the total valuation of the town. Of the 147 men from this town who enlisted in the Union Army, 59 were killed in battle, or died in Andersonville prison, or were discharged from further service on account of disability from wounds. Most of the remaining ninety-eight men returned home with broken health, and many of them died a lingering death in hospitals.[1]

[1] Mr. Henry L. Robinson, who served during the war and lived to write a history of "Pittsfield, New Hampshire, in the Great Rebellion," claims for his native town the following distinctions:

1. Pittsfield was the first town in the state, and perhaps in the entire

After leaving the monument, I walked down to the house in which my grandfather, Abraham French, lived and died. I found living there Captain Asa Bartlett, a veteran son of Pittsfield, who had served during the Civil War and had lived to write the history of the 12th New Hampshire Volunteers, a well-written book of nearly a thousand pages. He was slowly wasting away from illness contracted in army service. He died not many months after I saw him. His brother, Dr. Bradbury H. Bartlett, enlisted in Company E, 1st New Hampshire Heavy Artillery, and was assigned to hospital service. Then I called on my cousin, Charles French, who enlisted in Company G, 15th New Hampshire Volunteers, and served with a creditable record.

A Pleasant Interview

Two delightful days I passed on Jenness Hill at the home of my cousin Samuel Jenness, whose mother was Betsey (Swett) Jenness. The two brothers, Samuel Jenness, Senior, and John Jenness, Senior, were among the early settlers of Pittsfield from the town of Hampton.

North, to vote aid to soldiers' families, and that too without hope of being reimbursed from any source.

2. That the town raised more money according to its valuation to carry on the war than any other town.

3. That no other town sent a larger proportion of its inhabitants, — nearly twice its quota.

Mr. Robinson's war history of Pittsfield, a volume of 217 pages, contains a short sketch of the record of every enlisted man from that town, and is illustrated with pictures of forty-eight veterans. It is a volume of pathetic interest. The record of men shot dead on the field of battle, not including those mortally wounded who died in hospitals, shows as follows:

Gettysburg, 3; Chancellorsville, 3; Fort Wayne, 2; Port Hudson, 1; other battles, 2. Known to have died in Andersonville prison, 4.

They bought adjoining farms, built substantial farmhouses and barns, and soon had two of the best homesteads in the town. Both farms are owned and tilled by their descendants and are still productive. I called on the widow of John Jenness, then ninety-two years of age, and found her busy about light housework, apparently as erect and active as her daughter that was working with her. Her mind seemed unimpaired and her memory retentive. I asked her if she knew my father, and her reply was: "Did I know your father? Well, I should think I did. Why, he boarded with me in this very house one whole winter, when he was teaching our school."

"What kind of a teacher was he?"

"He was the best teacher we ever had. Everybody liked him. He was very popular and one of the nicest young men I ever knew."

"Did you know my mother?"

"Know her! Why, she helped me make up my wedding outfit."

From this charming old lady I learned many interesting incidents about my father and mother that I had never heard of before. I had several interviews with her afterwards, and we became well acquainted.

"Give me your arm," she said during one call. "I want to show you something." And then she took me into her parlor, that sacred sanctum of the New England housewife, and pointed out her wedding furniture, her samplers of needlework, family photographs, etc. Then as we were walking back, she laughed and said: "Now, here's my daughter — she never married. She never looked at a man. She wouldn't have married the angel Gabriel if he had come down and made love to her."

Dear old lady! She passed away two years after I saw her, as peacefully as a child going to sleep.

The White Mountains

After a six days' visit at Pittsfield, in company with my cousin John C. French, I passed a delightful week in the White Mountain region, making various excursions from Deer Park Hotel in the Pemigwasset Valley.

We ascended Mount Washington; saw the "Old Man of the Mountain" in the Franconia Notch; visited the Flume; and studied the effects of glacial denudation as far as limited time allowed. The Franconia Notch is a miniature Yosemite Valley; it bears unmistakable evidence of the enormous power of the great ice sheet which sculptured and eroded and ground down the mountains during the glacial period. On the carriage road that winds along the Franconia Notch we passed for two miles through a primeval forest of hardwood trees — maple, beech, and birch — untouched by the woodcutter's ax, save in the narrow clearing made for a carriage road. The effect of the summer sunlight as it trickled through the thick masses of green leaves upon the ground below, the play of sunshine and shadow, the grace of the slender tree trunks, impressed me as the most beautiful bit of woodland scenery my eye had ever beheld. I was glad to learn, two years afterwards, that the owner of the tract had set it apart as a woodland public reserve, and had placed it in trust in the hands of the state Society for the Preservation of Forests.

All too soon my stay in New Hampshire came to an end. I bade good-by to my cousin, Mr. French, and we parted, never to meet again. A year later he was thrown from his carriage by a runaway team, and received injuries from which he died, after lingering for some months. I remained in Boston for two weeks, passing my time in libraries and in companionship with Dr. Mayo, and then visited the home of my cousin, the Reverend John W. Lane, at North Hadley, in the valley of the Connecticut, from which I took short trips to Deerfield, Hadley, Holyoke, and other spots of historic interest.

A ten days' stay in New York city rounded out my vacation. While there I made arrangements for the publication of my book, "American Public Schools," and then turned my face homeward by way of the Great Northern Railway. I reached home in time to vote at the state election and to deliver an address, at the annual meeting of the California Teachers' Association, on the "Evolution of the American Common Schools."

CHAPTER XVIII

OUR HOME LIFE AT HILL GIRT FARM; MY CLASS IN HISTORY AND LITERATURE; AND INCIDENTAL EDUCATIONAL WORK

On many accounts I regretted to give up educational work and to leave the city which had been my home for forty years. But, on the other hand, I was glad to escape from the hard routine of official duties; glad to lead an active life out of doors; glad to have some leisure for reading, thinking, and writing; rejoiced to be in some measure my own master.

Our country home lies nestled among the hills of Contra Costa County, in the Alhambra Valley, thirty-five miles, by way of the Southern Pacific Railway, from San Francisco to Martinez, and two miles from Muir station on the Santa Fé Railway. There are also easy facilities for shipping fruit products to San Francisco on the steamboats that ply in the waters of the bay of San Francisco and up and down the Sacramento and San Joaquin rivers. We are four miles from Martinez, the county seat, on the water front of San Francisco Bay. Martinez is an incorporated town which has three thousand inhabitants, two banks, one daily and two weekly newspapers, a public library, a high school, and a large grammar-school building recently erected at a cost of $35,000. This town is lighted by electricity conducted by an electric cable from the power house a hundred miles distant on the Feather River, near the spot on which I was engaged in mining half a century ago.

Mrs. John Swett

For itself the Alhambra Valley is small in area, being only six miles in length and from one to two miles in variable width. Extending southward from an arm of San Francisco Bay known as the straits of Carquinez, it is hemmed in by nearly parallel ridges of picturesque hills that are covered with a luxuriant growth of oaks.

The average annual rainfall, of from twenty-five to thirty-five inches, is ample to secure crops without irrigation. The heat of summer is tempered by the cool and moist sea breezes that make the climate ideal.

It was in 1881, when visiting my friend John Muir, that I climbed one of the Alhambra hills and looked down on the level fertile valley watered by a winding creek fringed with sycamores and live oaks. The scenery seemed a bit of New Hampshire hill country transported to California. To the eastward Monte Diablo, four thousand feet high and ten miles distant, in air line, reminded me of Mount Kearsarge, which rose blue in the horizon in plain view from my father's farm in the old Granite State. Near at hand, the Briones hills, forming the southern wall of the valley, seemed a reproduction of Catamount, at the base of which lay the hill farm on which I was born. Captivated by this charming prospect, I immediately began negotiations for the purchase of a section of the widest part of the valley, and after some delay succeeded in buying it for $7000 cash payment. This tract included an area of 185 acres suitably divided into "tillage, pasturage, and woodland," after the manner of a New England farm. A mountain stream ran through the middle of the forty acres of rich bottom land. There were sixty acres of sloping hillsides suitable for vineyards, and eighty acres of woodland and pasturage. The place had long been rented as a stock and hay farm, and there were no improvements on it except a few fences, an old barn, and a house built of sundried brick, with walls three feet thick. There were no fruit trees, save one solitary fig tree.

"Hill Girt," as my wife named the farm, was bought neither for speculation nor for money-making, but as a kind of old-age home to which we could retire after school work was ended. Moreover, I had inherited a love of country life from six generations of Puritan farmers. Furthermore, my wife was fond of quiet life in the country.

Our farm was subject to a lease for one year, and we did not take formal possession of it until October, 1882, when we began improvements by hiring a foreman and planting out five acres of table grapes and a few acres of fruit trees. The following year the vineyard was enlarged by planting twenty acres with table grapes. Though my own direct supervision was limited to weekly visits on Saturdays and to school vacations, I managed to keep general run of affairs. I started out with a firm resolution to limit expenses to my income, and not to run in debt under any condition. Owing to my wife's prudent household management, at least one-half of my annual salary of three thousand dollars could be applied to farm expenses. Thus, year by year, Hill Girt was gradually improved, and we looked forward hopefully to the time when our income would equal expenses.

During these four years there was no income whatever from vines or fruit trees, as they had not yet come into bearing. In 1887 a part of the vineyard yielded a fair crop, amounting to $1335, but the expenses exceeded the income.

It was in July, 1889, that I retired from school and assumed personal charge of the farm. I found the condition of affairs such that I needed the help of my eldest son, who was then at the end of his sophomore year in the State University of California. Frank Tracy Swett began his education in the grammar schools of San Francisco, was graduated with credit from Lowell High School, where he proved himself a serious-minded student with steady habits and strong character. At the university he pursued an elective course, taking chemistry as a major, along with trigonometry, literature, botany, and viticulture, maintaining a good rank in his class. It was my hope that in a year he would be able to return and complete his course. I made him foreman of the farm with a salary of six hundred dollars a year and his board. We both worked hard to put the vineyard into better condition, so that it should pay running expenses. In the autumn of 1890, when I was elected superintendent of common schools in San Francisco, it became necessary for Frank to remain in charge of the farm and give up the remainder of his course in the State University.

I returned to my city house, which, meanwhile, had been occupied by my daughter and her husband, John W. Parkhurst. My wife, two sons, and my aged mother remained at Hill Girt, where I made them weekly visits on Saturday and Sunday. At times my wife's mother made her home with the family.

During the succeeding four years the products of the farm increased year by year, so that I was able to build an addition to the dwelling house, to enlarge the vineyard, and to make various other improvements.

At the expiration of my four years' term of office, I returned to Hill Girt with a fixed determination to remain there for life. We established the business firm of "John

My Mother in her Old Age

Swett and Son." My son was paid a fair salary for keeping the books and conducting the business correspondence, leaving me free to select the work best suited to my tastes. On a fruit farm of one hundred acres under cultivation there is always work all the year round, of a kind requiring constant watchfulness and care.

The even tenor of our family life was soon broken by the death of my mother, who fell from her chair stricken with partial paralysis. She lingered for three weeks, and then passed peacefully away on the 5th day of March, 1896, in the ninety-second year of her age. For twenty-five years she had been a loved and honored member of our family circle, watched over with tender care. We buried her by the side of her granddaughter, Mrs. Emily (Swett) Parkhurst, in the cemetery near Oakland. Four years previous to my mother's death our family circle had been broken by the death of my wife's mother, Mrs. Emily (Stone) Tracy, who had made her home with us for twenty years. She died at the age of seventy-seven years, in a health retreat in Napa Valley, whither she had gone for medical treatment. We laid her body to rest in Laurel Hill Cemetery, in the shadow of the granite shaft erected to the memory of her husband, Judge Frederic P. Tracy.

In 1897 Frank Tracy Swett, my eldest son, was married to Myrta Wallace More, stepdaughter of the Reverend August Drahms, and a graduate of the state normal school at San José. She taught the district school adjacent to Hill Girt, and entered our family as a boarder. Frank fell in love with her and he secured one of the best of wives, though the school lost a good teacher. As a wedding present to Frank we deeded him a one-fourth undivided interest in Hill Girt farm.

The year 1898 marked the beginning of a period of disaster on Hill Girt farm, for we discovered in the vineyard unmistakable evidence of the appearance of that most destructive of all vine pests, the *Phylloxera*, a graperoot aphis, barely discernible without the aid of a microscope, but destructive in its ravages on all varieties of European vinifera. Introduced into France on some American native grapevines, in the course of forty years it destroyed at least three-fourths of the French vineyards, which were renewed by planting out certain American wild vines, found to be resistant to the vine aphis, and by grafting this stock with European varieties. The Phylloxera has killed out thousands of acres of vineyard in California during the last thirty years, and it is still slowly but surely extending its ravages.

We at once secured from the State University a small stock of resistant cuttings from which to propagate vines for replanting our vineyard as fast as the old vines died out. We fortunately selected the *Rupestris St. George*, the variety that has been most extensively used in France, and which has proved best adapted to our own conditions.

For five years we were busily engaged in replanting, and at the end of that time the last of our old vines had been dug up and their places filled with European varieties grafted upon resistant roots. Our resistant vines began to come into bearing four years after planting, and the cost of planting and cultivating during that time we estimate at $125 an acre. Our loss in the gradual failure of crops, added to the cost of replanting, we estimate at $25,000. However, with our orchard products of Bartlett pears, prunes, and cherries, together with large sales of grafted and rooted resistant vines from our thirty-acre nursery at Ripon, in the San Joaquin Valley, we have been able to pull through without running into debt. We have succeeded by hard work, economical management, and a constant study of new conditions.

My son Frank is the business manager. Besides, he owns and cultivates a new twenty-acre vineyard contiguous to Hill Girt, living now in his own home with his wife and two children, Margaret and Elizabeth. He is employed at times by the State University to lecture at Farmers' Institutes on grape-growing and on resistant stock, on which subjects he is regarded as a practical expert.

Our granddaughter, Ruth Emelie Parkhurst, is a member of our household, attending the high school at Martinez, riding on horseback, or driving to and fro, eight miles a day. Her father, an employee in the Bank of California, comes up every Saturday night and stays over Sunday.

Our daughter Helen often visits us, bringing sunshine into our home. Her education was begun in the public schools in San Francisco, and continued in the state normal school at San José, from which she was graduated in 1895. She taught in a small rural school in Mendocino County for one term, and then entered Stanford University, from which she was graduated (1899) with high standing in biology, botany, and social science. Then she was engaged for three years in teaching biology in the Alameda high school and in directing nature study in the elementary schools. During this time she was betrothed to Ernest Schwartz, a graduate of Stanford, a teacher and law student. They were to be married in a few months, when suddenly Mr. Schwartz had an attack of appendicitis and died during a surgical operation. Helen gave up teaching to enter on a life of philanthropic work by engaging as an assistant in the office and field work of the Associated Charities of the city of Oakland.

After the earthquake and fire in San Francisco in 1906, she was transferred to that city for relief work, and was finally placed in a responsible position in directing the distribution of the large sum contributed by the New York City Chamber of Commerce for aiding needy people to make a new start in earning their own living, in which position she won a high reputation for executive ability.

My Class in History and Literature

During three long years, for two hours each day, I was engaged in teaching a private school limited to one pupil, and held in my own house at Hill Girt. In March, 1899, my youngest son, John French Swett, then near the end of his sophomore year in Stanford University, was taken down with the measles, which prevailed as an epidemic at that institution. After apparently recovering, he came home, stayed ten days, and then returned to his class. Three days later he was attacked with *retinitis* in a severe form. He came back with his eyes heavily bandaged, and entered a darkened room in which he was confined for seven weary months, never once going out of it during the daylight. The inflammation of the retina made sunlight unbearable, though his clearness of vision was not perceptibly affected. At the end of a year he was able, by wearing blue glasses, to go out of doors for exercise early in the morning or towards evening, but not in the middle of the day. The oculist who treated him said that recovery would be very slow. It had now become evident that he must give up all hope of ever being able to complete his course at the university, or to pursue the study of law, on which he had set his heart. His disappointment was great, but he bore up under it with the heroism of a martyr. As a boy in the common schools, and in the Lowell High School in San Francisco, he had ranked high in his classes. In Stanford University he took an elective course looking to the legal profession, and Professor E. A. Ross said of him that he was one of the three most promising students in his class of one hundred members. His health was good and his habits were exceptionally regular. When a child he learned to read under the old-style instruction of his two grandmothers, before he was five years old, and long before he went to school at six years of age he was a regular reader of the *St. Nicholas* magazine. He inherited a taste for books as strong as my own.

As the prospect of his recovering the use of his eyes for reading seemed far in the future, I determined to lend him my own eyes for the purpose of keeping him alive intellectually. I planned a systematic course of reading which seemed to be best adapted to his particular needs. I found by questioning him that he knew something about the history of Greece and Rome, picked up in his classical course in the high school, but about the history of our own country he knew little or nothing. Therefore I began the history lessons by reading one hour in the forenoon and one hour in the afternoon, until we had read the following list of books: John Fiske's Beginnings of New England; The Dutch and Quaker Colonies in America; Old Virginia and Her Neighbors; The American Revolution; Historical Essays; and The Discovery of America.

Next we took up Parkman's historical works, six or seven volumes in all. Parkman was followed by Nicolay and Hay's Abraham Lincoln; Lincoln's State Papers, in part;

Lincoln's Speeches in the Douglas Campaign; McMaster's Life of Daniel Webster; Webster's most notable orations; Webster's speeches in the Hayne debate in the senate; Memoirs of General Grant; Woodrow Wilson's History of the American People, five volumes, in part; Lodge's Story of the Revolution; Green's History of the English People; Motley's Dutch Republic, in part; Motley's Netherlands, in part; McMaster's History of the People of the United States, five volumes, in part; and in part, Hannis Taylor's Origin and Growth of the English Constitution.

In science and general literature, the following list includes a part of the books which we read: Huxley's works, in part; extracts from Tyndall and Darwin; Herbert Spencer, two volumes, in part; John Fiske's Excursions of an Evolutionist; Fiske's Darwinism and other lectures; Fiske's Destiny of Man, Idea of God, Life Everlasting, Through Nature up to Nature's God, and A Century of Science; David Starr Jordan's Care and Culture of Man, The Voice of the Scholar, Foot Notes in Evolution, and numerous other papers and lectures by the same writer; John Muir's Mountains of California, and Our National Parks; extracts from Ralph Waldo Emerson's works; and half a dozen books on political economy and social science. Added to the above list, there were a large number of articles, scientific and literary, from standard magazines.

Occasionally, by way of variety, I read short poems from Whittier, Longfellow, Holmes, and Lowell, — poems that delighted me when I was about the age of my boy. From the Bible we read the book of Job entire; selections from Proverbs, Genesis, the Psalms, and the New Testament.

Of the magazines from which I read many selections, my

pupil was most deeply interested in the *World's Work*, every number of which, from the beginning of its publication until the present time, has been read through from beginning to end, to the never-failing interest of the listener as well as that of the reader. From the other magazines which we take, such as the *Century*, *Harper's*, *McClure's* and the *Outlook*, I selected articles of special note, whether scientific, literary, or political. From the daily papers I gleaned the general news of the world and the current political news of our own country.

I have not given the preceding list as "the best books in the world that everybody ought to read." The books that seemed to me to be well suited to the needs of my particular pupil were selected without reference to the tastes of others.

During the long years of this reading course, my wife was an assistant teacher, who ably supplemented my own reading. She read wise selections from the works of Dickens and Thackeray, Bret Harte, and Mark Twain, and occasionally from the driftwood of recent fiction in magazines or in book form. Boswell's Johnson, Pepys' Diary, Hittell's History of California, four volumes, and numerous miscellaneous volumes of current literature. Whenever I was called away from home on business she more than filled my chair.

The eyes of our student gradually became strong enough to enable him to engage in light work about the farm in the morning and towards evening, and at length to work four or five hours a day, for which he was paid regular wages. In time he was able to read a few minutes daily, and to write short letters on the typewriter. Day dawned after the long cheerless arctic night. Recently he has received a deed of an undivided one-fourth interest in Hill Girt farm. Fortunately, his general health is good, and he keeps up a degree of cheerfulness that excites my admiration, because in my youthful days I also passed through the fiery furnace of affliction.

Earthquake and Fire

In April, 1906, our business was disturbed to some extent by the earthquake and fire which wrecked the business section of San Francisco. Our house in the city, which had been our home for more than twenty years, in which four of our six children had been born and in which two had died, was not damaged by the earthquake, because it was situated high on the eastern slope of Russian Hill, on Taylor Street, but it was reduced to ashes two days later by the wave of fire that swept up the long hill slope from the water front.

Incidental Educational Work

Though most of my own time has been occupied in farm work, I have taken an incidental interest in educational affairs. In 1897 I accepted an appointment as a member of the county board of education in my own county, for the purpose of securing a revision of the course of study, from which I retired after accomplishing my work. I have attended the annual county teachers' institutes and taken part in the proceedings.

By regular attendance at the annual meetings of the California Teachers' Association, I have kept up my acquaintance with teachers and renewed many old-time friendships. I began a revision of my book entitled "Methods of Teaching." When this work was completed it proved so unsatisfactory that I set it aside and wrote a volume entitled "American Public Schools." The introductory half of this book treated of the origin and development of the district and town schools of colonial times, of grammar schools, academies, and high schools, and the primitive textbooks which indicated their course of study. This involved an extended course of historical research, which led me to take a trip to New England for the purpose of getting access to numerous town histories, the original sources of information about the evolution of the common schools.

In 1901 I took an active part in the organization of the Alhambra Union High School, formed by the combination of five school districts, of which Martinez is the center. From the beginning, I have acted as chairman of the board of trustees. We carried an election for the issue of bonds for $10,000 and built a well-planned schoolhouse, which is not excelled in point of convenience, arrangement, and architecture by any small high-school building in the state.

I have kept in touch with the educators of the state by attending the quarterly meetings of The Schoolmasters' Club. I am also doing duty as one of five members of the advisory board of editors of the Western *Journal of Education*, the official organ of the state board of education.

In 1906 I was appointed by Governor Pardee as a member of the board of trustees of the state normal school at San Francisco, to fill a short term vacancy, and was reappointed by Governor Gillet in 1907. I am also known as an "honorary lecturer" before the Department of Education in the State University.

The meeting of the National Educational Association in

July, 1899, at Los Angeles, brought to the Pacific coast large numbers of distinguished educators from the East, among whom was Emerson E. White of Ohio, whom I had not seen since the Boston meeting of 1872. At the first general session, after the customary addresses of welcome, Mr. White read an able paper in response, and then went on to speak as follows:

Some thirty years ago I watched with interest the development of the school system of California. If my memory serves me, California was the first state in the Union to adopt a graded course of study for its rural schools. I examined this state course of study with much interest, and this was especially true of the accompanying manual prepared by the state school department for the guidance of teachers. While this early movement unduly emphasized the principle of uniformity in school administration, a principle that has everywhere been the source of serious evils in school affairs, the California experiment, as it was called, inspired efforts in different sections of the country to provide graded courses of study for rural schools, resulting here and there in the adoption of town or township courses, county courses, and, more recently, state courses.

In 1872 the National Educational Association met in Boston. In arranging the program for that meeting, I desired to see California represented by its foremost educator, and so I invited John Swett to give one of the principal addresses. He kindly accepted the invitation and came across the continent to render the service. In their appreciative notices of Mr. Swett's address the Boston papers referred to him as the "Horace Mann of the Pacific coast," a high and fitting honor. President Lyte at this point stated that he desired to introduce a man whose name was not on the program, an educator whose name was an inspiration to teachers throughout the land, a man who for a generation had stood preëminent in the profession — the Honorable John Swett.

When I heard this address, I learned for the first time why Mr. White had invited me to address the Boston meeting. This is what I said as I was called unexpectedly upon the stage in response to Mr. White's eulogium:

Members of the National Educational Association and fellow teachers of the United States of America, now, thank God, united never to be divided again: I appear before you as one of the few survivors of the old educational guard in California. I have no doubt the president introduced me as an awful example of the conservatism of the past, and the antediluvian condition of California years ago. I really don't know, myself, exactly where I do belong. Born in the Old Granite State, I once thought myself a Yankee. When I was twenty-two I drifted to California and soon became a native son. Last year I made a visit to my native state and in three months became a New Englander. When I recrossed the continent, I turned my coat and was transformed into a Californian. Now the only things I am quite certain about are that I am an American citizen and that I must be growing old.

Why, the other day I met on the street a bald-headed man who grabbed my hand and exclaimed, "Don't you know me? I used to go to school to you." I looked him over carefully and replied hesitatingly, "You must be mistaken, my good friend. It seems to me that you were the teacher, and that I was one of your boys." So we parted sorrowfully, not knowing exactly where we stood.

Well, I am willing to be taken as a fair sample of the teachers in the early days of California. We worked hard. We were ambitious. Most of us came here expecting to get rich in the mines. We failed in that, and then turned in and did harder work in the public schools.

It gave me great pleasure to listen to my friend, Mr. White. He gave us a statesmanlike paper, and we ought to thank him for his words of wisdom and caution. There is a growing tendency in California towards uniformity and state centralization of power, which, if continued, might lead us into a kind of Chinese civilization. I have no love for Chinese uniformity in education. Mr. White is of New England descent, and the old-time belief in democratic town government runs in his blood and will stick there until he dies.

I will not take up your time further, but if any member of this association thinks that I am going to disappear from the annual meetings because I belong to the age of Methuselah, he is altogether mistaken. You will see me, again and again, whenever I have money enough to cross the continent to attend them.

Not many months after the Los Angeles meeting, Mr. White closed his school life, leaving a name written high on the roll of honor of great American educators. Mr. White and Mr. William T. Harris were the two most notable educators that I met at the Boston meeting in 1872.

As I write this closing chapter, our course of life at Hill Girt is running smoothly. We are not getting rich, but we make a comfortable living in spite of some unfavorable conditions of the market for fruit. We are not encumbered by a mortgage. My wife, presiding over domestic affairs, seems, in spirit, as young as she was years ago, when we began to make the home of which she still remains the central sun. Though in my eightieth year, with my eyes turned to the setting sun, I find myself in fair health and in cheerful spirits. I take and read half a dozen school journals, and still consider myself as a volunteer private in the ranks of educational reformers. I rejoice in exceeding gladness that my life has been prolonged until my eyes behold the splendor of the dawning day of a newer and better education.

A few months ago, wishing to renew my youth, I visited the San Francisco State Normal School, and passed three whole days in quietly watching the six or seven hundred children in the training classes, all as busy as bees and happy as singing birds, because, under wise and skilled teachers, they were doing work suited to their ages and stages of development.

I left this school feeling that an educational millenium had begun to dawn. As I walked briskly down Market Street, a fragment from a class-day poem by Oliver Wendell Holmes kept running in my head.

> "Hang the almanac's cheat and the catalogue's spite,
> Old Time is a liar, we're twenty to-night!
> Gray temples at twenty? Yes, white if you please,
> Where the snowflakes fall thickest, there's nothing can freeze."

Not long after this school visit, Thanksgiving Day found our children and grandchildren gathered around the family altar fires at Hill Girt holding a musical concert. John plays the flute and the banjo, Helen the guitar, Ruth the piano accompaniments, my wife selects the songs, and I am an appreciative listener. When my soul is filled with music, I steal away into the spacious dining room in the old *adobe* wing, and sit before the smoldering wood fire in the large fireplace. In imagination I see my aged mother sitting by my side in her favorite rocking-chair. Emily, with her thoughtful face, glides noiselessly into the room as if looking for her little daughter, Ruth, whom she left as an infant to our care, and who now seems to fill her mother's place in our affections. Next, I seem to see, lying in his cradle, our first-born boy, Willie, that lived with us only four months and then died from pneumonia. And then I am holding in my arms our third child, Walter, that died, when one year old, under the treatment of a physician that failed to understand his case. For thirty days and nights we watched over him as he clung tenaciously to life. I remember how, on the day before he died, I held before him my open watch to see if he was still conscious. He feebly lifted his tiny finger until it rested over the revolving second hand, where he had so often been accustomed to place it, looked with a sad smile into my eyes, and then sank back upon his pillow. That hunting-case watch, which I still carry, reminds me daily of the dear little boy.

When the whitening embers on the hearth die out, I take with me the sacred memories of the dead and go back to the parlor into the presence of the dear ones living, whose faces, beaming with joy, turn my shadows into sunshine, and I join in the laughter and the song.

UNIVERSITY OF NEBRASKA LIBRARIES
UNIVERSITY OF NEBRASKA / LINCOLN